Communications
in Computer and Information Science　　　1871

Rationale

The CCIS series is devoted to the publication of proceedings of computer science conferences. Its aim is to efficiently disseminate original research results in informatics in printed and electronic form. While the focus is on publication of peer-reviewed full papers presenting mature work, inclusion of reviewed short papers reporting on work in progress is welcome, too. Besides globally relevant meetings with internationally representative program committees guaranteeing a strict peer-reviewing and paper selection process, conferences run by societies or of high regional or national relevance are also considered for publication.

Topics

The topical scope of CCIS spans the entire spectrum of informatics ranging from foundational topics in the theory of computing to information and communications science and technology and a broad variety of interdisciplinary application fields.

Information for Volume Editors and Authors

Publication in CCIS is free of charge. No royalties are paid, however, we offer registered conference participants temporary free access to the online version of the conference proceedings on SpringerLink (http://link.springer.com) by means of an http referrer from the conference website and/or a number of complimentary printed copies, as specified in the official acceptance email of the event.

CCIS proceedings can be published in time for distribution at conferences or as post-proceedings, and delivered in the form of printed books and/or electronically as USBs and/or e-content licenses for accessing proceedings at SpringerLink. Furthermore, CCIS proceedings are included in the CCIS electronic book series hosted in the SpringerLink digital library at http://link.springer.com/bookseries/7899. Conferences publishing in CCIS are allowed to use Online Conference Service (OCS) for managing the whole proceedings lifecycle (from submission and reviewing to preparing for publication) free of charge.

Publication process

The language of publication is exclusively English. Authors publishing in CCIS have to sign the Springer CCIS copyright transfer form, however, they are free to use their material published in CCIS for substantially changed, more elaborate subsequent publications elsewhere. For the preparation of the camera-ready papers/files, authors have to strictly adhere to the Springer CCIS Authors' Instructions and are strongly encouraged to use the CCIS LaTeX style files or templates.

Abstracting/Indexing

CCIS is abstracted/indexed in DBLP, Google Scholar, EI-Compendex, Mathematical Reviews, SCImago, Scopus. CCIS volumes are also submitted for the inclusion in ISI Proceedings.

How to start

To start the evaluation of your proposal for inclusion in the CCIS series, please send an e-mail to ccis@springer.com.

José Maria Fernandes · Guilherme H. Travassos ·
Valentina Lenarduzzi · Xiaozhou Li
Editors

Quality of Information and Communications Technology

16th International Conference, QUATIC 2023
Aveiro, Portugal, September 11–13, 2023
Proceedings

 Springer

Editors
José Maria Fernandes 🅾
University of Aveiro
Aveiro, Portugal

Guilherme H. Travassos 🅾
Federal University of Rio de Janeiro
Rio de Janeiro, Brazil

Valentina Lenarduzzi 🅾
University of Oulu
Oulu, Finland

Xiaozhou Li 🅾
University of Oulu
Oulu, Finland

ISSN 1865-0929   ISSN 1865-0937 (electronic)
Communications in Computer and Information Science
ISBN 978-3-031-43702-1   ISBN 978-3-031-43703-8 (eBook)
https://doi.org/10.1007/978-3-031-43703-8

This Springer imprint is published by the registered company Springer Nature Switzerland AG
The registered company address is: Gewerbestrasse 11, 6330 Cham, Switzerland

Paper in this product is recyclable.

Preface

The International Conference on the Quality of Information and Communications Technology (QUATIC) is a forum for disseminating advanced methods, techniques, and tools for supporting quality ICT engineering and management approaches. Practitioners and researchers meet at the conference to exchange ideas and approaches on how to adopt a quality culture in ICT process and product improvement and to provide practical studies in varying contexts.

QUATIC 2023 was held on September 11–13, 2023, in Aveiro, Portugal. The organizing chairs of this 16th edition of QUATIC were José Maria Fernandes and Ilídio Oliveira, who hosted it locally at their University of Aveiro. The Program Chairs were Guilherme Horta Travassos (Federal University of Rio de Janeiro, Brazil) and Valentina Lenarduzzi (University of Oulu, Finland). Xiazhou Li (University of Oulu, Finland) was the proceedings chair.

This volume collates the papers selected by the members of the Program Committee to be presented at the conference and published in the conference proceedings. QUATIC 2023 attracted many submissions from different areas spanning several thematic tracks, proposed in the call for papers in various cutting-edge technologies of specialized focus. The following five thematic tracks (together with their track chairs), together with a journal-first track, were considered in QUATIC 2023:

- ICT Process Improvement, Organization, and Governance (Andreia Malucelli, PUC-PR, Brazil; Karol Frühauf, INFOGEM AG, Switzerland)
- Quality Requirements (including Emerging Quality aspects) (Daniela Cruzes, NTNU, Norway; Michael Unterkalmsteiner, BTH, Sweden)
- Verification, Validation, and Testing (Domenico Amalfitano, University of Naples, Italy; Matteo Camilli, Politecnico de Milano, Italy)
- Quality Aspects of Digital Transformation (Antonio Guerrieri, ICAR, Italy; Claudio Micelli de Farias, UFRJ, Brazil)
- Quality Aspects of Human Factors in Software Engineering (Fabian Fagerholm, Aalto University, Finland; Maria Teresa Baldassarre, University of Bari, Italy)
- Journal-First and Special Issue (Andrea Janes, Vorarlberg University of Applied Sciences, Austria)

Technical Review Summary

The Technical Program Committee of QUATIC 2023 comprised 71 international academic and industrial domain experts from organizations in 20 different countries on five continents. The best quality papers were identified for presentation and publication based on a rigorous peer-review process by the Technical Program Committee members and external experts as reviewers. The review was done in a double-blind process, with at least three reviews per submission. Submitted papers came from over 21 countries, and accepted papers originated from 13 countries. Out of the submission pool of 37 papers, 17 (45.9%) were accepted as full papers after a discussion period and confirmation with the reviewers.

Apart from these papers, two 'Journal-first' papers were included in the QUATIC 2023 program. These papers correspond to articles published in 2022 in top-notch journals that did not have any prior publication as workshop or conference paper. These two papers were the following.

Gu, R., Jensen, P. G., Seceleanu, C., Enoiu, E., & Lundqvist, K. (2022). Correctness-guaranteed strategy synthesis and compression for multi-agent autonomous systems. *Science of Computer Programming*, *224*, 102894.

Gariano, I. O., Servetto, M., & Potanin, A. (2022). Using capabilities for strict runtime invariant checking. *Science of Computer Programming*, *224*, 102878.

Invited Talks

The conference this year included two outstanding keynote speakers.

The first keynote was Davide Taibi. He is a full Professor at the University of Oulu, Finland, and an Associate Professor at Tampere University, Finland, where he heads the M3S Cloud research group. His research is mainly focused on the migration to cloud-native technologies. He is investigating processes and techniques for developing Cloud Native applications, identifying cloud-native specific patterns and anti-patterns, and methods to prevent degradation. He has been a member of the International Software Engineering Network (ISERN) since 2018. Formerly, he worked at the Free University of Bozen-Bolzano, Italy, the Technical University of Kaiserslautern, Germany, Fraunhofer IESE - Kaiserslautern, Germany, and Università degli Studi dell'Insubria, Italy. In 2011 he was one of the co-founders of Opensoftengineering s.r.l., a spin-off company of the Università degli Studi dell'Insubria. In his talk "Microservices vs. Monolithic: an organizational and quality perspective," Davide addressed migrating from a monolithic system to microservices and its impact on the organization. He presented success and failure cases, providing the academic and practitioners' perspectives on the organizational and quality aspects, including cases of companies that started to revert their systems from microservice to monolithic having not achieved the expected benefits of microservices.

The second keynote speaker was José Carlos Almeida Santos. He holds a Licenciatura em Engenharia Informática (2004) and a Master's degree in Artificial Intelligence (2006), both from Faculdade de Ciências e Tecnologia da Universidade Nova de Lisboa, and a Ph.D. in Computer Science (Logic-based Machine Learning algorithms) from Imperial College, London (2010). José Santos has been a Software Engineer at Microsoft in the Bing division since 2011 and a Principal Software Engineer since 2020. José has worked on multiple Bing teams over the past 12 years: query alterations, autosuggest, shopping relevance, price insights, and, more recently, has been working on integrating generative pre-trained (GPT) language models in various product features. In his talk "AI-Assisted Programming: Revolutionizing the way we code?" He explored the exciting new world of AI-assisted programming and how it is revolutionizing the job of developers and software engineers. AI-assisted programming tools are underpinned by large language models trained on terabytes of source code from popular programming languages, e.g., Python, Javascript, C#, Java, and C++, among many others. He also included some live demonstrations of GitHub Copilot X, an advanced AI-pair programmer tool from Microsoft that integrates with the IDE and significantly improves the coding experience to solve complex programming problems and streamline the development and testing process.

Panels

This year's conference included two open panels between the academy and industry.

The first was entitled "Scaling Up Quality: from Startup to Corporate" and was moderated by Eduardo Miranda (Carnegie Mellon University, USA) with Eduardo Ribeiro (Critical Software, Portugal), Daniel Gonçalves (Wtvision, Portugal) and Valentina Lenarduzzi (University of Oulu, Finland).

This QUATIC panel explored potential synergies between the academic state of the art (SoA) and the real world, extending beyond technical and software development processes. Quality in ICT evolves from the early days of a tech-driven startup to a structured large corporate environment. Changes encompass pure technical implementation practices, strategic business continuity, QoS (Quality of Service) and client orientation. Diverse perspectives on Quality were explored from changing (and challenging) contexts in a tech company lifecycle.

The second panel was entitled "AI in building Software systems: Are we prepared yet?" and was moderated by Guilherme Horta Travassos (Federal University of Rio de Janeiro, Brazil) with José Carlos Santos (Microsoft, Portugal), Paulo Dimas (Unbabel, Portugal) and Davide Taibi (University of Oulu, Finland).

Departing from software engineering challenges posed by contemporary software systems, such as cyber-physical, smart environments, and those in the Internet of Things paradigm, the panel explored the potential use of Artificial Intelligence (AI) techniques to develop and ensure the Quality of such software systems to improve the software processes. Are we prepared to use AI to support Contemporary Software Systems Quality? Some challenging questions were used during the panel to lead the discussion and promote experience sharing: How are our primary quality concerns or desirable features tackled with AI techniques? How can software engineers incorporate terms such as responsibility, ethics and bias and mitigate potential dangers when using AI techniques?

SEDES Doctoral Symposium

In addition, there was a co-located doctoral student symposium chaired by Paula Ventura Martins (University of Algarve, Portugal) and Marielba Zacarias (University of Algarve, Portugal), the proceedings of which are expected to be included in ZENODO, a free and open platform backed by CERN Data Centre. ZENODO enables the discovery and citability of scientific papers by assigning a Digital Object Identifier (DOI) to every upload. We are particularly pleased to support this event, as doctoral students represent much of the future of our community.

As proceedings editors, we thank all the people and organizations that directly or indirectly supported this event. Thanks to the thematic track chairs and all members of the Program Committee for their many contributions and reviews that guaranteed the quality of the QUATIC 2023 conference.

Thanks to our colleagues from the University of Aveiro for all the organizational details required for hosting the conference and to colleagues at different levels in its organization. Thanks to the Steering Committee members for trusting us to organize the conference and for their guidance and support throughout this process. Thanks to the Comissão Setorial para as Tecnologias da Informação e Comunicações (Cs/03) from the Instituto Português da Qualidade that has been harboring and promoting QUATIC since its inception.

Also, a special thanks to all the organizations involved in this conference, including supporters at the University of Aveiro, Federal University of Rio de Janeiro, University of Oulu, University of Algarve, University of Coimbra, University Institute of Lisbon, NOVA School of Science and Technology, University of Porto, University of Minho, and Instituto Superior Técnico. We also thank the Ordem dos Engenheiros for their promotion and endorsement of QUATIC 2023, IEETA (Institute of Electronics and Informatics Engineering of Aveiro), an integrated member of the Associated Laboratory of Intelligent Systems (LASI), and Inova-Ria (Association of Companies for an Innovation Network in Aveiro).

Finally, a warm and kind mention to all the authors and participants of QUATIC 2023! Organizing the conference and producing these proceedings would be hard without their efforts. Thank you for contributing to the critical mass of researchers that keep the QUATIC history alive for what we expect to be many years to come.

September 2023

José Maria Fernandes
Guilherme H. Travassos
Valentina Lenarduzzi
Xiaozhou Li

Organization

Program Committee Chairs

Guilherme Horta Travassos   COPPE/UFRJ, Brazil
Valentina Lenarduzzi   University of Oulu, Finland

Thematic Track Chairs

ICT Process Improvement, Organization, and Governance

Andreia Malucelli   PUC-PR, Brazil
Karol Frühauf   INFOGEM AG, Switzerland

Quality Requirements (Including Emerging Quality Aspects)

Daniela Cruzes   NTNU, Norway
Michael Unterkalmsteiner   BTH, Sweden

Verification, Validation, and Testing

Domenico Amalfitano   University of Naples, Italy
Matteo Camilli   Politecnico de Milano, Italy

Quality Aspects of Digital Transformation

Antonio Guerrieri   ICAR, Italy
Claudio Micelli de Farias   UFRJ, Brazil

Quality Aspects of Human Factors in Software Engineering

Fabian Fagerholm   Aalto University, Finland
Maria Teresa Baldassarre   University of Bari, Italy

Journal-First and Special Issue

Andrea Janes   Vorarlberg University of Applied Sciences,
                                   Austria

Program Committee

Alberto Silva   Universidade de Lisboa, Portugal
Ana C. R. Paiva   Universidade do Porto, Portugal
Ana Rosa Cavalli   Institut Polytechnique de Paris/Télécom SudParis,
                                   France
Antonia Bertolino   National Research Council (CNR), Italy
Antonio Vallecillo   Universidad de Málaga, Spain
Fernando Brito e Abreu   Instituto Universitário de Lisboa, Portugal
Guilherme Horta Travassos   COPPE/UFRJ, Brazil
João Pascoal Faria   Universidade do Porto, Portugal
Joost Visser   Leiden University, The Netherlands
Mario Piattini Velthuis   University of Castilla – La Mancha, Spain
Martin Shepperd   Brunel University London, UK
Miguel Brito   Universidade do Minho, Portugal
Miguel Goulão   Universidade Nova de Lisboa, Portugal
Paulo Rupino da Cunha   Universidade de Coimbra, Portugal
Valentina Lenarduzzi   University of Oulu, Finland
Vasco Amaral   Universidade Nova de Lisboa, Portugal

Organizing Chairs

José Maria Fernandes   University of Aveiro, Portugal
Ilídio Oliveira   University of Aveiro, Portugal

Proceedings Chair

Xiaozhou Li   University of Oulu, Finland

Tutorials Chairs

José Pereira dos Reis   ISTAR-Iscte and ISTEC, Portugal
Antoine Craske   Grupo Lusiaves, Portugal

PhD Symposium Chairs

Paula Ventura Martins   University of Algarve, Portugal
Marielba Zacarias   University of Algarve, Portugal

Social Media Chairs

Simone Vasconcelos   Instituto Federal Fluminense, Brazil
Duarte Almeida   ISTAR-Iscte, Portugal

Contents

Scientific Workflow Management for Software Quality Assessment
Replication: An Open Source Architecture 1
*José Pereira dos Reis, Fernando Brito e Abreu, Glauco de F. Carneiro,
and Duarte Almeida*

Quality Assurance of Digital Twins: An Experience Report
in the Automotive Industry 15
Alican Tüzün and Georg Hackenberg

Continual Service Improvement: A Systematic Literature Review 30
Sanna Heikkinen, Marko Jäntti, and Markku Tukiainen

Elevating Software Quality Through Product Discovery Techniques: Key
Findings from a Grey Literature Review 45
Stefan Trieflinger, Lukas Weiss, and Jürgen Münch

Visual Milestone Planning in a Hybrid Development Context 60
Eduardo Miranda

Quantum as a Service Architecture for Security in a Smart City 76
Vita Santa Barletta, Danilo Caivano, Alfred Lako, and Anibrata Pal

A Retrospective Analysis of Grey Literature for AI-Supported Test
Automation 90
Filippo Ricca, Alessandro Marchetto, and Andrea Stocco

Process Improvement Using the Scientific Method: Demonstration
in Requirements Engineering 106
Isabel Lopes Margarido

Logs Based Verification Tool of Serious Game for Autistic Children 121
Arini Nur Rohmah and Nelly Condori-Fernandez

Beyond Dashboards: Operationalising a Measurement Framework
for Agile Teams 130
Gijsbert C. Boon, Christoph J. Stettina, Joost Visser, and Yassin El-Baz

Exploring Data Analysis and Visualization Techniques for Project
Tracking: Insights from the ITC 147
André Barrocas, Alberto Rodrigues da Silva, and João Saraiva

How a Professional Association Can Steer Digital Transformation: Case
Study of the Belgian Notary Industry 163
   Ziboud Van Veldhoven, Kani Kiliç, Divya Prakash,
   Ryan Michael Smith-Cooper, and Jan Vanthienen

DQBR25K: Data Quality Business Rules Identification Based on ISO/IEC
25012 178
   Ramón Galera, Fernando Gualo, Ismael Caballero,
   and Moisés Rodríguez

Pitching to the 'Big Fish': Elevating Presentation and Communication
Skills in a Software Quality Course 191
   Miguel Morales-Trujillo and Ismael Caballero Muñoz-Reja

Quantum Services Generation and Deployment Process:
A Quality-Oriented Approach 200
   Jaime Alvarado-Valiente, Javier Romero-Álvarez, Ana Díaz,
   Moisés Rodríguez, Ignacio García-Rodríguez, Enrique Moguel,
   Jose Garcia-Alonso, and Juan M. Murillo

External Dependencies in Software Development 215
   Aless Hosry and Nicolas Anquetil

Measuring Team Effectiveness in Scrum 233
   Kars Beek, Gerard Wagenaar, Laura Kester, Sietse Overbeek,
   and Evert de Rooij

Author Index 249

Scientific Workflow Management for Software Quality Assessment Replication: An Open Source Architecture

José Pereira dos Reis[1,2(✉)], Fernando Brito e Abreu[2], Glauco de F. Carneiro[3], and Duarte Almeida[2]

[1] Instituto Superior de Tecnologias Avançadas (ISTEC), Lisboa, Portugal
`josevicente.reis@my.istec.pt`
[2] Instituto Universitário de Lisboa (ISCTE-IUL), ISTAR-IUL, Lisboa, Portugal
`{jvprs,fba,dsbaa}@iscte-iul.pt`
[3] Federal University of Sergipe (UFS), Aracaju, Brazil
`glauco.carneiro@dcomp.ufs.br`

Abstract. Replication of research experiments is important for establishing the validity and generalizability of findings, building a cumulative body of knowledge, and addressing issues of publication bias. The quest for replication led to the concept of scientific workflow, a structured and systematic process for carrying out research that defines a series of steps, methods, and tools needed to collect and analyze data, and generate results.

In this study, we propose a cloud-based framework built upon open source software, which facilitates the construction and execution of workflows for the replication/reproduction of software quality studies. To demonstrate its feasibility, we describe the replication of a software quality experiment on automatically detecting code smells with machine learning techniques.

The proposed framework can mitigate two types of validity threats in software quality experiments: (i) internal validity threats due to instrumentation, since the same measurement instruments can be used in replications, thus not affecting the validity of the results, and (ii) external validity threats due to reduced generalizability, since different researchers can more easily replicate experiments with different settings, populations, and contexts while reusing the same scientific workflow.

Keywords: scientific workflow · software quality · quality assessment · replication · code smells · open source

1 Introduction

1.1 Replication

In Science, replication refers to *"a conscious and systematic repeat of an original study"* [16]. Replication is an important process in Software Engineering

J. M. Fernandes et al. (Eds.): QUATIC 2023, CCIS 1871, pp. 1–14, 2023.
https://doi.org/10.1007/978-3-031-43703-8_1

research, and many authors have emphasized its relevance [14]. For instance, Kitchenham [15] claims that *"replication is a basic component of the scientific method, so it hardly needs to be justified."*. For Shull et al. [24], replication allows to *"better understand Software Engineering phenomena and how to improve the practice of software development. One important benefit of replications is that they help mature Software Engineering knowledge by addressing internal and external validity problems"*. The same authors also mention that in terms of external validation, replications help to generalize the results, demonstrating that they do not depend on the specific conditions of the original study. Regarding internal validity, replications also help researchers show the range of conditions under which experimental results hold.

However, replication is not consensual. Some authors like Shepperd [23] argue that *"replication is often used to gain confidence in empirical findings, as opposed to reproduction where the goal is showing the correctness, or validity of the published results."* Thus, almost all replications are confirmatory because the prediction intervals are wide. Shepperd suggests to *"limit replications to matters of reproducibility (where warranted)"* [23].

One of the framework's objectives presented in this paper is to enhance the replication/reproduction of studies repeating a previously performed experiment.

1.2   Software Quality Assessment

In software development and maintenance, especially in complex systems, the existence of code smells jeopardizes the quality of the software and hinders several operations, such as the reuse of code.

Code smells are not bugs since they do not prevent a program from functioning, but rather symptoms of software maintainability problems [30]. They often correspond to the violation of fundamental design principles and negatively impact its quality.

Software development and maintenance is a complex task that can be hindered by the presence of code smells [26,30], causing code misunderstanding, therefore reducing maintenance efficiency and promoting defects injection. Their removal can be achieved through refactoring operations, thereby improving software quality, such as reusability, ease of maintenance, and readability [9].

Code smells detection is not an easy task because it requires a lot of effort if the process is entirely manual [17]. Depending mainly on the size and complexity of the source code and the developer's experience, the greater the experience of the latter, the easier it is to detect code smells, as well as the greater the complexity of the detected code. [18,19].

Although there has been some progress in recent years in the detection and visualization of code smells [22], the main problems remain the same: 1) the subjectivity of the detection process, which makes it very manual, 2) difficulties in process automation, with lacking in data for models calibration, 3) absence of detection and visualization tools in the IDE to help developers.

In recent years we have seen an evolution in the automatic detection of smells, with various automation techniques based on machine learning, to be applied

[2,8,9,17,20,21,26], but remains its detection difficult because of two main problems: 1) there is no formal definition of code smell, according to Wang, "Automatic detection of code smells has been studied to help users find which parts of their application codes should be refactored. However, code smells have not been defined in a formal manner" [27]; 2) the calibration of detection algorithms is a key point to good accuracy, and for such the existence of reliable data is needed.

In this context, we focus on software quality, namely the automatic detection of code smells with machine learning.

1.3 Scientific Workflows

Scientific workflows provide a visual representation of the research process, including data inputs, processing steps, and outputs, and enable researchers to organize and automate complex tasks. Enacting scientific workflows can help to improve the reproducibility, efficiency, collaboration, quality control, and reusability of research, leading to more reliable and impactful research results.

Defining scientific workflows has several advantages in research:

- Reproducibility: Scientific workflows define a clear and systematic process for carrying out research, which enables others to reproduce the research results. By making the workflow explicit and transparent, researchers can ensure that others follow the same steps and obtain the same results.
- Efficiency: Scientific workflows provide a structured and efficient way to carry out research. By breaking down the research process into smaller, manageable steps, workflows enable researchers to identify bottlenecks, optimize resource utilization, and reduce the time and effort required to complete the research.
- Collaboration: Scientific workflows facilitate collaboration among researchers by providing a common framework for data and information exchange. By standardizing the data and methods used in the research, workflows enable researchers to share data and result more easily and collaborate on common research objectives.
- Quality Control: Scientific workflows help to ensure the quality and accuracy of research results. By standardizing methods and data collection, workflows can help to minimize errors and inconsistencies and enable researchers to identify and correct errors more easily.
- Reusability: Scientific workflows can be reused for different research projects, saving time and effort in future research. By standardizing methods and data collection, workflows can be adapted for use in different research contexts and as a starting point for future research projects.

The Taverna workflow tool suite was designed to combine distributed Web Services and/or local tools into complex analysis pipelines [28]. Taverna Workflows can be designed and executed on local desktop machines through the *Taverna Workbench*, or they can be executed through other clients or web interfaces using the *Taverna Server*. *Taverna Workbench* connects to *myExperiment*, allowing us to import and export workflows directly from this collaborative environment. *myExperiment* is a Virtual Research Environment for collaboration and sharing workflows and experiments [5].

1.4   Contribution

In this study, we present a framework supported by two open source software, *Taverna Server/Taverna Workbench* [28] and *JGU WEKA REST Service*[1], which allows the construction of workflows for the replication/reproduction of quality studies based on machine learning. To demonstrate the availability of the framework, we present the replication of a study that aims to understand the best machine learning algorithm in code smells detection. It should be noted that other applications can be used to create this framework. For example, we can use *Pegasus* [7] instead of using *Taverna Server* to manage the workflows.

Our goal is to contribute to a solution to the problem presented by Ivie and Thain [13] where they claim, "For a workflow that can run on a single machine, solutions exist for replicability, but for distributed systems, and/or for reproducibility, existing systems are generally inadequate for scientists who are experts in their scientific domain and not experts on computer systems."

The paper is organized through the following Sections: in 2, we introduce some related works; in 3, we describe our framework based on *Taverna and Weka Servers*; in 4, we present an example of replication based on our framework. Finally, Sect. 5 provides some conclusions and future work.

2   Background

Although replication/reproduction of studies is widely considered an essential requirement of the scientific process and plays an important role in building knowledge in Software Engineering, several serious concerns have recently been raised. Thus, in Software Engineering, the use of workflows for the replication/reproduction of studies is still limited and far from standard practice.

Unlike in other areas, e.g., bioinformatics and biomedical sciences, where the use of Scientific workflows management systems are increasingly used [3,29], in Software Engineering is not yet a common practice. For example, searching at *myExperiment*, workflows for Software Engineering, we found very few in the universe of nearly 4.000 workflows in this collaborative environment.

Ivie and Thain [13] describe a set of problems that make replication difficult, such as technical barriers. These authors claim that, in principle, it should be possible to specify a computation to sufficient detail that anyone should be able to reproduce the study exactly. But in practice, there are fundamental, technical, and social barriers to doing so. They also present how various authors have defined reproducibility and the need for more consensus on this subject. Another significant contribution of this study is the chapter "technical barriers to reproducing a workflow", which presents the advantages of using scientific workflows and presents a set of recommendations for their use.

De Magalhães et al. [4] performed a systematic mapping study where they analyzed 37 papers reporting studies about replication published in the last 17

---

[1] This application is developed by the Institute of Computer Science at the Johannes Gutenberg University Mainz, inserted in the *openrisk* project.

years. The purpose of this paper is to understand the current state of work on replication in empirical Software Engineering research. These authors have concluded that for replication to be a frequently used means of achieving robust results, it still has a long way to go. In replication, there is not yet a set of standardized concepts and terminology, so it is important that the Software Engineering research community engage in an effort to create and evaluate taxonomy, frameworks, guidelines, and methodologies to support replications' development fully.

Regarding the replication of studies, there are other important works on this subject, which emphasize the importance of replication, defined concepts, and guidelines for performing replication [1, 11, 12, 14, 23].

Regarding the use of scientific workflows, several works point out the challenges and recommendations for their use [6, 25, 29].

There are some applications that allow machine learning workflows to be created for users who are not experts on computer systems. Still, these applications are not free or are not for server system architectures. Some of these systems will be presented below.

Azure Machine Learning Studio[2] is a web-based integrated development environment (IDE) for developing data experiments. It is a collaborative, drag-and-drop tool to build, test, and deploy predictive analytics solutions on your data. The user can develop a predictive analytics model by creating a machine learning workflow only by drag-and-drop blocks.

Weka[3] is, according to the authors, "a collection of machine learning algorithms for data mining tasks. It contains tools for data preparation, classification, regression, clustering, association rules mining, and visualization.". Weka is a local open source software.

RapidMiner[4] presents a concept similar to Azure Machine Learning Studio for creating machine learning workflows. Provides products for local operation, such as RapidMiner Studio (visual workflow designer for predictive models), and for servers with RapidMiner Server (Share and re-use predictive models, automate processes, and deploy models into production). RapidMiner is not open source software.

Orange[5] is an open source machine learning and data visualization that uses the same concept as Azure and RapidMinder to create machine learning processes. Orange only works locally.

H20.ai[6] offers a full suite of products designed to make it easy for every user and every enterprise to accelerate the adoption of Machine Learning and artificial intelligence, providing a web-based platform.

None of the above solutions cumulatively has the flexibility of our framework in terms of 1) costs, as we only use free software; 2) possibilities of use, since

---

[2] https://studio.azureml.net/.

[3] https://www.cs.waikato.ac.nz/ml/index.html.

[4] https://rapidminer.com/.

[5] http://orange.biolab.si/.

[6] https://www.h2o.ai/.

we can build our interface if we do not intend to use *Taverna Workbench*; 3) It is not a local solution, and can be all installed in microservices; 4) ease of availability of scientific workflows in *myExperiment*.

3   Description of the Proposed Framework

3.1   Introduction

The model we present is based on creating workflows of the experiences performed in the studies and making these workflows publicly available. In this way, we allow the entire community to replicate the experiences and confirm the results obtained.

The proposed framework is based on the use of *Taverna* for creating scientific workflows and *JGU WEKA REST Service* for creating machine learning models.

To create a workflow, we first use *Taverna Workbench* (Fig. 1) to design the workflows and perform the first tests, ensuring that the workflow works. Our workflow is essentially a task set that interacts with *Weka Server* through Web Services, in this case, RESTful Web Services.

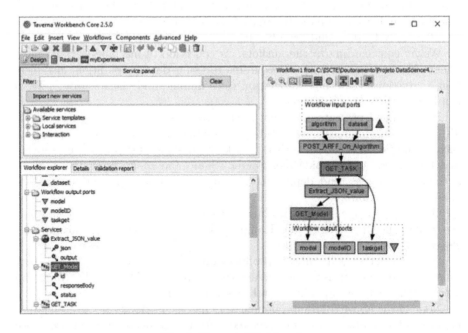

Fig. 1. Taverna Workbench.

Figure 2 shows an example of a workflow that produces the training of a Weka machine learning algorithm by creating its model. This workflow has as inputs the algorithm to be used (e.g., "J48", "RandomForest", "libsvm", etc.) and the training dataset. The outputs are the model, model ID, and task ID. Creating workflows in *Taverna Workbench* consists of choosing the components you want to add to the workflow from the menus since the interface is graphical.

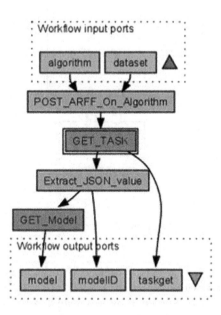

Fig. 2. Workflow to create the Machine Learning model.

Taverna Workbench. Works in local mode, i.e., on local desktop machines, so using very large datasets can cause the machine to slow down or even not have enough resources for Workflow processing. In the second phase, we use *Taverna Server* to solve this problem. The process is to create workflows in *Taverna Workbench* and then import and run them in *Taverna Server*. As the *Taverna Server* is in the cloud and the *Weka Server*, we have no problems with processing speed or lack of resources.

With this architecture, we are convinced that we contribute to solving the problem presented by Ivie and Thain [13] when they say, "For a workflow that can run on a single machine, solutions exist for replicability, but for distributed systems, and/or for reproducibility, existing systems are generally inadequate for scientists who are experts in their scientific domain and not experts on computer systems.".

3.2   Architecture of the Framework

The framework is based on two docker containers, one for *JGU WEKA REST Service* and another for *Taverna Server*, communicating through RESTful API (Application Program Interface), as illustrated in Fig. 3.

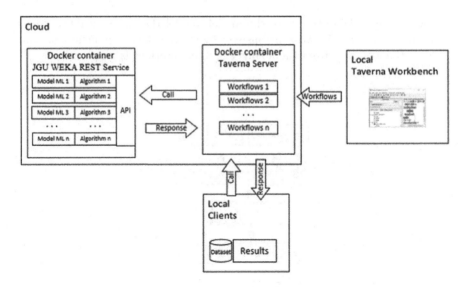

Fig. 3. Framework architecture.

As already mentioned, *Taverna Workbench* works in local mode and serves to produce the workflows that are then loaded into the *Taverna Server*. Once the models are in *Taverna Server*, they are available to be called by different local clients. When a client calls a Workflow in the *Taverna Server*, it interacts with *JGU WEKA REST Service*, which is in another docker container, through the API provided by *Weka Server*.

The workflows we created are for software quality assessment replication using Machine Learning techniques (see Fig. 2), although the same principle holds true for other experiments. Thus, the operating principles are as follows:

a) The workflow that is in the *Taverna Server* receives the ML algorithm and the training dataset as input. These parameters are stored in the *Taverna Server*;

b) Invoking the *JGU WEKA REST Service* API, we pass Weka the two parameters from the previous point, and Weka performs the training of the algorithm with the dataset;

c) *JGU WEKA REST Service* returns the result in a JSON format containing various information, such as training success, model ID, etc.;

d) In *Taverna Server* we will extract the various information from JSON;

e) Obtain from *JGU WEKA REST Service* the created ML model and its evaluation, passing as a parameter the model ID;

This framework presents a scalable solution where it is possible to add more docker containers with other services, thus creating the possibility to produce more elaborate workflows with more functionalities.

We are currently developing a Java graphical user interface so that users can easily interact with the *Taverna Server*. Currently, the workflows placement in the *Taverna Server* is performed manually, and the results are consulted in the server directories, also manually, through a browser. However, it should be noted that it is always possible to invoke a Workflow directly from the *Taverna Workbench* (see Fig. 1), particularly when datasets are small and do not require large computational resources.

4 Replication Example

To exemplify our framework, we have replicated an article that compares various machine learning algorithms to determine the best algorithm for detecting code smells.

4.1 Study to Be Replicated

We chose to replicate Fontana's paper *"Code Smell Detection: Towards a Machine Learning-based Approach"* [10]. This paper has conducted a study where the authors use six different machine learning algorithms to detect four code smell types, i.e., Data Class, Large Class, Feature Envy, and Long Method.

This study aims to compare and benchmark code smell detection with supervised machine learning techniques. For this purpose, four datasets were created, one for each code smell, to train the machine learning algorithms. The application used in this experiment to train and evaluate machine learning algorithms was Weka (open source software from Waikato University), and the following algorithms available in Weka were implemented:

- J48 is an implementation of the C4.5 decision tree, and its three types of pruning techniques: pruned, unpruned, and reduced error pruning;
- JRip implements a propositional rule learner;
- Random Forest consists of a large number of individual decision trees that operate as an ensemble;
- Naïve Bayes is a probabilistic model based on the Bayes theorem;
- SMO is a Sequential Minimal Optimization algorithm widely used for training support vector machines;
- LibSVM is a library for Support Vector Machines (SVMs), integrated software for support vector classification.

Experiments were performed to evaluate the performance values of the machine learning algorithms with their default parameters for each type of code smell. Cross-validation was the statistical technique applied to test the performance of Machine Learning models, and three standard performance measures were used: accuracy, F-Measure, and Area Under ROC (Receiver Operating Characteristics).

The results show that the experienced algorithms obtained high performances, regardless of the type of code smell. On the other hand, the SVM algorithms tend to perform worse than the other algorithms, with the J48 and Random Forest classifiers obtaining the highest accuracy (>96 %).

4.2 Replication Using the Framework

With our framework, it is easy and accessible for everyone to replicate this type of study because the use of scientific workflows avoids repetitive work and having to understand the application used in the training and evaluation of different machine learning algorithms, Weka, in this case.

The replication facility is essentially in the fact that we use the workflow shown in Fig. 2, having as input parameters the desired algorithm and the training dataset and as output parameters the model with its performance measures. Thus, to obtain the results for the different algorithms, just change the two input parameters. For example, to test the performance of the J48 algorithm in detecting the code smell Data Class, it is only necessary to invoke the workflow, passing as inputs the algorithm identifier - in this case, "J48" - and the training dataset previously prepared for this code smell in ARFF format. An ARFF (Attribute-Relation File Format) file is an ASCII text file that describes a list of instances sharing a set of attributes. ARFF files were developed by the Machine Learning Project at the Department of Computer Science of The University of Waikato for use with the Weka machine learning software[7].

Some of the possible values for the first workflow parameter, i.e., the algorithm identification, are RandomForest, J48, J48/adaboost, NaiveBayes, NaiveBayes/adaboost, NaiveBayes/bagging, libsvm, libsvm/adaboost, libsvm/bagging, SMO.

Note that the JRip algorithm is not implemented in our version of *JGU WEKA REST Service*, so it is impossible to compare this algorithm's results.

Regarding the second workflow parameter, i.e., the dataset, the four datasets provided by the paper authors were used, one for each code smell. The dataset is at the class level for Data Class and Large Class code smells, and for Feature Envy and Long Method code smells, the datasets are at the method level.

Each dataset contains the identification of the Java project used, the package, class, and method (the method for code smell only at this level), the code metrics - of class or method - and the value of whether or not it is a code smell.

The results presented in Fontana's paper [10] show that J48, Random Forest, JRip, and SMO have accuracy values greater than 90% for all datasets, and on average, they have the best performances. Naive Bayes has slightly lower performances on Data Class and Feature Envy than on the other two smells. LibSVM performances are lower than the others (far lower in three cases out of four).

---

[7] https://www.cs.waikato.ac.nz/ml/weka/arff.html.

Table 1. Performance results for Data Class code smell.

Classifier	Accuracy	F-measure	ROC Area
J48	0.981	0.981	0.975
Random Forest	0.974	0.974	0.999
Naive Bayes	0.786	0.792	0.935
SMO	0.952	0.952	0.945
LibSVM	0.738	0.677	0.609

Table 2. Performance results for God Class code smell.

Classifier	Accuracy	F-measure	ROC Area
J48	0.969	0.969	0.961
Random Forest	0.979	0.979	0.990
Naive Bayes	0.931	0.932	0.976
SMO	0.955	0.954	0.943
LibSVM	0.667	0.533	0.500

Table 3. Performance results for Feature Envy code smell.

Classifier	Accuracy	F-measure	ROC Area
J48	0.938	0.938	0.943
Random Forest	0.919	0.919	0.983
Naive Bayes	0.850	0.850	0.912
SMO	0.900	0.898	0.870
LibSVM	0.676	0.566	0.520

Tables 1, 2, 3, 4 present our results for the different machine learning algorithms for each of the 4 code smells. We do not configure any of its parameters in these algorithms, having used the default settings. To evaluate the performance of each model, we used 10-fold cross-validation as the study authors.

We can see slight differences in values when comparing our results with those of the original study. But when we compare the original study's findings, we can confirm them.

The first result obtained by the authors of the original study was that the J48, Random Forest, and SMO algorithms have accuracy values greater than 90% for all datasets, and on average, they have the best performances. We confirm this first result. The second result is that the Naive Bayes algorithm has slightly lower performances for all four code smells. We also confirm this result. The final result is that LibSVM's performance is lower than the other algorithms (much lower in three cases out of four). As we can see in Tables 1, 2, 3 and 4, the worst performing algorithm is LibSVM, and for God Class, Feature Envy

Table 4. Performance results for Long Method code smell.

Classifier	Accuracy	F-measure	ROC Area
J48	0.995	0.995	0.999
Random Forest	0.993	0.993	1.000
Naive Bayes	0.936	0.937	0.964
SMO	0.976	0.976	0.971
LibSVM	0.686	0.576	0.529

and Long Method code smell, results are much lower than the other algorithms. Thus, we also confirm this last result.

5   Conclusions

This study presents a framework that allows the replication/reproduction of studies based on scientific workflows.

Unlike in other areas, e.g., bioinformatics and biomedical sciences, where the use of Scientific workflows management systems has been long used [3, 29], in Software Engineering is not yet a common practice. With this framework, we aim to present a simple and scalable way to create and reuse scientific workflows.

This framework is based on two open source software systems: *Taverna Server/Taverna Workbench* [28] and *JGU WEKA REST Service*. This architecture allows workflows to be performed on the local computer that does not require large computational resources. Remote execution on the cloud-based architecture allows the processing of large datasets. Workflows are created in the *Taverna Workbench*, where they can also be run, and loaded into the *Taverna Server*, so they are available to be run by multiple users.

To exemplify the feasibility of the proposed framework, we have replicated the study named *"Code Smell Detection: Towards a Machine Learning-based Approach"* published in [10], which compares six machine learning algorithms to determine the best one for detecting 4 code smell types, i.e., *Data Class, Large Class, Feature Envy* and *Long Method*. Comparing our results with the study's, we confirm its findings.

With this framework, we think we have contributed to facilitating the application/reproduction of studies, thus contributing to Software Engineering development.

Acknowledgement. This research was partially funded by ISTAR's projects FCT UIDB/04466/2020 and UIDP/04466/2020.

References

1. Abbuhl, R.: Why, when, and how to replicate research. In: Research Methods in Second Language Acquisition: A Practical Guide, pp. 296–312 (2012). https://doi.org/10.1002/9781444347340.ch15

2. Bryton, S., Brito e Abreu, F., Monteiro, M.: Reducing subjectivity in code smells detection: experimenting with the Long Method. In: Proceedings of the 7th International Conference on the Quality of Information and Communications Technology (QUATIC), pp. 337–342. IEEE (2010). https://doi.org/10.1109/QUATIC.2010.60
3. Cohen-Boulakia, S., Chen, J., Missier, P., Goble, C., Williams, A.R., Froidevaux, C.: Distilling structure in taverna scientific workflows: a refactoring approach. BMC Bioinformatics **15**(Suppl 1), 1–14 (2014). https://doi.org/10.1186/1471-2105-15-S1-S12
4. De Magalhães, C.V., Da Silva, F.Q., Santos, R.E., Suassuna, M.: Investigations about replication of empirical studies in software engineering: a systematic mapping study. Inf. Softw. Technol. **64**, 76–101 (2015). https://doi.org/10.1016/j.infsof.2015.02.001
5. De Roure, D., Goble, C., Stevens, R.: The design and realisation of the Experimentmy virtual research environment for social sharing of workflows. Futur. Gener. Comput. Syst. **25**(5), 561–567 (2009). https://doi.org/10.1016/j.future.2008.06.010
6. Deelman, E., et al.: The future of scientific workflows. Int. J. High-Perform. Comput. Appl. **32**(1), 159–175 (2018). https://doi.org/10.1177/1094342017704893
7. Deelman, E., et al.: Pegasus, a workflow management system for science automation. Future Gener. Comput. Syst. **46**, 17–35 (2015). https://doi.org/10.1016/J.FUTURE.2014.10.008
8. Fokaefs, M., Tsantalis, N., Stroulia, E.: JDeodorant: identification and application of extract class refactorings. In: Proceedings of the 33rd International Conference on Software Engineering, (ICSE). ACM/IEEE (2011). https://doi.org/10.1145/1985793.1985989
9. Fontana, F.A., Mangiacavalli, M., Pochiero, D., Zanoni, M.: On experimenting refactoring tools to remove code smells. In: Proceedings of the XP'15 Workshops, pp. 1–8. ACM Press, New York (2015). https://doi.org/10.1145/2764979.2764986
10. Fontana, F.A., Zanoni, M., Marino, A., Mäntylä, M.V.: Code smell detection: towards a machine learning-based approach. In: Proceedings of the International Conference on Software Maintenance (ICSM). IEEE (2013). https://doi.org/10.1109/ICSM.2013.56
11. Gómez, O.S., Juristo, N., Vegas, S.: Understanding replication of experiments in software engineering: a classification. Inf. Softw. Technol. **56**(8), 1033–1048 (2014). https://doi.org/10.1016/j.infsof.2014.04.004
12. Harman, M., McMinn, P., de Souza, J.T., Yoo, S.: Search based software engineering: techniques, taxonomy, tutorial. In: Meyer, B., Nordio, M. (eds.) LASER 2008-2010. LNCS, vol. 7007, pp. 1–59. Springer, Heidelberg (2012). https://doi.org/10.1007/978-3-642-25231-0_1
13. Ivie, P., Thain, D.: Reproducibility in scientific computing. ACM Comput. Surv. **51**(3), 1–36 (2018). https://doi.org/10.1145/3186266
14. Juristo, N., Gómez, O.S.: Replication of software engineering experiments. In: Meyer, B., Nordio, M. (eds.) Empirical Software Engineering and Verification. Lecture Notes in Computer Science, vol. 7007, pp. 60–88. Springer, Berlin (2012)
15. Kitchenham, B.: The role of replications in empirical software engineering-a word of warning. Empir. Softw. Eng. **13**(2), 219–221 (2008). https://doi.org/10.1007/s10664-008-9061-0
16. La Sorte, M.A.: Replication as a verification technique in survey research: a paradigm. Sociol. Q. **13**(2), 218–227 (1972). https://doi.org/10.1111/j.1533-8525.1972.tb00805.x

17. Liu, H., Ma, Z., Shao, W., Niu, Z.: Schedule of bad smell detection and resolution: a new way to save effort. IEEE Trans. Softw. Eng. **38**(1), 220–235 (2012). https://doi.org/10.1109/TSE.2011.9
18. Mantyla, M., Lassenius, C.: Subjective evaluation of software evolvability using code smells: an empirical study. Empir. Softw. Eng. **11**(3), 395–431 (2006). https://doi.org/10.1007/s10664-006-9002-8
19. Mantyla, M., Vanhanen, J., Lassenius, C.: Bad smells - humans as code critics. In: Proceedings of the 20th International Conference on Software Maintenance (ICSM), pp. 399–408 (2004). https://doi.org/10.1109/ICSM.2004.1357825
20. Palomba, F., Bavota, G., Penta, M.D., Oliveto, R., Poshyvanyk, D., Lucia, A.D.: Mining version histories for detecting code smells. IEEE Trans. Software Eng. **41**(5), 462–489 (2015). https://doi.org/10.1109/TSE.2014.2372760
21. Pessoa, T., Brito e Abreu, F., Monteiro, M.P., Bryton, S.: An eclipse plugin to support code smells detection. In: Proceedings of INFORUM 2011 (Simpósio de Informática). p. 12 (2011). https://arxiv.org/abs/1204.6492
22. Pereira dos Reis, J., Brito e Abreu, F., de Figueiredo Carneiro, G., Anslow, C.: Code smells detection and visualization: a systematic literature review. Arch. Comput. Methods Eng. **29**(1), 47–94 (2022). https://doi.org/10.1007/s11831-021-09566-x
23. Shepperd, M.: Replication studies considered harmful. In: Proceedings of the International Conference on Software Engineering (ICSE), pp. 73–76. ACM/IEEE (2018). https://doi.org/10.1145/3183399.3183423
24. Shull, F.J., Carver, J.C., Vegas, S., Juristo, N.: The role of replications in empirical software engineering. Empir. Softw. Eng. **13**(2), 211–218 (2008). https://doi.org/10.1007/s10664-008-9060-1
25. Taylor, I.J., Deelman, E., Gannon, D., Shields, M.S.: Workflows for E-science: Scientific Workflows for Grids. Springer, Cham (2007). https://doi.org/10.1007/978-1-84628-757-2
26. Tsantalis, N., Chaikalis, T., Chatzigeorgiou, A.: JDeodorant: identification and removal of type-checking bad smells. In: Proceedings of the 12th European Conference on Software Maintenance and Reengineering (CSMR), pp. 329–331 (2008). https://doi.org/10.1109/CSMR.2008.4493342
27. Wang, C., Hirasawa, S., Takizawa, H., Kobayashi, H.: Identification and elimination of platform-specific code smells in high performance computing applications. Int. J. Networking Comput. **5**(1), 180–199 (2015). https://doi.org/10.15803/ijnc.5.1_180
28. Wolstencroft, K., et al.: The taverna workflow suite: designing and executing workflows of web services on the desktop, web or in the cloud. Nucleic Acids Res. **41**(Web Server issue), 557–561 (2013). https://doi.org/10.1093/nar/gkt328
29. Wolstencroft, K., Fisher, P., Goble, C.: Scientific workflows overview. Connexions **26**, 1–6 (2009)
30. Yamashita, A., Moonen, L.: To what extent can maintenance problems be predicted by code smell detection? - An empirical study. Inf. Softw. Technol. **55**(12), 2223–2242 (2013). https://doi.org/10.1016/j.infsof.2013.08.002

Quality Assurance of Digital Twins: An Experience Report in the Automotive Industry

Alican Tüzün[1]([✉]) and Georg Hackenberg[2]

[1] Josef Ressel Centre for Data-Driven Business Model Innovation, University of Applied Sciences Upper Austria, Wehrgrabengasse 1-4, 4400 Steyr, Austria
`alican.tuzuen@fh-wels.at`
[2] School of Engineering, University of Applied Sciences Upper Austria, 4600 Wels, Upper Austria, Austria
`georg.hackenberg@fh-wels.at`

Abstract. Digital twins are becoming increasingly important for the efficient and effective development and operation of cyber-physical systems. However, digital twins are only useful if they reflect the real-world system accurately enough, i.e. their quality is high enough. This claim entails the question, of what the term quality in the context of digital twins means and how it can be measured. In this article, the authors presented their experience with the quality assurance of a digital twin for an assembly line in the automotive industry. Authors explained the preliminary definition of digital twin quality, which authors derived from classical quality models for general software systems. Furthermore, authors described quality issues, which they were able to detect in a digital twin of an assembly line in the automotive industry. Finally, authors concluded how to leverage their experience in different contexts and how to generalize the underlying approaches.

1 Introduction

The notion of the digital twin, which has gained popularity in recent years, is often subject to vague and ambiguous envisions [30]. The mispresenting of this notion began with the physical twin of the Apollo 13 spacecraft. The twin of Apollo 13 was merely a tangible replication of the spacecraft that has been utilized in physical simulations. Even though the digital aspect was expected to be present, there wasn't [16]. Another physical twin is the historic D-Day map (also known as the Big Board) in Southwick House England, which was used simultaneously before and during the operation, and can be argued to be similar. The board was a twin of the operation, and it included models of battalions and ships that reflected the actual locations of the corresponding formations. Furthermore, synchronization was implemented to give directives from the real system to control the operation flow and to update the physical twin state [10]. In contrast, a digital twin is virtual information of a possible or constructed real system, which can be synchronized with a selected frequency and fidelity [25, 30, 37].

The envision of a digital twin emerged from Grieves'es conceptual model, which was called mirrored spaces model in 2002 [15], and later referenced in a 2005 journal article [14]. Furthermore, he introduced the information mirroring model, which was his ideal form of product lifecycle management at that time with only one goal. The goal was to gather as much relevant and useful information about the real system and leverage that information to trade the required energy, time, and material sources for the system operations. Initially, this model had four main parts. The real system, virtual system, connection between the real and virtual system and virtual simulations [13]. Later, Grieves removed the latter, to simplify the model [15]. Lastly, after co-authoring with Vicker in 2010, Grieves decided to use the NASA-invented 'Digital Twin' word, instead of the information mirroring model [15].

In recent years, there is evidence that digital twins play a crucial role in the manufacturing industries, life sciences, healthcare, infrastructure and smart cities [25]. For example, a digital wind farm from General Electric is a good illustration of how building a digital twin helped to design a better turbine, which was used to collect and analyze the data from the real system for making the process of the real system more efficient [9]. Another fascinating example of the use of digital twins is Philips' virtual heart model. The twin of the heart evolves with the data generated by ultrasonic sensors to calculate how well the real heart is pumping the blood. This information can be used to predict a potential heart failure, allowing for early intervention and potentially life-saving treatment [34]. Lastly, FELICE is another interesting example of a digital twin application in manufacturing. In the project, twin models of machines/equipment and agents are utilized to support real-time decision-making and to conduct what-if analysis and experiments [21].

The previous studies predominantly focused on the design and implementation of digital twins [25, 30]. However, a crucial aspect that remains unclear is how to achieve quality in these highly intricate and evolvable systems. Therefore, ascertaining the requisite level of quality of a digital twin is an arduous undertaking that requires further research.

This paper aims not only to review the digital twin artifacts utilized in the FELICE project and evaluate the quality issues associated with them [21], but also, targets to enhance the scientific understanding of the quality of digital twins. The artifacts analyzed in this study include process videos showing the current assembly procedure, a scope definition, a requirements specification, a general and operational conceptual model, and a discrete event simulation module. To evaluate these artifacts, we considered five crucial quality attributes: correctness, completeness, fidelity, efficiency, and evolvability.

2   Related Work on Quality

The notion of quality is defined in many forms in the literature. Some scholars defined quality as conformance to specifications and requirements [5, 12, 29], while others saw it as a value [1] or the fitness for use [18]which evolved to fitness for purpose later [26], or an abstain of loss [11], and meeting or exceeding customer expectations [17]. Even the ISO9000 standard defines the quality differently, which is an inherent characteristic of the entity [23]. These definitions endeavors to provide an universal understanding of quality and assess it subsequently. However, they come with some strengths and weaknesses. For example, conforming to the requirements and specifications can be useful for assessing the quality of the system but may not always reflect the needs of the stakeholders, hence the quality of the system depends on how accurately these requirements were set [6].

The first serious discussions of subcategorization of quality trace back to the beginning of the 20th century with the emergence of product-focused quality management practices in manufacturing [4]. Later on, with the development of new technologies, subcategorization of quality was evolved and extended to other areas, such as software, which appeared in the 19701970ss [43]. With this emergence, assessing the software quality became inevitable and as a result, a considerable amount of software quality models and characteristics have been established [7, 8, 42]. As an example, ISO/IEC:25010 has standardized eight software quality characteristics, including functional suitability, performance efficiency, compatibility, usability, reliability, security, maintainability, and portability, to determine software quality [40].

It was not until the late 19501950ss that another important subcategory for the context of this paper 'computer simulation quality' was considered [35]. Surprisingly, R. W. Conway et al.identified several potential problems with computer simulation systems in this era, which are still relevant today. To find and evaluate these problems, validation and verification techniques have emerged [3, 36, 39]. Validation is the process of evaluating the simulation quality in comparison to the real system from the perspective of its intended applications. On the other hand, verification is a procedure to evaluate the implementation of the simulation model and its associated data concerning the conceptual description and specifications of the model developer [36, 39]. These techniques are broadly categorized into six areas: informal, static, dynamic, symbolic, constraint, and formal techniques [2, 3]. Formal techniques involve mathematical formality, whereas informal techniques rely on human intervention and reasoning. Although mathematical techniques are more precise, informal techniques are more commonly used [3].

2.1 Digital Twin Quality

To analyze the state of the digital twin quality, a literature analysis was executed. The analysis especially focused on how the digital twin quality is mentioned and assessed within the academic dissertations. Therefore, various tools, such as Scopus and Google Scholar were used to perform an extensive literature analysis on digital twin publications. However, due to the vast amount of available literature, the scope of the research was narrowed down, resulting in the identification of 150 dissertations linked to digital twin quality, verification and validation. After a thorough review of these, only 17 were considered relevant for this paper, and as a result following findings were revealed.

First, He Zhang et al. developed a consistency evaluation approach for digital twin models, which can be used to assess their quality. The authors also discuss essential concepts, such as consistency between real and virtual systems and ultra-fidelity models [45].

In yet another insightful article, He Zhang et al. introduced the updating method for digital twin models. Once more, the accuracy and coherence of the model concepts were addressed [20].

Furthermore, Selch et al. presented a machine-learning approach based on Bayesian networks to track the quality of the digital twin. The unique aspect of this study is that the authors determined the contributions of subsystems to forecast the overall quality of the digital twin, rather than just analyzing it as a single system. The digital couplings, which are linkages between the subsystems, are also identified as a source of extra uncertainty. However, since only one digital twin has been used in practice, multiple subsystem digital twins have not been validated [38].

Additionally, the stability of digital twin models was assessed by another study using the Kolmogorov-Smirnov statistical test, which measures the degree of similarity between the probability distribution of the model's predictions and the distribution of the actual data [41].

Edward Y. Hua et al. identify five open problems with digital twin model validation, including modeling realism, data uncertainty, system dynamics, use-case alignment, and reporting invalid modes. To address these challenges, the authors propose a digital-twin model validation framework. The paper also highlights three areas for future research, including uncertainty and sensitivity analysis, model validation of system-of-systems, and combining expert knowledge and collected data [22].

Finally, Shotaro Hamato et al. demonstrated successful real-time anomaly detection using the Unscented Kalman Filter with the digital twin model. However, determining the appropriate threshold for anomaly detection remains problematic [19].

These dissertations provide valuable insights into various aspects of digital twin quality assessment, including model consistency, stability, and validation, as well as machine learning-based approaches and real-time anomaly detection. However, the identified open problems, including modeling realism, data uncertainty, system dynamics, use-case alignment, and reporting invalid modes, call for further research in the field to improve the quality and reliability of digital twins. Moreover, the lack of well-defined quality parameters for digital twins puts forward a significant challenge in ensuring their quality, which necessitates the development of appropriate quality metrics and standards for digital twins.

3   Method

The form of FELICE's digital twin was the digital twin instance [31], which implies that the real system was already constructed. It is important to note that, for the sake of convenience, the authors utilized the term 'Digital Twin' in the subsequent chapters instead of 'digital twin instance'.

Moreover, since the digital twin was still in the design phase, the methodology of assessing its quality consists of several key steps, including identification of the artifacts, manual reviews of these artifacts, mapping quality attributes to the identified findings, an evaluation of the artifact quality, and ultimately, an evaluation of the digital twin's overall quality.

3.1   Artifacts

The current stage of review encompassed five key artifacts, including process videos displaying the current assembly procedure without an adaptive workstation and cobot, a scope definition outlining the objects on the shop floor requiring tracking or twinning, a requirements specification summarizing functional and non-functional requirements for the digital twin, a general and an operational conceptual model elucidating the high-level structure of the assembly procedure, and a discrete event simulation module that implements the structures prescribed by the conceptual models.

Process Videos have been utilized to explain the manual assembly procedures performed at each of the three workstations. From the three videos initially provided by the project partner, the sequence of assembly steps was extracted at least for one product variant. The tools and the parts needed for each assembly operation were observed. Additionally, the approximate duration of each assembly step was estimated, and some ergonomic characteristics of each operation were derived. The derivable ergonomic characteristics mainly included the poses and motions performed by the operators.

Scope Definition was determined using a methodology based on hierarchical task analysis and process videos provided by the project partner, which aids in better understanding the context and focus of the digital twin. This resulted in a scope definition that identified entities to be twinned, entities to be tracked, and important areas in the scene. Entities to be twinned needed to be represented accurately in the simulation models, including their position, pose, speed, fatigue, and other state variables. Entities to be tracked, on the other hand, only required position information. The scope definition was based on a floor plan of the production facility, with the three workstations marked as gray rectangles. The human workers, cobot, and adaptive workstation were identified as entities to be twinned, and therefore required accurate representation, monitoring, and simulation. Other entities, such as an AGV, carts with doors, and screwdrivers used for assembly operations, were designated as entities to be tracked.

Requirements Specification for the digital twin was defined with a unique ID, a natural language description, an origin, a category, a priority, and a rationale. The ID was used as a reference point for other project artifacts, while the specification described the requirement in a way that allowed for testing of the digital twin implementation. The origin of the requirement was noted to identify the project partner responsible for its creation. The category is distinguished between functional and non-functional requirements, as well as constraints and standards. The priority of each requirement was classified into four levels (must-, should-, could-, and would-have) to help prioritize development efforts. Finally, the rationale provided a clear explanation for each requirement's implication in the specification.

Conceptual Model was comprised of two parts: a general conceptual model and an operational conceptual model. Both models described the assembly line processes however the operational conceptual model focused on the specific steps of the assembly process, while the general conceptual model focused on higher-level processes and workflows. The general conceptual model was represented using a general flow chart notation which distinguishes a root node, activity nodes, and decision nodes. The operational conceptual model consisted of three spreadsheets, each displaying the sequence of assembly operations performed at one workstation. The assembly operations were divided into macro- and micro-operations, with each macro-operation referring to one part of the final product being assembled, and the micro-operations referring to the individual steps needed to complete the respective macro-operation.

Discrete Event Simulation Model consisted of seven sections, including two animation sections, two input sections, one output section, one process logic section, and a database section. The animation sections provided a two-dimensional and a three-dimensional representation of the system, which aided in understanding the simulation and debugging purposes. The input sections allowed for the management of inputs to the simulation model, and the output section displayed summary performance indicators about the simulation run. The process logic section contained the process building blocks, such as queues and assembly operations. Lastly, the database section provided an interface to data sources and sinks.

3.2 Manual Artifact Reviews

During the initial stages of the project, when the target system was not yet available, there was a lack of observable data about system behavior that could be utilized for validation. Instead, informal and potentially incomplete, inconsistent, or incorrect system descriptions had to be relied upon. Therefore, manual reviews were deemed the most suitable tool to account for the characteristics of this situation. The manual review included audits, inspections, reviews, structural analysis and walkthroughs with the project partners which was inspired by Balci's manual review works [2].

3.3 Digital Twin Quality Attributes

To identify the digital twin quality attributes, the following standards, including ISO/IEC:25010, IEE730-2014, ISO9000, and ISO9001, as well as the Oxford dictionary was consulted to synthesize our findings [6, 23, 24, 33, 40].

Correctness is a derived word from the adjective *correct*, which means that the entity is error-free regarding fact or truth. In the context of the digital twins, the fact or truth is the real system hence, *correctness* is a grade of quality, that indicates an error between the real system and a digital twin system (Fig. 1). Meanwhile, the quality of being *correct* is measured by the metric accuracy [33].

Completeness is a derived word from the word *complete*, which can be described as an adjective, attribute, or verb [33]. The adjectival form used in the study denotes *complete* as a state of having all the necessary or appropriate parts according to the real system (Fig. 1). Additionally, sub aspects of completeness, which are *incompleteness* and *overcompleteness* were inspected but identified as a completeness issue.

Fidelity refers to the degree of exactness with which the real system is copied and represented. Low fidelity indicates a simplified representation, while high fidelity refers to an accurate and detailed representation of the real system [25] (Fig. 2). The concept of fidelity has garnered significant attention in recent years and continues to be an important focus in Digital Twin research [25,30].

Efficiency refers to the quality of being efficient [33]. Therefore, *efficiency* is achieving maximum productivity with minimum wasted resources (Fig. 2). It is worth mentioning that the concept of *efficiency* is tightly coupled with the notion of productivity, although *efficiency* differs from the latter's definition, which is defined as the capability to produce large amounts of goods [33]. For example, time efficiency indicates that, with less amount of time as an input, more output with the minimum waste during the process is desired (Fig. 2).

Evolvability is a system's capability to enhance its suitability to its environment through alterations to both its internal and functional structure [32]. Another term to describe the response to changes in the environment is adaptability. However, this concept differs from *evolvability* in that it only affects a system's internal or functional structure temporarily. For instance, a digital twin, which is an evolvable virtual system, can be designed to be more flexible and scalable, allowing for easy updates and the addition of new features [20]. Furthermore, the evolvability of the digital twin was assessed based on the quantity of effort, which is a necessary resource to initiate transformation within the system (Fig. 3).

3.4 Mapping Digital Twin Attributes to Manual Review Results

To evaluate the quality of the artifact, the issues were mapped to digital twin attributes. To begin this process, the findings were collected from the manual review, followed by an inspection of the findings to determine which digital twin qualities were absent. Finally, the findings were mapped to the relevant missing quality attribute(s) and submitted for artifact quality evaluation (Fig. 4).

3.5 Artifact Quality Evaluation

To evaluate the quality of the digital twin artifacts, the mapped findings were scrutinized and evaluated. The process started by identifying which quality attribute(s) were mapped. Once identified, the missing attribute(s) was incremented by 1 to determine the total quality of missing attributes of the artifact(Fig. 4).

(a) Incorrect **Digital Twin**

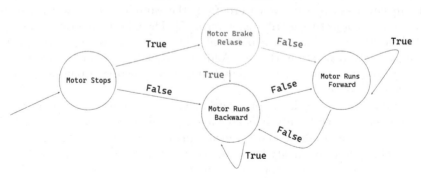

(b) Incomplete **Digital Twin**

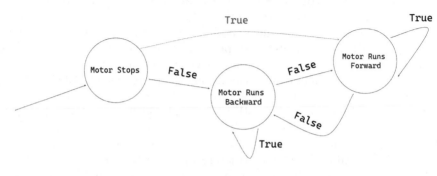

Real System

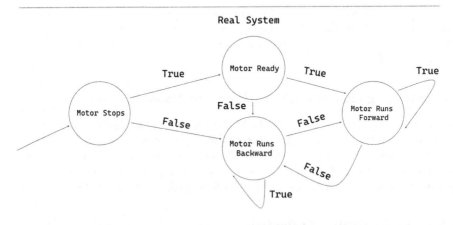

Fig. 1. Incorrect (a) and incomplete (b) status has been demonstrated with a simplified finite state machine. Incorrectness can be observed in the behavior of the machine after 2 state transitions. Incompleteness, on the other hand, can be observed in the missing state. It should be noted that, even though the second state machine is missing a component, it shows the right behavior, hence it is correct.

Fig. 2. Fidelity and Efficiency levels have been demonstrated with simplified CAD drawings. For the assessment of Efficiency, quantitative metrics, rendering time, and model size have been utilized.

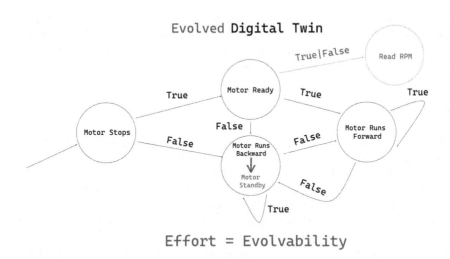

Fig. 3. Figure represents the demonstration of evolvability with the comparison between the first state machine(represented in black), and the evolved state machine(represented in green). The required effort to evolve from the black state machine to the green state machine could be evaluated as *Evolvability*. (Color figure online)

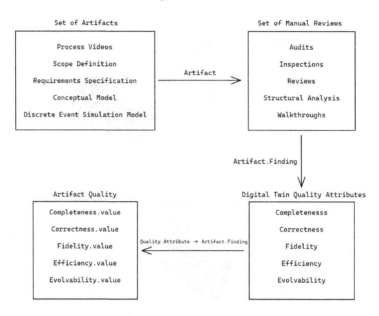

Fig. 4. Method for the evaluation of the digital twin artifact quality: 'Artifact.finding' indicates that the finding belongs to the artifact, while '->' indicates mapping

3.6   Digital Twin Quality Evaluation

To determine the quality of the digital twin, the values obtained from evaluating each artifact's quality were collected and summed. Furthermore, the value of the sum was assigned to the related digital twin quality attribute. As a result, the digital twin quality was demonstrated with quality attribute values (Fig. 5).

4   Results

First, to assess digital twin quality, manual reviews for each artifact were conducted (Fig. 6). As a result, a total of twenty-one quality related issues were identified, listed, and finally mapped to the digital twin quality attributes (Table 1) (Fig. 6). The mapping process revealed that a total of thirty-eight digital twin quality attributes were lacking in the artifacts (Fig. 6). Specifically, 23% of the quality issues of the digital twin were related to correctness, which indicates an error between the real- and digital twin system. Furthermore, 36% were related to completeness, proving that some necessary or appropriate parts were missing. Moreover, 8% were related to fidelity, indicating a lack of detail. In addition, 5% were related to efficiency, indicating poor performance or excessive resource usage. And finally, 28% were related to evolvability, indicating that the system was unresponsive to the environment and was not flexible or scalable.

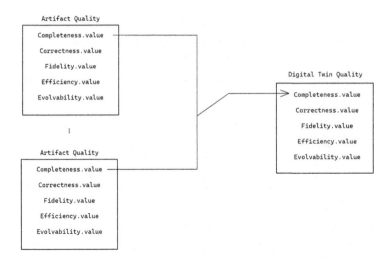

Fig. 5. Method for the evaluation of the digital twin quality

4.1 Example Findings

Two examples (Finding 12, Finding 18) are given to the reader to illustrate the results of the manual review as well as the mapping to the digital twin quality attributes.

Conceptual Model-Finding 12: The duration of the micro-operations in the conceptual model was calculated using a simple calculation scheme based on the duration of the corresponding macro-operations, which were well-known from a prior well-conducted study. However, relying on estimated, simplified calculations for the micro-operation durations, suggests that the digital twin conceptual model suffers from issues of correctness and completeness (Table 1).

Simulation Model-Finding 18: The discrete event simulation model enforced a strictly sequential execution of micro-operations, which precludes the support of parallel execution. However, machine-human collaboration on a task, needs a parallel execution, especially when the cobot overtakes certain micro-operations. Thus, the exclusion of parallel executions indicates that the simulation model was incomplete, at the same time, using the wrong type of execution highlights its inaccuracies (Table 1).

Table 1. Mapping of digital twin attributes to the results of the manual reviews: Cases where an attribute is mapped, were marked by 'X'.

Findings	Correctness	Completeness	Fidelity	Efficiency	Evolvability
Artifacts					
└ Process Videos					
└ Finding 1	0	X	0	0	0
└ Scope Definition					
└ Finding 2	0	X	0	0	0
└ Requirement Specs					
└ Finding 3	X	X	0	0	0
└ Finding 4	X	X	0	0	0
└ Finding 5	0	0	0	0	X
└ Finding 6	0	X	0	0	0
└ Conceptual Model					
└ Finding 7	X	X	X	X	X
└ Finding 8	0	X	X	0	X
└ Finding 9	0	0	0	0	X
└ Finding 10	X	X	X	0	X
└ Finding 11	0	0	0	0	X
└ Finding 12	X	X	0	0	0
└ Simulation Model					
└ Finding 13	0	X	0	0	X
└ Finding 14	X	X	0	0	0
└ Finding 15	X	X	0	0	0
└ Finding 16	0	0	0	0	X
└ Finding 17	X	X	0	0	0
└ Finding 18	0	X	0	X	0
└ Finding 19	0	X	0	0	X
└ Finding 20	0	0	0	0	X
└ Finding 21	0	0	0	0	x

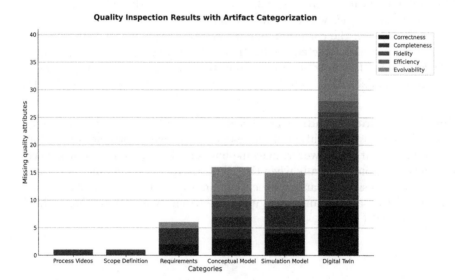

Fig. 6. Quality Inspection Results Categorized with Artifacts: X-Axis represents artifacts in Sect. 3.1, Y-Axis represents the number of missing quality attributes found for each artifact, and lastly, each digital twin quality attribute is shown by the colors.

5 Discussion

This paper aimed to evaluate the quality issues with the given digital twin system in the FELICE project while enhancing the scientific understanding of the quality of digital twins. As a result, this study demonstrates the idea of doing a manual review and mapping quality attributes to issues as a suitable approach for evaluating the quality of digital twins in the design phase. Furthermore, the study suggests that this evaluation is an effective way to collect information about the strengths and weaknesses of the digital twin system. Although the findings should be interpreted with caution, collected information can be used to improve the upcoming design decisions, consequently to higher-quality digital twin systems.

However, manual reviews are a time-consuming endeavor, and even with a reasonable investment of resources, it is not feasible that all relevant data will be covered. Additionally, the completeness of manual reviews is questionable due to the inherent limitations of the process. Moreover, the reliance on human judgment in manual reviews presents an additional challenge, as it is subject to individual interpretation and bias. For example, during the walkthrough, the author's assessment of the system could be flawed due to limited information about the designed digital twin system, resulting in false issue identification and mapping. Additionally, those explaining the system to the authors may be biased, whether due to political or economic reasons or lacking explanation ability. Consequently, the data gathered from the walkthroughs is highly subjective and lacks objectivity. Lastly, this issue not only shows the severity of the data but also raises concerns about the overall quality of the review process.

Taken together, the quality assessment of the digital twin encountered limitations due to the exility of information about the real system. Some artifacts provided less information, such as process videos, which gave a limited perspective of the shop floor based on the camera's field of view and the skills of the video maker. In contrast, the simulation and conceptual model offer a plethora of aspects to examine and assess, which resulted in a higher probability of discovering the issues (Fig. 6). Furthermore, not only the exility but also the visibility of the information was the limiting factor. Therefore, evolvability, completeness, and correctness were easier to map and detect, rather than fidelity and efficiency.

For further enhancement, the risk mapping approach including the severity and priority variables, with the perspective of the stakeholders can be conducted [27, 28]. As a result, quality attributes can be weighted regarding the stakeholder needs. This aspect might be important, because of observer dependent nature of the quality [44].

Acknowledgement. The financial support by the Austrian Federal Ministry for Digital and Economic Affairs, the FELICE project, the National Foundation for Research, Technology and Development, and the Christian Doppler Research Association is gratefully acknowledged.

References

1. Abbott, L.: Quality and Competition: An Essay in Economic Theory. Columbia University Press, New York (1955)
2. Balci, O.: Validation, verification, and testing techniques throughout the life cycle of a simulation study. In: Proceedings of Winter Simulation Conference, pp. 215–220 (1994)
3. Balci, O.: Principles and techniques of simulation validation, verification, and testing. In: Proceedings of the 27th Conference on Winter Simulation, WSC '95, pp. 147–154. IEEE Computer Society, USA (1995)
4. Bennett, S.: A History of Control Engineering 1930–1955. The Institution of Engineering and Technology (1993)
5. Crosby, P.B.: Quality is Free: The Art of Making Quality Certain: How to Manage Quality - so that it Becomes a Source of Profit for Your Business. McGraw-Hill, New York (1979)
6. C/S2ESC/730WG: IEEE standard for software quality assurance processes. Standard, Institute of Electrical and Electronics Engineers (2014)
7. Deissenboeck, F., Wagner, S., Pizka, M., Teuchert, S., Girard, J.F.: An activity-based quality model for maintainability. In: 2007 IEEE International Conference on Software Maintenance, pp. 184–193 (2007)
8. Deissenboeck, F., Juergens, E., Lochmann, K., Wagner, S.: Software quality models: Purposes, usage scenarios and requirements. In: 2009 ICSE Workshop on Software Quality, pp. 9–14 (2009)
9. Electric, G.: Meet the digital wind farm, GE renewable energy. Accessed 5 Mar 2023
10. Eyre, J.: Untangling the requirements of a digital twin (2020)
11. Taguchi, G., Chowdhury, S., Wu, Y.: Taguchi's Quality Engineering Handbook, 1st edn. Wiley, Hoboken (2004)
12. Gilmore, H.L.: Product conformance cost. Qual. Prog. **7**, 16–19 (1974)
13. Grieves, M.: Product Lifecycle Management: Driving the Next Generation of Lean Thinking. McGraw-Hill Education Ltd, New York (2005)
14. Grieves, M.: Product lifecycle management: the new paradigm for enterprises. Int. J. Prod. Dev. **2**, 71–84 (2005)
15. Grieves, M.: Origins of the digital twin concept. Florida Institute of Technology/NASA (2016)
16. Grieves, M.: Physical twins, digital twins, and the Apollo myth. Digital Twin Institute (2022)
17. Groenroos, C.: Strategic Management and Marketing in the Service Sector, 1st edn. Marketing Science Institute, Cambridge (1983)
18. Gryna, J.J.M.F.M., Bingham, R.S.: Quality Control Handbook, 3rd edn. McGraw Hill Higher Education, New York (1974)
19. Hamato, S., Tsutsumi, S., Yamashita, H., Shiohara, T., Hirotani, T., Kato, H.: Study on model-based real-time anomaly detection in a 6.5 m 5.5 m low-speed wind tunnel. In: SICE (2022)
20. Zhang, H., et al.: An update method for digital twin multi-dimension models. Roboti. Comput.-Integr. Manuf. **80**, 102481 (2023)
21. Felice flexible assembly manufacturing with human-robot collaboration and digital twin models. Accessed 26 Feb 2023
22. Hua, E., Lazarova-Molnar, S., Francis, D.: Validation of digital twins: challenges and opportunities. In: MITRE Corporation (2022)

23. ISO/TC176, T.C.: Quality management systems - fundamentals and vocabulary. Technical report, International Organization for Standards (2015)
24. ISO/TC176, T.C.: Quality management systems-requirements. Standard, International Organization for Standards (2015)
25. Jones, D., Snider, C., Nassehi, A., Yon, J., Hicks, B.: Characterising the digital twin: a systematic literature review. CIRP J. Manuf. Sci. Technol. **29**, 36–52 (2020)
26. Juran, J.M.: Juran's Quality Handbook: The Complete Guide to Performance Excellence, 6th edn. McGraw-Hill Professional Pub, New York (2010)
27. JTC1/SC7, T.C.I.: Software and systems engineering - software testing. Technical report, International Organization for Standards - Institute of Electrical and Electronics Engineers - International Electrotechnical Commission (2022)
28. Kaner, C., Bach, P.: Lessons Learned in Software Testing: A Context-Driven Approach, 1st edn. Wiley, Hoboken (2001)
29. Levitt, T.: Production-line approach to service. Harvard Business Review (1972)
30. Liu, M., Fang, S., Dong, H., Xu, C.: Review of digital twin about concepts, technologies, and industrial applications. J. Manuf. Syst. **58**, 346–361 (2021). digital Twin towards Smart Manufacturing and Industry 4.0
31. Michael Grieves, J.V.: Transdisciplinary Perspectives on Complex Systems. Springer, Cham (2017)
32. Mobus, G.E.: Systems Science: Theory, Analysis, Modeling, and Design, 1st edn. Springer, Cham (2022)
33. Oxford: Oxford Dictionary of English. Oxford University Press (2010)
34. Philips: How a virtual heart could save your real one, Philips. Accessed 5 Mar 2023
35. Conway, R.W., Johnson, B.M., Maxwell, W.L.: Some problems of digital systems simulation. Manag. Sci. **6**(1), 92–110 (1959)
36. Sargent, R.: Verification and validation of simulation models. In: Engineering Management Review, vol. 37, pp. 166–183. IEEE (2011)
37. Sean Olcott, C.M.: Digital twin consortium defines digital twin (2022)
38. Selch, M., et al.: Quality monitoring of coupled digital twins for multistep process chains using Bayesian networks. In: Conference on Production Systems and Logistics (2021)
39. Stewart, R.: Simulation The Practice of Model Development and Use. PALGRAVE MACMILLAN, London (2014)
40. Technical Committee ISO/IEC JTC1, I.T.S.S.: Systems and software engineering - systems and software quality requirements and evaluation(square) - system and software quality models. Standard, International Organization for Standardization - International Electrotechnical Commission (03 2011)
41. Timoshenko, A., Perlov, A., Khodataev, N., Kazantsev, A., Lvov, K.: Algorithm for validation of the radar digital twin based on the results of diagnostic control data processing. IEEE (2022)
42. Boehm, B.W.: Characteristics of Software Quality. Elsevier Science Ltd (1978)
43. Weinberg, G.M.: The Psychology of Computer Programming. Litton Educational Publishing, New York (1971)
44. Weinberg, G.M.: Quality Software Management: Systems Thinking. Dorset House, New York (1991)
45. Zhang, H., Qi, Q., Tao, F.: A consistency evaluation method for digital twin models. J. Manuf. Syst. **65**, 158–168 (2022)

Continual Service Improvement: A Systematic Literature Review

Sanna Heikkinen[1]([⊠]), Marko Jäntti[2], and Markku Tukiainen[3]

[1] Istekki Oy, P.O 4000, 70601 Kuopio, Finland
`sanna.heikkinen@istekki.fi`
[2] School of Computing, University of Eastern Finland, P.O Box 1627, 70211 Kuopio, Finland
`marko.jantti@uef.fi`
[3] School of Computing, University of Eastern Finland, P.O. Box 111, 80101 Joensuu, Finland
`markku.tukiainen@uef.fi`

Abstract. Continual Service Improvement (CSI) is an ongoing activity to identify and improve organization practices and services to align them with changing needs. CSI is one of the core elements of IT Service Management (ITSM) frameworks. However, as a research topic it is still an emerging research area of service science. This study explores implementation of CSI and its seven-step improvement process in the context of ITSM. The goal of this paper is to present results of systematic literature review increasing understanding about the CSI and seven-step improvement process, and provide topics for future research. A Systematic Literature Review (SLR) was carried out to analyse CSI-related academic articles. Our main finding is that CSI-related terminology needs clarification and consistency both in academia and in practice to guide the future CSI research for example clarify roles and internal practices of CSI; provide a staged approach for continual improvement; and identify models that support improving and automating the seven-step improvement process.

Keywords: IT service management · ITSM · ITIL · CSI · seven-step improvement process · Systematic Literature Review

1 Introduction

Continual improvement of services plays a crucial role from the point of view of competitive advantage [1]. It is important for the IT service providers to continually evaluate and improve their IT services and IT service management processes [2]. IT services are transitioned to the service operation phase after design, and finally to the CSI phase [3]. The CSI phase includes a seven-step improvement process with following activities [1]: Identify the strategy for improvement; Define what you will measure; Gather the data; Process the data; Analyze the information and data; Present and use the information; Implement improvements. ISO/IEC 20000-1:2018 standard for service management [4] requires service providers to have activities for managing improvement. ISO 20000-1:2018 requirements for the improvement process can be characterized following 6

J. M. Fernandes et al. (Eds.): QUATIC 2023, CCIS 1871, pp. 30–44, 2023.
https://doi.org/10.1007/978-3-031-43703-8_3

practices defined as performance indicators for Improvement [5]: 1) Establish commitment to continual improvement, 2) Determine evaluation criteria for opportunities for improvement, 3) Identify and record opportunities for improvement, 4) Prioritise and approve opportunities for improvement, 5) Implement improvements, and 6) Evaluate and report the effectiveness of implemented improvements.

According to ISO/IEC 20000-1:2018 standard for service management [4], improvements can include reactive and pro-active actions. Crain and Yetton [6] present improvement attributes such as; improvements are made to existing processes, improvements are identified continuously, improvement's level of change is incremental, improvements require little of time, and risk for improvements is moderate.

Customers' dependency on IT has been growing, forcing IT service providers to have more effective management [7]. According to Cater-Steel [8] "If IT service providers fail to provide a reliable customer-centric focus, it will impact on their organizations by limiting the potential for IT to add value". This has shifted the IT service providers' focus from a technology-oriented IT department to deliver IT services in a more service-oriented way [9, 7]. However, modern technology is becoming more diverse and complex. This drives IT service providers to spend a significant part of their time just maintaining the IT service and leaving little time for improvements and innovations that drive the IT service forward.

In order to make IT operations effective IT service providers are turning to the best practices and standards in the field of IT service management [10]. IT Service management (ITSM) is a set of objectives and processes used to direct and control the service provider's activities and resources for the design, transition, delivery, and improvement of services in conducting and fulfilling the service requirements [11]. The goal of ITSM is to manage the IT service infrastructure that delivers and ensures continuous operation of IT services to a customer [12]. To direct and control service management activities, it is essential to put a service management system (SMS) in a place to help organizations efficiently to deliver and support services to their customers [13]. Several frameworks are available to manage IT services and software development, such as COBIT [14], IT Infrastructure library (ITIL) [12], DevOps [15], and Scrum [16]. ITIL provides the practical service management knowledge to build IT service operation from lifecycle phases (service strategy, service design, service transition, service operation, and continual service improvement) [17].

In this systematic literature review, the goal is to find research papers related to ITIL Continual Service Improvement (service lifecycle phase) and particularly its seven-step improvement process. The rest of the paper is organized as follows. Section 2 describes the research method. Section 3 presents the findings of the literature review. Section 4 provides a discussion, and conclusions are given in Sect. 5.

2   Research Method

In this study, we used a Systematic Literature Review (SLR) to answer the research problem: How could IT service providers manage continual improvement in a systematic way? The goal of this study is to increase understanding about the CSI and provide topics for future research. The SLR presented in this study has carried out a structured research process of Kitchenham et al., [18, 19] including three phases: 1) Planning the Review, 2) Conducting the Review, and 3) Reporting the Review. Following research questions are formulated: 1) What is the current state of a seven-step improvement process in literature?; 2) What kind of ITSM process improvement have been identified from literature?; 3) How to identify and manage improvements related to IT services and ITSM processes?; and 4) What opportunities could an automation bring to a seven-step improvement process?

2.1 The Search Process

The search process was organized according to guidelines of Petticrew and Roberts [20]. They suggest using the PICOC as criteria to frame research problem to construct search string for use with electronic databases. The identified synonyms for words are linked using the Boolean operators (OR, AND) to scope the question elements as following:

- Population (P): process (seven-step), practice or framework in which IT service providers are implemented to identify and manage improvement ideas in practice. Boolean attributes: *process OR practice OR model OR framework OR procedure OR method OR continual service improvement OR continual improvement OR CSI process OR 7-step OR seven-step improvement process OR improvement process OR continual service improvement process OR continuous improvement process*
- Intervention (I): clarify the continual improvement activities to perform specific tasks such as requirements specification of ISO/IEC 20000-1:2018 standard to continual improvement. Boolean attributes: *continuous OR continual*
- Comparison (C): describe how service provider performs ideas, initiatives or improvements in practice. Boolean attributes: *idea OR initiative OR change OR improvement*
- Outcomes (O): impact on service operation for example customer satisfaction, effectiveness or value. Boolean attributes: *satisfaction OR effectiveness OR quality OR prediction OR value*
- Context (C): context in IT service management and IT service providers in IT-business (industry). Boolean attributes: *IT service management OR ITIL OR ISO/IEC 20000 OR IT service provider*

2.2 Inclusion and Exclusion Criteria

The selected research problem on CSI guided us to identify and specify which articles are included and excluded. A predefined protocol is necessary to reduce the possibility of researcher's bias [19]. In this study research protocol includes following selection for including and excluding studies:

- Inclusion criteria: 1) Source type: Journal, book series, conference proceeding, 2) Published between 2010–2021, 3) Language: English, and 4) Articles related to discipline of service science, engineering and management.
- Exclusion criteria: 1) Papers are not peer-reviewed, 2) Papers are not available from University of Eastern Finland library, 3) Author's own articles, 4) Articles presenting research in progress, 5) Articles that did not match the inclusion criteria, 6) Posters and tutorials, 7) IEEE Xplore, ACM, Scopus, ScienceDirect, and Google Scholar first 30 results were reviewed, and 8) duplicates studies.

2.3 Data Collection

The systematic literature review was conducted on 11.11.-20.12.2021. Data collection was conducted in two phases and multiple databases were used to find relevant research articles (see Table 1). The first phase included six databases and word "IT service management" was a mandatory word in an abstract field which limited the results. After the first phase, authors decided to add a new database (SpringerLink) and keywords were merged together with the AND operation to increase results. Additionally, "IT service management" as a mandatory word in the abstract was deleted. The second phase expanded the search results (see Table 1).

Table 1. Databases and search results

No.	Database name	Phase 1	Phase 2
1	IEEExplore	8	265
2	Association for Computing Machinery (ACM)	12	77
3	Scopus	33	192
4	Web of Science	6	1
5	ScienceDirect (Elsevier)	0	88
6	Google scholar	17573	2550
7	SpringerLink	-	10

By reading a title, an abstract, and keywords of an article the researcher evaluates whether the research was related to the research scope. Data search was documented into Microsoft Excel (database, year, topic area, research question/issue, summary of paper, whether the study referenced a research problem, reported quality bias, and cite) and analyzed whether the study supported or was closely related to the research problem. Overall, we identified 29 relevant studies: 8 journals and 21 conference articles. Findings are presented in Chapter 3 and on the tables in Chapter 4.

3 Findings

3.1 What is the Current State of a Seven-Step Improvement Process in Literature?

According to literature review, the concept of continual service improvement (CSI) was just mentioned to be part of the ITIL v3 life cycle. There is a lot of research on how ITIL processes and IT service management can be improved using other methodology such as Six Sigma. Donko [21] presents the improvement of the service quality using Six Sigma methodology. According to Donko [21], CSI interacts with the Plan-Do-Check-Act (PDCA) cycle, and the same idea can be recognized in Six Sigma methodology's steps in DMAIC (Define, Measure, Analyse, Improve, Control) cycle. Additionally, Herrera and van Hillegersberg [22] present Lean, Six Sigma, and Lean Six Sigma approaches which have gained popularity to improve manufacturing and processes.

In this paper, the focus is to study how CSI and the seven-step improvement process have been studied in IT service management literature. As a result, a few studies have examined CSI in more detail. According to Lamichhane [23]: "Most of us have heard and read about continual service improvement but still don't know from where to start its implementation process". Lima et al., [24] present that in an IT Service Management setting, current approaches to support CSI suffer from many deficiencies and CSI activities typically rely on unstructured procedures based on weak data.Trinkenreich et al., [25] investigate how IT service managers define, measure, and monitor IT service goals and strategies, and the difficulties they have faced in this context such as: a) Lack of available time to work on measurement results, b) Lack of discipline to provide measurement data, c) Lack of process to deal with people's behavioral issues, d) Lack of understanding on what to do with measurement results.

Yamamoto [17] checks the seven-step process activity items and identifies following maturity level problem: service management operations are not assessed to achieve business objectives. Kummamuru [26] proposes a CSI framework including phases: 1) capturing service improvement objectives in a holistic point of view, 2) prioritizing improvement objectives, 3) executing ideas through an appropriate implementation strategy, and measuring the managing improvement process. According to Kummamuru's [26] study, using six sigma methods to implement improvements in production only helped to solve the identified problem, rather than identifying problems and improvements systematically.

3.2 What Kind of ITSM Process Improvement Have Been Identified from Literature?

During the literature review, several studies on ITSM process improvements were found. Articles focused on specific process challenges where data is analyzed to better identify the root cause of the problem and discover how the ITIL processes can be improved. Arisenta et al., [27] identify change management process maturity and improvements related to it. Lamichhane [23] focused on identifying potential of the improvements in the course business planning and realization processes of decisions. Lineberry [28] identifies that by implementing knowledge management (KM) practices IT organizations can have an opportunity to leverage understanding of their environment and tools to improve performance metrics, customer service, and collaboration.

Macías et al., [29] identify that most institutions in the public sector do not have their IT services catalog implemented. Indra and Hendra [30] present that a project team was ready to implement CSI on the project perspective, but challenges related to software support the CSI activities.

Ilvarianto and Legowo [31] study provide solution to a ticket reporting record system: 1) a ticket system need to be implemented in all business units, not only certain areas, 2) utilization of staff available to the number of incidents handled should be further analyzed and reviewed periodically so that the balance of resources can be met, and 3) maturity level measurement should be done periodically in every organization to trigger innovation and continual development.

Yuan et al., [32] identify that a lot of companies want customers to provide feedback, but companies do not pay the customers for their time as customers did in user studies.

Therefore, customers are getting smarter and ignoring such surveys. In the study, they integrate gamification into the IT service desks to create a loop of knowledge collaboration. In the process flow (users' journey), the customers will be rewarded, and they can earn points, and get gifts by providing useful feedback to IT service teams.

Dos Santos et al., [33] present that ITSM processes can contain segments where the human becomes a bottleneck and slows down the entire process. Karkošková [34] identify lack of comprehensive and efficient methodology for management of cloud computing services from a consumer' point of view. Related to CSI, they propose a new concept to CSI which is a "continual cloud service improvement management process" which focuses on improving long-term performance of cloud service by collecting data.

According to Kajbaf et al., [35] measurement and reporting are the key requirements of service improvement, which in turn are required for value creation and success in a competitive market. They propose an IT service reporting framework to help organizations implementing IT service improvement process in relation to ISO/IEC 20000 PDCA-cycle and identified the following report types which could be used to identify service improvements: 1) Reporting routine task, 2) reporting assigned task, 3) reporting on events 4) reporting on service, 5) reports on review meeting, and 6) management reports.

3.3   How to Identify and Manage Improvements Related to IT Services and ITSM Processes?

Kirilov and Mitev [36] propose a pattern of ITIL integration activities consisting of 4 stages: assessment of ITSM processes, creating a roadmap for ITIL implementation, managing the transition and evaluation, and continual service improvement. Additionally, Abdelkebir et al., [13] propose three tasks to support ITIL usage: defining goals through a Process Maturity Framework (PMF), auditing Quality Management System (QMS), Project Management and a Continuous Service Improvement Program (CSIP). According to Kirilov and Mitev [36], after successful IT management framework implementation, the continual improvement starts. Kirilov and Mitev present that improvement can be based on the experienced results such as ideas noticed during the transition (implies that some best practices are applied appropriately) or during regular audits (conducted yearly to optimize the IT management process).

Jaadla and Johansson [37] state that the assessment of process maturity is commonly used as the starting point of identifying improvements that would be the most beneficial to perform. According to them, the continual improvement of service management processes can be measured by performing a process maturity assessment and comparing the organization's process performance against a best-practice reference set of processes.

Several assessment frameworks exist; however, the most existing assessments are qualitative in nature, which makes them expensive to apply, especially repeated regularly. Shrestha et al., [38] developed a Software-mediated Process Assessment (SMPA) approach that enables the assessment of ITSM processes. The SMPA approach includes process selection; an online survey to collect assessment data; a measurement of process capability; and a report of process improvement recommendations. The SMPA approach supports decision-making on process improvements.

Cortina et al., [39] present the Tudor IT Process Assessment (TIPA) framework to improve ITSM process assessment which can be used to increase the business value of IT services. According to Silva et al., [40] TIPA-framework does not have any relationship between Enterprise Architecture (EA) principles that are useful in understanding organizations and the business. Silva et al., [40] create graphical notation which closes the gap between Enterprise Architecture (EA) and TIPA making it easier for organizations to improve (visualize) their processes and achieve desired process maturity levels.

The research of Abdelkebir et al., [13] aims to identify the important aspects that propose a practical agile framework for ITSM. Their study enables decision-makers to improve and measure agility enhancements and hence, compare the agility of Information Systems before and after Agile Process Maturity Framework (APMF) deploying. Cater-Steel and Lepmets [41] present IT service quality measurement framework in industry to propose feasibility of measuring of interlinked IT service quality aspects. Findings of Cater-Steel and Lepmets support systemic approach to IT service measurement because various service areas are interlinked and stability of IT service impacts on process performance and customer satisfaction.

Jäntti [42] describes the KISMET (Keys to IT Service Management Excellence Technique) model for process improvement. Phases are: 1) Create a process improvement infrastructure, 2) Perform a process assessment, 3) Plan process improvement actions 4) Improve/Implement the process based on ITSM practices, 5) Deploy and introduce the process, 6) Evaluate process improvement, and 7) Continuous process/service improvement. From the CSI point of view, KISMET model's phases could be used to form a structure to the seven-step improvement process's Implement improvement phase.

3.4 What Opportunities Could an Automation Bring to a Seven-Step Improvement Process?

Shiono et al., [43] propose a graphic visualization of the relationship between processes and documents. Their approach helps to improve work efficiency and management processes. Related to documentation, Ahmad et al., [44] present proper documentation and effective process design can give directions to organizations to implement ISO/IEC 20000 in an effective way. According to Krishnan and Ravindran [45] digital transformation forces the organization to implement automation solutions to meet demands of the digital services. Krishnan and Ravindran reviewed the automation scope of ITIL process perspective and identified that in service operation processes have the highest scope for automation opportunities (75% to 85%) and CSI 20% to 25%. Guzman et al., [46] present in their study that Twitter messages (tweets) contain important information for software improvement and requirements evolution (e.g., feature requests, bug reports and feature shortcoming descriptions). The study of Rouhani [47] focused on ITSM software selection to achieve successful ITSM implementation. She/he proposed ITIL-based framework present ITSM software selection criteria such as functional and non-functional requirements.

4   Discussion

4.1   Aspect of Continual Service Improvement in Literature

In the academic literature, studies on the systematic implementation of the CSI or seven-step improvement process in the ITSM context is a rarely studied topic. There is a lot of research on how ITIL processes and service management can be improved using other industry methodology such as Six Sigma and Lean. Six Sigma refers to a statistical measure to indicate the defect within a process [22] and Lean can be applied in situations where the process is already in use but need for improvements [48]. From this point of view, Six sigma and Lean would have brought a slightly different perspective focusing more on fixing problems than creating a process to improve service continually [48]. The way, how the improvement to the IT service is produced, contains a weak visibility of impacts, modeling, and metrics [24, 23]. According to the literature, CSI is an important phase, but articles mainly focus on describing the CSI as a part of ITIL framework. Terminologically, CSI is discussed in academia confusingly: various concepts are used without a clear definition such as CSI process, CSI activities, CSI program, 7-step process activity items, and Continuous Service Improvement Program (CSIP). In this case, forming a perception is challenging due to missing and vague definitions. Summary of literature contribution is presented on Table 2.

Table 2. Aspect of CSI in literature

No.	Researcher	Contribution
1	Donko (2014)	Present results of using Six Sigma methodology
2	Herrera & van Hillegersberg (2019)	Propose an integrated approach of Lean Six Sigma for Continuous Improvement (CI) to IT Services
3	Lamichhane (2019)	Present that it is unclear how to start to implement the ITIL CSI process
4	Lima et al., (2012)	Present that CSI improvement suffer of weak visibility of impacts, modeling, and metrics
5	Trinkenreich et al., (2018)	Identify that IT service managers faced difficulties related to define and monitor IT service goals and strategy
6	Yamamoto (2017)	Identify maturity level problem related to 7-step process activity items
7	Kummamuru (2011)	Propose a CSI framework to ensuring systematic service improvement

4.2   Identify and Manage Improvements Related to IT Service and ITSM Processes

According to the literature, improvements could be identified to have two focuses: 1) the service that is provided and 2) the way (process) that the service is provided. A large number of studies focus on making a resolution of an IT service provider's specific ITSM process problem. In those studies, case organization's challenges were analyzed to identify the root cause of the problem and then discover how the ITIL processes can be improved. These studies support the search for solutions to identify similar problems, for example in the development of an incident management process. However, through these studies, it is challenging to clarify a systematic and repeatable seven-step improvement management process which could be implemented to the IT service provider organization. Abdelkebir et al., [13] study presents that ITSM maturity is low (Level 1–2) which could indicate why only few CSI related papers are found in literature review. A process is an agreed way to accomplish something including steps, inputs, outputs and process monitoring which can be used to verify the outcome of the process. For example, ISO/IEC 20000-1:2018 [4] defines requirements to continual improvement where the process consists of the following steps: improvements are documented, improvement's goal have been set (e.g., quality, value, cost, productivity, and risk reduction), improvements are prioritized, improvements are planned, improvements are implemented, improvements are measured, and improvements are reported. To support the implementation of improvements related to IT services and ITSM processes, future research could explore the possibility of adding a new step to the seven-step improvement process (e.g., evaluate the effectiveness of implemented improvements). Summary of literature contribution is presented on Table 3.

Table 3. Identify and manage improvements related to IT service and ITSM processes

No.	Researcher	Contribution
8	Arisenta et al., 2020	Change management process
9	Lineberry (2019)	Knowledge management
10	Macías et al., (2018)	Service catalogue management
11	Indra & Hendra (2018)	Project management
12	Ilvarianto & Legowo (2017)	Incident management process
13	Yuan et al., (2017)	Feedback management and knowledge management
14	Karkošková (2018)	Continual cloud service improvement management process
15	Dos Santos et al., (2011)	ITSM processes and people perspective
16	Kajbaf (2011)	Report types (reporting process)
17	Kirilov & Mitev (2021)	Improvements can be identify from experienced results or during regular audits

(continued)

Table 3. (*continued*)

No.	Researcher	Contribution
18	Jaadla & Johansson (2019)	Design a quotative measuring tool to a recurring maturity self assessment
19	Shrestha et al., (2016)	Develop a Software-mediated Process Assessment (SMPA) approach that enables assessment of ITSM processes
20	Cortina et al., (2013)	Present Tudor IT Process Assessment (TIPA) framework to improve ITSM process assessment
21	Silva et al., (2015)	Create graphical notation between Enterprise Architecture (EA) and TIPA
22	Abdelkebir et al., (2017)	Propose Agile Process Maturity Framework (APMF)
23	Cater-Steel & Lepmets (2014)	Systemic approach to IT service measurement
24	Jäntti (2012)	Keys to IT Service Management Excellence Technique (KISMET) model for process improvement

4.3 Improving and Automating the Seven-Step Improvement Process

Related to literature, the scope of the seven-step improvement process automation is 20–25% [45]. These results could be increased if the maturity of the seven-step improvement process increases. The maturity of the seven-step improvement process shall be more to support other ITSM process capability and overall organizational maturity. The assessment of process maturity is commonly used as the starting point to identify improvements that would be the most beneficial to perform [37]. From the continual improvement point of view, the seven-step improvement process should be applicable at any ITSM processes and organizational levels. Otherwise, it would not support improvements and increasing maturity in immature IT service provider organizations where it is needed most. Summary of literature contribution is presented on Table 4.

Table 4. Improving and automating the seven-step improvement process

No	Researcher	Contribution
25	Shiono et al., (2021)	Propose graphic visualization of the relationship between processes and documents to understand ITSM structure
26	Ahmad et al., (2020)	Identify challenges related to the ISO/IEC 20000 implementation (e.g., senior management support, justification of investment, cooperation among IT support teams, documentation and effective process design)

(*continued*)

Table 4. (continued)

No	Researcher	Contribution
27	Krishnan & Ravindran (2017)	Identify that CSI automation opportunities are 20% to 25%
28	Guzman et al., 2017)	Propose analysis techniques to summarizing, classifying, and prioritizing tweets
29	Rouhani (2017)	Present ITSM software criteria to achieve successful ITSM implementation

5 Conclusion

This study aimed at answering the research problem: How could IT service providers manage continual improvement in a systematic way? The goal of this paper was to present results of systematic literature review increasing understanding about the CSI and seven-step improvement process, and provide topics for future research. The research is related to ITIL-based CSI and its seven-step improvement process because ITIL is a widely used framework for managing IT services and its vocabulary and practices are familiar to IT service providers. Our main finding is that CSI-related terminology needs clarification and consistency both in academia and in practice to guide the future CSI research for example clarify roles and internal practices of CSI; provide a staged approach for continual improvement; and identify models that support improving and automating the seven-step improvement process.

The study consisted of four research questions. Regarding the first research question "What is the current state of a seven-step improvement process in literature" we focused on present CSI related studies in the context of IT service management. Our findings indicate that, in the literature, there was not much research on the CSI phase and its seven-step improvement process which could be used to improve IT services and ITSM processes systematically.

Our findings from the second research question "What kind of ITSM process improvement have been identified from literature?" revealed that process improvement has been studied, especially from the point of view of Lean and Six Sigma methods. From this point of view, Six sigma and Lean would have brought a slightly different perspective focusing more on fixing problems than creating a process to improve service continually [48].

The third research question "How to identify and manage improvements related to IT services and ITSM processes?" focused on study models which support to improve and implement ITSM process and IT services. Maturity and quality aspects in IT services and ICT systems could not be improved without systematic management of improvements. We observed that identifying and managing improvements may need for example: 1) frameworks for process assessment, quality auditing and Enterprise Architecture to defining planned goals for improvement, 2) prioritization and roadmap for improvement implementation, 3) managing the transition such as Project Management, and 4) the evaluation of improvement.

The fourth research question "What opportunities could an automation bring to a seven-step improvement process?" focused on aspects of how to use automation and process visualization to implement the seven-step improvement process. Automation can be used, for example, to increase visualization of the relationships between processes and documents [43], and to analyze service management records and tweets [46].

The following limitations are related to this study: First, the literature review was conducted by one researcher, the first author. Several researchers would have helped in the analysis of the literature review results. Second, the study was conducted within a limited time. A longer research period would have resulted in more studies and deepened analysis. We aimed at improving the validity of the study by using Kitchenham [19] guidelines for performing Systematic Literature Reviews. Reliability was improved by utilizing datastore and maintaining the chain of evidence. Future studies could focus on examining the seven-step improvement process in more detail and identifying the interfaces to other ITSM processes and ISO/IEC 20000-1:2018 standard requirements for continual improvement as part of the whole process.

References

1. Lloyd, W., Lacy, S., Hanna, A.: ITIL Continual Service Improvement. 2nd edn. The Stationery Office (TSO), London (2011)
2. Shrestha, A., Cater-Steel, A., Toleman, M., Rout, T.: Towards transparent and efficient process assessments for IT service management. In: Mitasiunas, A., Rout, T., O'Connor, R.V., Dorling, A. (eds.) Software Process Improvement and Capability Determination. CCIS, vol. 477, pp. 165–176. Springer, Cham (2014). https://doi.org/10.1007/978-3-319-13036-1_15
3. Kemppainen, J., Tedre, M., Sutinen, E.: IT service management education in Tanzania: an organizational and grassroots-level perspective. In: Proceedings of the 13th Annual Conference on Information Technology Education, pp. 99–104. ACM, New York (2012)
4. ISO/IEC: ISO/IEC 20000-1:2018, Information technology. Service management. Part 1: Service management system requirements, International Organization for Standardization (2018)
5. International Assessor Certification Scheme (Intacs.info): SPICE for IT-Services - Process Reference and Assessment Model, 11 June 2022. https://intacs.info/index.php/component/rsfiles/download-file/files?path=SPICE%2BDocuments%252FSPICE%2Bfor%2BIT-Services%252FSPICE-for-IT-Services-V4.0-released.pdf&Itemid=750. Accessed 7 July 2023
6. Craig, J., Yetton, P.: Business process redesign: a critique of process innovation by Thomas davenport as a case study in the literature. Aust. J. Manag. 17(2), 285–306 (1992)
7. Keel, A., Orr, M., Hernandez, R., Patrocinio, E., Bouchard, J.: From a technology-oriented to a service-oriented approach to IT management. BM Syst. J. 46(3), 549–565 (2007)
8. Cater-Steel, A.: IT service departments struggle to adopt a service-oriented philosophy. Int. J. Inf. Syst. Serv. Sect. (IJISSS) 1(2), 69–77 (2009)
9. Tan, W., Cater-Steel, A., Toleman, M.: Implementing it service management: a case study focussing on critical success factors. J. Comput. Inf. Syst. 50(2), 1–12 (2009)
10. IT Governance Institute (ITGI): Global Status Report on the Governance of Enterprise It (Geit - 2011) (2011)
11. Van Bon, J.: IT Service Management: An Introduction, 3rd edn. Van Haren Publishing, Zaltbommel (2007)
12. Adams, S., Cartlidge, A., Hanna, A., Range, S., Sowerby, J., Windebank, J.: ITIL V3 Foundation Handbook. TSO Information and Publishing Solutions, London, UK (2009)

13. Abdelkebir, S., Maleh, Y., Belaissaoui, M.: An agile framework for ITS management in organizations: a case study based on DevOps. In: Proceedings of the 2nd International Conference on Computing and Wireless Communication Systems (ICCWCS 2017), pp. 1–8, New York, ACM (2017)

14. Boonen, H., Brand, K.: IT Governance Based on COBIT 4.1 - A Management Guide. Van Haren Publishing (2007)

15. Ebert, C., Gallardo, G., Hernantes, J., Serrano, N.: DevOps. IEEE Softw. **33**(3), 94–100 (2016)

16. Agh, H., Ramsin, R.: Scrum metaprocess: a process line approach for customizing Scrum. Software Qual. J. **29**(2), 337–379 (2021)

17. Yamamoto, S.: A continuous approach to improve IT management. Procedia Comput. Sci. **121**, 27–35 (2017)

18. Kitchenham, B., Dypa, T., Jorgense, M.: Evidence-based software engineering. In: Proceedings of the 26th International Conference on Software Engineering, pp. 273–281. IEEE Computer Society, Los Alamitos CA (2004)

19. Kitchenham, B., Charters, S.: Guidelines for performing systematic literature reviews in Software Engineering. Version 2.3, EBSE Technical Report EBSE-2007-01. Keele University and University of Durh (2007)

20. Petticrew, M., Roberts, H.: Systematic Reviews in the Social Sciences: A Practical Guide. Blackwell Publishing, USA (2006)

21. Donko, D.: Improvement of the process quality in the service provider organization. In: Proceedings of the 2014 X International Symposium on Telecommunications (BIHTEL), pp. 1–5. IEEE, Sarajevo (2014)

22. Herrera, M., van Hillegersberg, J.: Using metamodeling to represent lean six sigma for IT service improvement. In: Proceedings of the 21st Conference on Business Informatics (CBI), pp. 241–248. IEEE, Moscow (2019)

23. Lamichhane, N.: Implementing continual service improvement in business enterprises: a proposal to improve business effectiveness of Nepal. Int. J. Adv. Res. Publ. (IJARP) **3**, 238–251 (2019)

24. Lima, A., Sauve, J., Souza, N.: Capturing the quality and business value of IT services using a business-driven model. IEEE Trans. Netw. Serv. Manage. **9**(4), 421–432 (2012)

25. Trinkenreich, B., Conte, T., Barcellos, M., Santos, G.: Defining, measuring and monitoring IT service goals and strategies: preliminary results and pitfalls from a qualitative study with IT service managers. In: Proceedings of the 12th ACM/IEEE International Symposium on Empirical Software Engineering and Measurement (ESEM 2018), pp. 1–10. ACM, New York (2018)

26. Kummamuru, S.: Framework for continuous service improvement (CSI): optimizing by dovetailing different systemic frameworks. In: Proceedings of the International Conference on Quality and Reliability (ICQR 2011), pp. 307–311. IEEE (2011)

27. Arisenta, R., Suharjito, A., Sukmandhani, A.: Evaluation model of success change management in banking institution based on ITIL V3 (Case Study). In: Proceedings of the International Conference on Information Management and Technology (ICIMTech), pp. 470–475. IEEE (2020)

28. Lineberry, R.: Solve and evolve: practical applications for knowledge-centered service. In: Proceedings of the 2019 ACM SIGUCCS Annual Conference (SIGUCCS 2019), pp. 70–75. ACM, New York (2019)

29. Macias, C., Alonso, I., Vélez, D.: Valuation of the management of the information technology services catalog in public organizations in the province of Manabí, Ecuador. In: Proceedings of the 2018 10th International Conference on Information Management and Engineering (ICIME 2018), pp. 193–199. ACM, New York (2018)

30. Indra, R., Hendra, P.: Strategy implementing continual service improvement with ITIL framework at PT. Anabatic Technologies Tbk. Int. Res. J. Comput. Sci. (IRJCS) **5**(2), 70–76 (2018)
31. Ilvarianto, D., Legowo, N.: Incident management implementation using continual service improvement method at PT AOP. In: Proceedings of the International Conference on Applied Computer and Communication Technologies (ComCom), pp. 1–7. IEEE (2017)
32. Yuan, Y., Qi, K., Marcus, A.: Gamifying HPE service manager to improve IT service desks' knowledge contribution. In: Proceedings of the 10th EAI International Conference on Simulation Tools and Techniques (SIMUTOOLS 2017), pp. 141–148. ACM, New York (2017)
33. Dos Santos, C., Granville, L., Cheng, W., Loewenstern, D., Shwartz, L., Anerousis, N.: Performance management and quantitative modeling of IT service processes using mashup patterns. In: Proceedings of the 7th International Conference on Network and Services Management (CNSM 2011), Laxenburg, AUT, International Federation for Information Processing, pp. 10–18 (2011)
34. Karkošková, S.: Towards cloud computing management model based on ITIL processes. In: Proceedings of the 2nd International Conference on Business and Information Management (ICBIM 2018), pp. 1–5. ACM, New York (2018)
35. Kajbaf, M., Madani, N., Suzangar, S., Nasher, S., Kalantarian, S.: An IT service reporting framework for effective implementation of ITIL continual service improvement process conforming to ISO/EC 20000. In: Proceedings of the Fifth International Conference on Digital Society (ICDS 2011), IARIA, pp. 18–23 (2011)
36. Kirilov, L., Mitev, Y.: An approach for implementing the information technology infrastructure library. Comptes Rendus de l'Académie Bulgare Des Sciences : Sciences Mathématiques et Naturelles. **74**(5), 729–737 (2021)
37. Jaadla, H., Johansson, B.: A self-assessment tool for estimation of IT maturity. In: Proceedings of the 15th European Conference on Management, Leadership and Governance (ECMLG 2019), pp. 207–2016. Academic Conferences and Publishing Limited (2019)
38. Shrestha, A., Cater-Steel, A., Toleman, M.: Virtualising process assessments to facilitate continual service improvement in IT service management. In: Proceedings of the Australasian Conference on Information Systems, arXiv.org, pp. 1–15 (2016)
39. Cortina, S., Renault, A., Picard, M.: TIPA process assessments: a means to improve business value of IT services. Int. J. Strateg. Inf. Technol. Appl. (IJSITA) **4**(4), 1–18 (2013)
40. Silva, N., da Silva, M., Barafort, B., Vicente, M., Sousa, P.: Using ArchiMate to model a process assessment framework. In: Proceedings of the 30th Annual ACM Symposium on Applied Computing, pp. 1189–1194. ACM, New York (2015)
41. Cater-Steel, A., Lepmets, M.: Measuring IT service quality: evaluation of IT service quality measurement framework in industry. J. Serv. Sci. Res. **6**(1), 125–147 (2014)
42. Jäntti, M.: Improving IT service desk and service management processes in finnish tax administration: a case study on service engineering. In: Dieste, O., Jedlitschka, A., Juristo, N. (eds.) Product-Focused Software Process Improvement. LNCS, vol. 7343, pp. 218–232. Springer, Heidelberg (2012). https://doi.org/10.1007/978-3-642-31063-8_17
43. Shiono, Y., Yoshizumi, T., Goto, T., Tsuchida, K.: Fuzzy database and interface to analyze management system operations. In: Proceedings of the 8th International Virtual Conference on Applied Computing & Information Technology (ACIT), pp. 19–26. ACM, New York (2021)
44. Ahmad, N., Rabbany, M., Ali, S.: Organizational and human factors related challenges to ISO 20000: implications for environmental sustainability and circular economy. Int. J. Manpow. **41**(7), 987–1004 (2020)

45. Krishnan, G., Ravindran, V.: IT service management automation and its impact to IT industry. In: Proceedings of the International Conference on Computational Intelligence in Data Science (ICCIDS), pp. 1–4 (2017)

46. Guzman, E., Ibrahim, M., Glinz, M.: Prioritizing user feedback from Twitter: a survey report. In: Proceedings of the 4th International Workshop on CrowdSourcing in Software Engineering (CSI-SE 2017), pp. 21–24. IEEE Press (2017)

47. Rouhani, S.: A fuzzy superiority and inferiority ranking based approach for IT service management software selection. Kybernetes **46**(4), 728–746 (2017)

48. Ruostesaari, S.: Implementing continual service improvement process for Aberdeen standard ITSS division (2019). https://www.theseus.fi/bitstream/handle/10024/208709/Thesis_S-Ruostesaari_%20F2019.pdf?sequence=2&isAllowed=y. Accessed 2 Dec 2021

Elevating Software Quality Through Product Discovery Techniques: Key Findings from a Grey Literature Review

Stefan Trieflinger$^{(\boxtimes)}$, Lukas Weiss, and Jürgen Münch

Reutlingen University, Alteburgstraße 150, 72762 Reutlingen, Germany
{stefan.trieflinger,juergen.muench}@reutlingen-university.de,
lukas.weiss@student.reutlingen-university.de

Abstract. In the era of digital transformation, the notion of software quality transcends its traditional boundaries, necessitating an expansion to encompass the realms of value creation for customers and the business. Merely optimizing technical aspects of software quality can result in diminishing returns. Product discovery techniques can be seen as a powerful mechanism for crafting products that align with an expanded concept of quality—one that incorporates value creation. Previous research has shown that companies struggle to determine appropriate product discovery techniques for generating, validating, and prioritizing ideas for new products or features to ensure they meet the needs and desires of the customers and the business. For this reason, we conducted a grey literature review to identify various techniques for product discovery. First, the article provides an overview of different techniques and assesses how frequently they are mentioned in the literature review. Second, we mapped these techniques to an existing product discovery process from previous research to provide concrete guidelines for establishing product discovery in their organizations. The analysis shows, among other things, the increasing importance of techniques to structure the problem exploration process and the product strategy process. The results are interpreted regarding the importance of the techniques to practical applications and recognizable trends.

Keywords: product management · product discovery · user experience · software quality · digital transformation

1 Introduction

The environment for creating new products, services, and features is getting increasingly complex. This means that increasing market dynamics, rapid technology changes, and changing customer behaviors make it difficult to predict which products, features, or services will satisfy the customers' needs, especially in the long-time horizon. In addition, customers and users are seeking not just products and services but more experience [1]. These factors pose new challenges for companies when considering software quality. The IEEE Standard Glossary of Software Engineering Terminology defines software quality 1) as the degree to which a system, component, or process meets specified requirements

J. M. Fernandes et al. (Eds.): QUATIC 2023, CCIS 1871, pp. 45–59, 2023.
https://doi.org/10.1007/978-3-031-43703-8_4

and 2) the degree to which a system, component, or process meets customer or user needs or expectations [2]. These two definitions are combined in the quality pyramid (see Fig. 1) developed by Gojko Adzic [3].

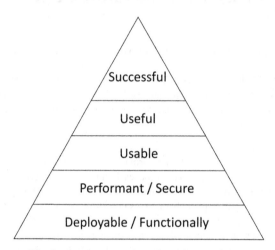

Fig. 1. Quality pyramid according to Adzic [3]

The lowest level (deployable/functionally) in the pyramid describes that the software must be deployable and meet the minimum functional requirements. Subsequently, the level "performant/secure" aims to ensure that non-functional requirements such as performance, reliability, security, etc., are fulfilled. After the software works well and fulfills non-functional requirements, usability aspects get relevant (usable). This means ensuring that customers or users can easily operate the features. However, this level does not address the issue of whether the features are used by customers or not. Therefore, in order to reach the level of useful, it is necessary to understand whether the software also satisfies real customer needs and helps them to make progress related to their customer goals. If attention is not paid to this, a development organization can run the risk of developing features that the customer does not need or want. Such features can incur further costs, e.g., for maintenance. Finally, care must be taken to ensure that software is successful in the sense that it contributes to economic goals. This is the top level of the quality pyramid. In practice, it can often be observed that companies focus on fulfilling the two lowest levels of the quality pyramid. This often results in software that is functional but either not needed by customers (i.e., no or low value is delivered to customers) or too complicated to use (i.e., there is insufficient usability). For these reasons, more and more companies are struggling to develop products that deliver value to customers and thus contribute to the achievement of high product quality [3].

Regardless of whether an elevated understanding of software quality is described in a quality pyramid, as here, or whether another model is used, digital transformation requires an expanded understanding of the concept of software quality that enables features or entire products to be linked to value creation. Product discovery can be understood as a mechanism for developing products that correspond to such an expanded concept of quality [4]. Product discovery is the ability of a company to identify and validate products that either solve an existing problem for which there is currently no solution or that enable customers to solve a problem more efficiently and effectively than with existing solutions [5]. Therefore, product discovery focuses on the identification and exploration of problems of potential customers as well as finding solutions that are useful, feasible, and economically viable. In simple terms, product discovery aims to quickly separate the good ideas from the bad to answer the question of which products, features, or services should be developed to fulfill the customers' needs. However, in practice, most companies do not conduct product discovery, and experts or management determine which products should be developed and delivered to the customers [6]. The main reason is that most companies do not know how to conduct product discovery systematically. This means that companies need to better understand which phases a product discovery process includes and which techniques can be applied in each phase [7]. With regards to the former, a study conducted by Münch et al. [7] revealed that a typical product discovery process includes the phases 1) **alignment** (align various stakeholders on the most important cornerstones of the product development project), 2) **research** (gain an understanding of user and customer problems), 3) **ideation** (develop creative ideas based on learnings of the conduction of previous phases), 4) **creation** (translate the ideas into tangible products or features), 5) **validation and refinement** (build prototypes to collect customer feedback). However, the authors do not answer the question of which methods companies can perform in each of these phases. In order to close this gap, this paper aims to identify suitable techniques for each phase of the product discovery process defined by Münch et al. [7]. Therefore, this study can be considered as an extension of the research by Münch et al. [7] and is intended to provide companies with guidelines for the establishment of product discovery techniques.

2 Related Work

A comprehensive description of related work can be found in Münch et al. [7]. For space limitations, we focus on selected aspects.

In scientific literature, product discovery is often referred to as continuous experimentation. Fagerholm et al. [8] mention that a suitable experimentation environment requires at least the ability to create minimum viable products (MVPs). Moreover, the environment for experimentation must also enable the creation and management of experimentation plans, include experiment findings in a product roadmap, and manage a flexible business strategy. Bosch [9] presents the concept of an innovation experiment system. This concept includes first the development of a hypothesis based on customer paints points or business goals. Subsequently, metrics to measure the hypothesis must be defined. After these steps, a minimum viable product can be created in order to collect data. This data is analyzed and serve as input for accepting or rejecting the hypothesis. If the hypothesis is confirmed, the strategy can proceed, and the product or feature can be fully implemented. Otherwise, the impact of the invalid hypotheses must be analyzed, which could lead to an adjustment of the product strategy. Finally, Münch et al. [7] conducted a grey literature review in order to gain a better understanding of product discovery in practice. In this context, the authors identified motivations and challenges and proposed a process to conduct product discovery. As mentioned in the introduction, Münch et al. [7] propose several phases to apply product discovery. However, this research lacks insights into which techniques are suitable for the conduction of each phase. From our point of view, the provision of concrete techniques is a crucial aspect of providing appropriate guidelines to practitioners. Therefore, the study at hand aims to identify suitable product discovery techniques and maps them to the phases proposed by Münch et al. [7].

3   Research Approach

This paper aims to identify specific techniques for the application in the various phases of the product discovery process. To achieve this, the practical experience and knowledge of practitioners are required. To collect such experience and knowledge systematically and repeatably, grey literature reviews (GLRs) have emerged as a promising approach in recent years. A GLR is a structured process in order to analyze sources of the grey literature such as blogs or white papers. We decided to conduct a grey literature review since practitioners often use grey literature to report their experiences. In order to structure the GLR, we apply the guidelines from Garousi et al. [10], which consist of the three main phases 1) planning the review, 2) conducting the review, and 3) reporting the review (see Table 1). It should be noted that we applied the approach of a grey literature review in previous studies. Therefore, the following description of the research method is based on the following studies [e.g., 11, 12, 13].

Table 1. Design of the grey literature review

Planning the Review	• Identification of the need for a GLR
	• Formulation of the research questions and scope of the study
	• Definition and refinement of the search string
	• Determination of the inclusion and exclusion criteria
Conducting the review	• Usage of the search string
	• Conduction of a quality assessment
	• Data extraction
Reporting the review	• Writing down the findings as documentation

3.1 Planning the Review

Identification of the Need for a Grey Literature Review: First, we considered whether a GLR is suitable for our research. Therefore, we applied the checklist provided by Garousi et al. [10], which consists of seven questions. Garousi et al. [10] propose conducting a GLR if one or more questions can be answered positively. Otherwise, a systematic literature review is more suitable. Our answers related to this paper are shown in Table 2.

To answer the first and third question, a systematic literature review was conducted on product roadmapping, which is closely related to the topic of product discovery. This review showed that the conduction of product discovery is highly relevant for the success of product roadmapping. However, none of the identified papers discuss techniques for conducting the various phases of the product discovery process. To answer questions six and seven served, an expert interview study [14] that indicates that the question of which techniques should be conducted in the different product discovery phases is of great interest to practitioners. For these reasons, a grey literature review contributes to transferring practical knowledge to the scientific community and the industry.

Table 2. Checklist to Garousi et al. [10]

ID	Question	Answer
1	Is the subject "complex" and not solvable by considering only the formal literature?	Yes
2	Is there a lack of volume or quality of evidence or a lack of consensus on outcome measurement in the formal literature?	No
3	Is the contextual information relevant to the subject under study?	Yes
4	Is it the goal to validate or corroborate scientific outcomes with practical experience?	No
5	Is it the goal to challenge assumptions or falsify results from practice using academic research or vice versa?	No
6	Would a synthesis of insights and evidence from the industrial and academic communities be useful to one or even both communities?	Yes
7	Is there a large volume of practitioner sources indicating high practitioner interest in a topic?	Yes

Scope of the Study and Formulation of the Research Questions: In particular, companies that are operating in the software-intensive business are facing the challenge of high market dynamics with the associated uncertainties. This situation complicates the development of products, features, or services that fulfill the needs of the customers, and thus specific techniques are required that can be executed efficiently and effectively. Therefore, the objective of our study is to identify techniques that can be conducted in the various phases of the product discovery process. Based on this goal, we have defined the following research questions:

- **RQ1:** Which product discovery techniques are mentioned in the grey literature, and how often?
- **RQ2:** How can these techniques be mapped to a product discovery process?

We answer RQ2 based on the product discovery process of Münch et al. [7]. It should be noted that, in general, various recommendations for the conduction of a product discovery process exist. We chose the product discovery process proposed by Münch et al. [7] since it was developed based on insights from the grey literature.

Identification of the Search String: For the search of articles, we developed a search string in a brainstorming session in which all authors participated. In this context, we first defined a set of search terms, tested them with an initial search, and then iteratively adjusted them. Afterward, we connect the final terms with Boolean operators. We defined the following search terms (ST):

ST1: product discovery; ST2: process, ST3: method; ST4: tool.

The complete search string used for our search was: ST1 AND (ST2 OR ST3 OR ST4).

Definition of the Inclusion/Exclusion Criteria: In order to separate relevant from irrelevant articles, we used the inclusion and exclusion criteria as shown in Table 3.

Table 3. Inclusion and exclusion criteria

Inclusion	• The article discusses a technique to conduct product discovery
	• The article was published in English
	• The URL is working and freely available
Exclusion	• The source is non-text-based
	• The article contains the duplicated content of a previously examined article

3.2   Conducting the Review

Data Collection and Study Selection Process: The data collection process was conducted by using the search string mentioned above and applying it to the Google search engine (google.com). Previously, search history and cookies were deleted to minimize the impact of history and cookies on search results. Moreover, the language of the results was set to English, and the selection of any region was enabled. To increase the number of possible results, the Google option to include similar results was activated. The search was conducted in January 2023 and resulted in 401 hits. In addition, we conducted a snowballing process (i.e., considering further articles that are recommended in an article), which led to ten additional articles. Then we applied a study selection process consisting of the steps 1) delete duplicates, 2) scan the articles and 3) apply the defined inclusion and exclusion criteria. This leads to a final set of 36 relevant articles.

Quality Assessment: Since grey literature is not peer-reviewed like scientific papers, we subjected the relevant articles to a quality assessment. Therefore, we used the proposed quality assessment procedure by Garousi et al. [10]. This means that each relevant article was assessed based on the assessment criteria of the author's authority, the description of the objective and methodology of the articles as well as its novelty and impact. Each of these assessment criteria contained specific questions, such as whether the author is associated with a reputable organization or is the conclusion supported by the data. The entire assessment includes 16 questions that are rated based on a three-point Likert scale as follows: 1 point was assigned if the article fully met the assessment question, 0,5 points were awarded if the article partially met the assessment question, and 0 points were given if the article did not meet the assessment question. After all questions were answered, the points were summed up, and a total score was calculated. The maximum score that can be achieved is 16 points, while an article is considered trustworthy if it achieves a total score of 8 points. To answer the questions regarding the author's authority, we conduct additional investigations via Google. In addition, the assessment includes the question of how many backlinks an article contains to assess the impact of the article. To answer this question, we use the tool "Backlink Checker" (see https:// ahrefs.com/de/backlink-checker). Our detailed quality assessment was too extensive to attach to this paper. Therefore, it can be found on Figshare [15].

4 Results

4.1 Product Discovery Techniques

In order to answer RQ1, we analysed the relevant articles and identified 28 different techniques for conducting the different phases of the product discovery process. It should be noted that usually, several techniques are discussed in one article. Figure 2 shows the 15 most frequently mentioned articles we identified in our review. The most frequently mentioned techniques are 1) prototyping, 2) conducting customer interviews, and 3) the development of personas.

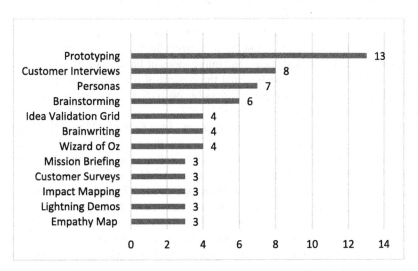

Fig. 2. Frequency of product discovery techniques in the identified articles.

Based on the experience of the authors, a few techniques that have gained importance in practice in recent years are selected and described below. Due to space limitations, we could not include all identified techniques in this paper. A list of all relevant articles can therefore be found on Figshare [16].

Wizard of Oz Prototyping: The goal of the method Wizard of Oz is to create the illusion of a functional product to allow testing before producing the final version. The idea behind this concept is that the user of a product interacts with a system that they believe to be autonomous but, in reality, is controlled by an invisible person (the wizard). Once the key features have been identified, refinement can take place through more in-depth user testing. One example of a Wizard of Oz prototype is from the company Aardvark which aims to connect people with questions with people best qualified to answer via a digital interface over the internet. The creation of such a network, including the algorithms, involves a lot of coding effort. However, the product team wanted to test the reactions of the users to the interface well before the coding was completed. For this reason, they used an instant messaging system and a team of people behind the scenes to physically reroute questions and answers to the right people. The result is that the product team learned a lot and developed their concept without investing in programming resources. The Wizard of Oz is often used in rapid development to improve the user experience. It is also helpful for AI-driven experiences because the range of system responses is virtually impossible to replicate with traditional prototyping tools [17–20].

Empathy Map: This method is designed to help product teams better understand their users or customers by capturing knowledge about their behaviour and attitudes. Therefore, empathy maps provide four quadrants: 1) says, 2) thinks, 3) does, and 4) hear. The quadrant "says" shows what the user says out loud, for example, in an interview. The "thinks" quadrant captures what the user is thinking about their experiences with the product. Example questions could be 1) what occupies the user's thoughts or 2) what matters to the user?". The "does" quadrant shows the actions that the user is currently performing. For example, refreshing web pages several times or shopping around to compare prices. Finally, the quadrant "hear" reflects the factors that influence the user. This can be, for example, statements and impressions of families or friends. An important aspect of using this approach is that the content of the individual sections is not filled arbitrarily but is based as much as possible on evidence (e.g., through interviews, observations, or results from workshops) [21, 22].

Gray and Osterwalder presented an extension of the Empathy Map called Empathy Map Canvas (see Fig. 3) [21]. The main extension was that in addition to the four Sects. 1) says, 2) thinks, 3) does, and 4) hears, the section goals was added to the Empathy Map Canvas. This should help product teams better understand the context of the customers or users. Moreover, the sections "pains" and "gains were added. The intention of this change is to emphasize that pains and gains (inside the box) can only be guessed or inferred, while the elements outside the user box (say, think, does, hear) can be answered through the conduction of interviews or observations. Product people can apply the Empathy Map Canvas by starting with the section "goals" and then working through the Canvas in a clockwise direction.

Lightning Demos: This method is a structured group session to gather ideas and inspiration on how to solve an identified problem. First, a facilitator should be designated to lead and moderate the Lightning Demo session. Then, the participants have 20–30 min to identify three products or services that have solved related problems to the one problem for which the participants are seeking ideas. Afterward, each participant presents his findings to the group. In this context, it is important that each presenter explains how the

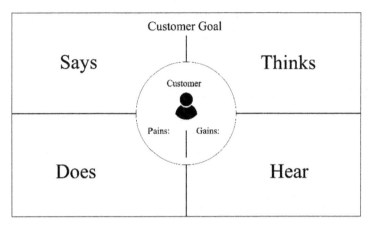

Fig. 3. Empathy Map Canvas, based on [22]

identified solution to a similar problem contributes to the solution of the current problem. Moreover, it is recommended to limit the duration of each presentation to 10–15 min to avoid dragging them out. After each participant has presented his three products or services, the result is an idea board that serves as inspiration for developing a solution to the identified problem [23, 24].

Mission Briefing: Herbig [25] suggests using the method of mission briefing within the phase alignment. This method consists of five parts 1) context, 2) higher intent, 3) team intent, 4) key implied tasks, and 5) boundaries. The mission briefing creates alignment by having the entire product team discuss the content of each section and agree on which aspects to include for each section. In this context, it is important to come to an agreement on every section before moving to the next one. The reason, therefore, is that decisions made in one section may have an impact on the content of the other sections.

Impact Mapping: Impact Mapping aims to align product teams to business objectives, test mutual understanding of objectives and expected outcomes, focus teams toward the highest value feature to deliver, and enable collaborative decision-making. In order to achieve this, this technique shows assumptions and connections between business goals, impacts on users and stakeholders, and team deliverables. Figure 4 shows an example of an impact map of an online gaming platform. In this context, the business goal is to increase the number of active players to 1 million. An example of an important actor is players. On the one hand, players can help to achieve to increase the number of players by posting about the games on social media platforms, recommending the games to their friends, or sending their friends an invitation to the games directly. In order to influence the behavior of the players so that they perform the aspects mentioned above, several deliverables can serve. For instance, semi-automated invitations can help to make sending invitations more comfortable, a more personalized gaming experience can increase the probability that players will invite friends, and reaching new levels should motivate players to share their gaming achievements on social media [26, 28].

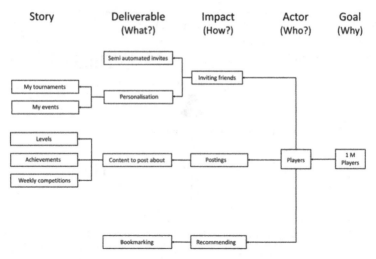

Fig. 4. Example of an Impact Map, based on [27]

Opportunity Solution Tree: Torres [29] suggests using Opportunity Solution Trees (see Fig. 5) to visually represent possible paths to reach a desired outcome. The construction of an Opportunity Solution Tree starts with defining a quantitative business outcome. This is followed by the discovery of opportunities that will drive that desired outcome. Below the opportunities, possible solutions that may contribute to the achievement of the respective opportunity are defined. The validation of whether a possible solution really leads to the fulfilment of the opportunity takes place in the space of assumption testing. According to Torres, the application of an Opportunity Solution Tree provides several benefits. For example, 1) resolving the tension between business needs and customer needs, 2) building and maintaining a shared understanding of how to achieve a desired outcome, 3) unlocking better decision-making and learning cycles, as well as 4) building confidence in knowing what steps to take next.

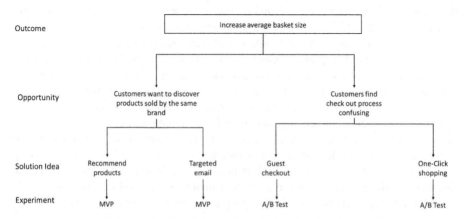

Fig. 5. Example of an Opportunity Solution Tree, based on [29]

4.2 Mapping the Product Discovery Techniques to the Phases of the Product Discovery Process

In order to answer RQ2, we mapped the identified product discovery techniques to the product discovery process proposed by Münch et al. [7]. As mentioned, the product discovery process by Münch et al. [7] consists of the stages of research, ideation, creation, validation, and refinement (see columns in Table 4). First of all, it should be mentioned that the techniques that we identified in our review can be applied in several phases of the discovery process. The reason, therefore, is that many techniques take a holistic approach and thus address many phases of the discovery process. A good example of this is the development of an Opportunity Solution Tree. This technique starts with the identification of outcomes that serve as input for the generation of opportunities, such as customer problems (phase research). Subsequently, a variety of solution ideas are defined (phase ideation), and a prioritization is conducted as to which opportunities should be tackled (phase creation). Finally, it is determined how (e.g., the development of a prototype) the high-priority ideas should be validated (phase validation and refinement). In more detail, we identify one technique that focuses on the creation of alignment. Ten techniques can be applied in the phase research, i.e., finding out what problems the customers have. Fifteen ideas can be applied to generate ideas (ideation), while nine techniques address the translation of the ideas identified into concrete outputs. Finally, six techniques consider the validation process in order to identify if the outputs contribute to solving the customer problems.

5 Threats to Validity

We use the framework according to Wohlin et al. [30, 31] in order to discuss the trustworthiness and validity of our study. **Construct validity:** First, the construct validity is threatened by the Google search engine in terms of the accessibility of the returned results. This means that after entering our search string Google, the search engine returns 648.000.000 articles. However, we have only access to 401 articles. We cannot verify that these 401 articles are representative of the total search results of 648.000.000. A second threat concerns the reproducibility of our study. In particular, a Google search using our search terms could produce results that do not exactly match the search results found in this study. Third, our defined search string presents a threat to the construct validity. There may be articles that discuss the topic of product discovery techniques but use different keywords than those our search string captured. Therefore, we cannot be excluded that we missed some relevant articles. **Internal validity:** To increase the criterion of internal validity, we subjected our relevant articles to a quality assessment. We use this measure to filter out those articles that have a high probability of providing untrustworthy content. **External validity:** The techniques we identified are particularly relevant in a dynamic market environment with associated uncertainties. Therefore, the finding of this study is not directly applicable to other industry sectors, such as mechanical engineering. However, it cannot be excluded that some aspects may bring benefits to other industries. **Conclusion validity:** In order to increase the conclusion validity, we

Table 4. Mapping product discovery techniques to the phases according to Münch et al. [7]

Method	Alignment	Research	Ideation	Creation	Validation and Refinement
Prototyping					X
Customer Interviews		X			
Personas				X	
Wizard of Oz					X
Brainstorming			X		
Empathy Map		X			
Idea Validation Grid					X
Brainwriting			X		
Lightning Demo			X		
Mission Briefing	X				
Customer Surveys		X			
Impact Mapping		X	X	X	
Opportunity Solution Tree		X	X	X	X
Job Story			X	X	
Jobs to be Done		X	X		
Customer Journey Mapping		X	X	X	
Opportunity Assessment			X	X	
Usability Testing					X
The Five Whys		X			
Assumption Mapping					X
User Story Mapping			X	X	
Value vs. Complexity Matrix			X		
Value Proposition Canvas			X	X	
Product Vision Board			X	X	
Product Analytics		X			
Ideation Risk Matrix		X			

(continued)

Table 4. (*continued*)

Method	Alignment	Research	Ideation	Creation	Validation and Refinement
Actor-Job-Outcome Mapping			X		
Uncertainty-Impact Matrix			X		

discuss our findings with one practitioner who has several years of experience in conducting product discovery activities. These discussions have not revealed any ambiguities or inconsistencies.

6 Conclusion

In this paper, we conducted a grey literature review and identified 28 product discovery techniques and assigned them to the discovery phases of 1) alignment, 2) research, 3) ideation, 4) creation, and 5) validation and refinement. Conducting product discovery is critical to identify and validate risky assumptions before starting product development. The analysis showed that in addition to classic instruments such as interviews and surveys, techniques regarding the validation phase are on the rise. Examples are techniques such as Idea Validation Grid, Wizard of Oz, or Assumption Mapping. In addition, techniques for structuring the research process, such as Opportunity Trees or Impact Mapping, are gaining more and more attention. This indicates that practitioners are increasingly concerned with the importance of conducting product discovery and seeking ways to implement it. From the industry point of view, practitioners can use our findings as guidelines and best practices to establish product discovery activities in their organization. The establishment of product discovery activities is critical to developing high-quality products that satisfy the needs of the customers. From a scientific point of view, we transfer practical knowledge in the field of software engineering research. Until now, only a few researchers have focused on exploring the topic of product discovery. Therefore, we hope that our work inspires research to position research in the area of product discovery.

References

1. Kim, E., Beckman, S., Agogino, A.: Design roadmapping in an uncertain world: implementing a customer-experience-focused strategy. Calif. Manage. Rev. **61**(1), 43–70 (2018)
2. IEEE Standards Committee: IEEE standard glossary of software engineering terminology. IEEE std 610 (1990): 12
3. Adzic, G. https://gojko.net/2012/05/08/redefining-software-quality/. Accessed 29 May 2023
4. Torres, T.: Continuous Discovery Habits: Discover Products that Create Customer Value and Business Value. Product Talk LLC (2021)

5. Cagan, M.: How to Create Tech Products Customers Love. Wiley, Hoboken, New Jersey (2017)
6. Münch, J., Trieflinger, S., Lang, D.: DEEP: the product roadmap maturity model: a method for assessing the product roadmapping capabilities of organizations. In: Proceedings of the International Workshop on Software-Intensive Business (SiBW): Start-ups, Platforms, and Ecosystems, pp. 19–24. ACM (2019)
7. Münch, J., Trieflinger, S., Heisler, B.: Product discovery–building the right things: insights from a grey literature review. In: Proceedings of the International Conference on Engineering, Technology, and Innovation (ICE/ITMC), pp. 1–8. IEEE (2020)
8. Fagerholm, F., Guinea, A.S., Mäenpää, H., Münch, J.: Building blocks for continuous experimentation. In: Proceedings of the 1st International Workshop on Rapid Continuous Software Engineering, pp. 26–35. ACM (2014)
9. Bosch, J.: Building products as innovation experiment systems. In: Cusumano, M.A., Iyer, B., Venkatraman, N. (eds.) Software Business. LNBIP, vol. 114, pp. 27–39. Springer, Heidelberg (2012). https://doi.org/10.1007/978-3-642-30746-1_3
10. Garousi, V., Felderer, M., Mäntylä, V.: Guidelines for including grey literature and conducting multivocal literature reviews in software engineering. Inf. Softw. Technol. **106**, 101–121 (2019)
11. Münch, J., Trieflinger, S., Bogazköy, E., Eißler, P., Roling, B.: Product roadmap formats for an uncertain future: a grey literature review. In: Proceedings of the Euromicro Conference on Software Engineering and Advanced Applications (SEAA), pp. 284–291. IEEE (2020)
12. Trieflinger, S., Münch, J., Bogazköy, E., Eißler, P., Schneider, J., Roling, B.: How to prioritize your product roadmap when everything feels important: a grey literature review. In: Proceedings of the International Conference on Engineering, Technology and Innovation (ICE/ITMC), pp. 1–9. IEEE (2021)
13. Trieflinger, S., Münch, J., Petrik, D., Lang, D.: Why traditional product roadmaps fail in dynamic markets: global insights. In: Taibi, D., Kuhrmann, M., Mikkonen, T., Klünder, J., Abrahamsson, P. (eds.) Proceedings of the International Conference on Product-Focused Software Process Improvement (PROFES), pp. 21–23, Springer, Cham (2022). https://doi.org/10.1007/978-3-031-21388-5_26
14. Münch, J., Trieflinger, S., Lang, D.: What's hot in product roadmapping? Key practices and success factors. In: Franch, X., Männistö, T., Martínez-Fernández, S. (eds.) Product-Focused Software Process Improvement. LNCS, vol. 11915, pp. 401–416. Springer, Cham (2019). https://doi.org/10.1007/978-3-030-35333-9_29
15. Figshare: Quality assessment, conducted by the authors. https://figshare.com/s/42d67f711 67be5988a21. Accessed 29 May 2023
16. Figshare: List of all relevant articles including in this review. https://figshare.com/s/a9d195 d9d282074cdd35. Accessed 29 May 2023
17. McGovern, N.: https://blog.prototypr.io/wizard-of-oz-prototyping-process-blog-a20ffc e8886. Accessed 29 May 2023
18. AnswerLab. https://www.answerlab.com/insights/wizard-of-oz-testing. Accessed 29 May 2023
19. Breaker. https://futureofstuffchallenge.org/download/prototype/bootleg-wizardofoz.pdf. Accessed 29 May 2023
20. UX4Sight. https://ux4sight.com/blog/wizard-of-oz-prototyping. Accessed 29 May 2023
21. UX Booth. https://www.uxbooth.com/articles/empathy-mapping-a-guide-to-getting-inside-a-users-head/. Accessed 9 May 2023
22. Niels Norman Group, Empathy Mapping. https://www.nngroup.com/articles/empathy-mapping/. Accessed 29 May 2023
23. Relab Academy. https://relab.academy/design-sprint/lightning-demo-a-fast-way-to-ignite-inspiration-in-a-design-sprint/. Accessed 29 My 2023

24. Swiss innovation academy. https://store.swissinnovation.academy/view/courses/basics-of-ideation-for-innovation/200984-a-selection-of-ideation-techniques/586967-lightning-demos. Accessed 29 May 2023
25. Herbig, T.: https://herbig.co/product-discovery/. Accessed 29 May 2023
26. Neuri Consulting LLP. https://www.impactmapping.org/. Accessed 29 May 2023
27. Aktia. https://aktiasolutions.com/getting-started-with-product-discovery/. Accessed 29 May 2023
28. Adzic, G., Marjory, B.: Impact Mapping: Making a Big Impact with Software Products and Projects. Provoking Thoughts Limited (2012)
29. Torres, T: https://www.producttalk.org/2016/08/opportunity-solution-tree/. Accessed 29 May 2023
30. Wohlin, C., Runeson, P., Höst, M., Ohlsson, M.C., Regnell, B., Wesslen, A.: Experimentation in Software Engineering: An Introduction. Kluwer Academic Publishers (2000)
31. Runeson, P., Host, M.: Guidelines for conducting and reporting case study research in software engineering. Empir. Softw. Eng. **14**, 131–164 (2009)

Visual Milestone Planning in a Hybrid Development Context

Eduardo Miranda(✉) (iD)

Carnegie Mellon University, Pittsburgh, PA 15213, USA
mirandae@andrew.cmu.edu

Abstract. This paper explains the Visual Milestone Planning (VMP) method using an agile vocabulary to facilitate its adoption by agile practitioners as a front end for a hybrid development process. VMP is a visual and collaborative planning approach which promotes a shared understanding of the work approach and commitment through the direct manipulation by team members of the reified planning constructs involved in the development of the plan. Once the product backlog has been established and relevant milestones identified, a novel construct called the milestone planning matrix is used to document the allocation of product backlog items to milestones. The milestones due dates are later determined by grouping sticky notes representing the work to be performed into timeboxes called work packages and accommodating them on a resource and time scaled scheduling canvas very much as it would be done in a Tetris game.

Keywords: Milestone planning · Hybrid development · Agile project management

1 Introduction

Prominent agile authors have long advocated the need for a project to have an artifact to guide the work of a team through it. Cohn [1], for example, suggests the use of a release plan, without which "teams move endlessly from one iteration to the next"; Cockburn [2], adds "a coarse-grained project plan, possibly created from a project map or a set of stories and releases to make sure the project is delivering suitable business value for suitable expense in a suitable time period"; Highsmith [3], postulates a Speculate Phase, in which "a capability and/or feature-based release plan to deliver on the vision is developed as well as a wave (or milestone) plan spanning several iterations used as major synchronization and integration points"; and Brechner [4] writes "it's important to have a vision and a plan for achieving your project goals. Even crowdsourcing projects need an organizing principle and structure to allow everyone to contribute toward the shared outcome".

Although these authors discuss the characteristics these plans must show, e.g. that the plan must be formulated, not in terms of the tasks to be performed but rather in terms of the outcomes the project must deliver and how they must be elaborated, e.g.

J. M. Fernandes et al. (Eds.): QUATIC 2023, CCIS 1871, pp. 60–75, 2023.
https://doi.org/10.1007/978-3-031-43703-8_5

collectively by the team and not by a solitary project manager who later hands it down to it for execution, they do not provide a method for doing it.

This approach to planning was first proposed by Andersen [5] who called it Milestone Planning. In his seminal article, Andersen defines a milestone "as result to be achieved … a description of a condition or a state that the project should reach by a certain point in time. A milestone describes what is to be fulfilled, but not the method to fulfil it". In a subsequent work [6], he describes milestone planning as an activity to be performed by the group stating "We strongly emphasize the motivational and inspirational aspects of planning. They are often neglected in practice so that planning becomes a tedious chore carried out on the project manager's desk or PC. This results in a lack of ownership of the plan by the parties involved in the project and consequently the plan is never actively used. This is one reason for the failure of so many projects", but also like in the case of the agile authors, he failed to provide a method to construct such plans. The gap was addressed by Miranda [7] who proposed a participatory and visual approach to construct milestone plans he called the Visual Milestone Planning (VMP).

By their own nature, good milestone plans are robust, comprehensive, easy to understand, and confer great flexibility in terms of how to achieve the milestones, all of which makes them a good fit to organize agile endeavors.

This paper casts the VMP approach in the context of planning a project which will be executed using an agile approach like Scrum. Creating what is commonly defined as a hybrid approach [8]. The execution aspects of the project are only cursory covered due to page count limits and the interested reader is directed to [9, 10] for an in-depth treatment.

The rest of the paper is organized as follows: Sect. 2 describes milestone plans, Sect. 3, briefly describe the execution of the plan, Sect. 4 explains the proposed method, Sect. 5 provides a detailed example that illustrates the use of the method and serves as validation and Sect. 6 provides a summary and reference to the initial evaluation of the method.

2 Milestone Plans

Figure 1 shows a conventional milestone plan. As can be observed, the plan is concise, typically confined to a size which will allow it to be grasped at once and written using a vocabulary stakeholders can understand. The plan comprises the sequence of states the project will go through, from its inception to its successful conclusion, and not the activities the team needs to perform to achieve those states which will be proposed as work progresses. For example, the "Design concept approved" milestone defines a state where the project team has presented an idea that satisfies the needs of the sponsor, and she has acquiesced to it. The plan does not estipulate how the team will get there. Will they show wireframe diagrams to her? Develop high fidelity prototypes? Make a PowerPoint presentation? These issues will certainly have to be addressed by the team, for example during sprint planning, but they have no place in the milestone plan.

The focus on states rather than on activities results in a more robust plan since, independent of what tasks need to be performed to get there, when and by whom, it is unlikely, the project sponsors' desire to approve the design concept before it is implemented, will change.

The dependencies between milestones are typically "Finish to Finish" relations, meaning that if "Milestone B" depends on "Milestone A", "Milestone B" cannot be completed until "Milestone A" has been completed. Finish to Finish relations are easy to spot and provide flexibility as to when the activities leading to the realization of the milestone could start.

Milestones could be hard or soft. Hard milestones are milestones, that if not accomplished by a set date, lose all or most of its value or results in severe penalties. The date a government resolution which the system under development is supposed to address goes into effect and the start of the holidays shopping season are examples of hard milestones a project might encounter. Soft milestones, on the other hand, have completion dates that result from the planning process. They might be associated with penalties or other liabilities after a statement of work is agreed, but in principle are discretionary.

State¹	Planned date	Forecasted date	Team	Client	Description	Responsible
	Oct 1st				Project kick-off	
	Oct 20th				UX concept approved	
	Nov 1st				Cloud infrastructure selected	
	Nov 10th				Ux design completed	
	Jan 10th				Cloud infrastructure available	
	Jan 15th				Release 1: CL, BD, AC, CO, Data Base	
	Jan 20th				Beta testing launched	
	Feb 10th				Release 2: CBL, RC, SM	
	Feb 25th				Beta testing results reviewed	
	Mar 10th				Release 3: Customer feedback + emergent features	
	Mar 15th				Acceptance testing procedure approved	
	Apr 1st				Acceptance test completed	
	May 1st				System deployed	
	May 15th				Customer sign-off	
	May 15th				Project closed	

¹State: C – Completed, P – In progress, Blank – Not started

○ - Hard milestone   ⟨ ⟩ - Soft milestone

Fig. 1. A typical milestone plan showing due dates, responsibilities and milestones' descriptions

Miranda [10], supplemented Andersen's original technique, with the concept of "Work Packages Schedule" (see Fig. 2). A Work Packages Schedule consists of a number of timeboxes within which all the work associated with a given milestone, called its work package, will have to be executed for the plan to hold. The purpose of the Work Packages Schedule is twofold: 1) to determine the earliest day by which a milestone can be completed in the context of other project work that might need to be performed, and 2) to drive the scheduling of work during project execution.

Within the constraints imposed by the hard milestones' due dates and the dependencies identified in the plan, the Work Packages Schedule will be decided by the team according to its technical, business and staffing strategies, such as: this needs to be done before that, do as much work as possible at the onset, start slow to minimize risk and then aggressively ramp up, maintain a constant workforce, work must be completed within six months, do not use more than five people, and so on. In constructing it, we will assume, the distribution of competencies in the team matches the work's needs. This is a sensible assumption in an agile context which assumes either generalists or balanced, cross-functional, teams. In cases where this assumption would not hold, it would be possible to break the resource dimension into competency lanes and assign the corresponding effort to each lane. The same approach could be used to scale up the method to be used in projects with multiple teams.

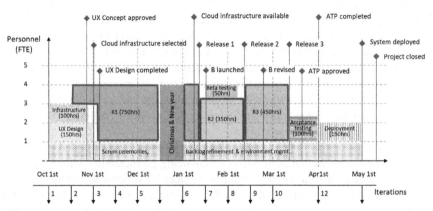

Fig. 2. Work Packages Schedule. This represents one possible arrangement of work packages corresponding to the milestone plan in Fig. 1. Each shaded area corresponds to the work associated with the milestone immediately to its right. The resource-time frame enclosing the work package is its timebox. During iteration 1 and part of iteration 2, one team member will work on UX Design and another in the selection of infrastructure. Other team members can help as needed. From iteration 2 to 6, the team will mainly work on the items included in the first release; from iteration 7 to 9, the team will work on the features included in the second release and in Beta testing. Adapted from [7]

3 Executing the Plan

In the course of the project, the team progressively refines items in the backlog to meet their definition of ready and decomposes them into the tasks necessary for its realization during the iteration/sprint planning meeting, as dictated by the timeboxes depicted by the Work Packages Schedule instead of the biweekly concerns of the product owner. As development progresses, the plan is updated to reflect new circumstances arising from the work completed or from changes in the project context, but since milestones are basically states or goals to be attained, and the plan does not specify when tasks must begin, how long they should take, nor who should perform them, it tends to be pretty stable.

4   The Visual Milestone Planning (VMP) Method

Figure 3 depicts the VMP Method. The first step in the process is to create a product backlog defining the project scope. Each backlog item in it will have associated the estimated effort required for its realization. These estimates will be later used to establish the timeboxes in which the anticipated work could be performed.

VMP proposes the adoption of a hierarchical product backlog, see Fig. 4, which is an enumeration of all the outputs to be delivered to the customer to meet the project objectives: functionality, documentation, infrastructure, gadgets, and services, decomposed into smaller chunks, until they reach the user story level, which defines backlog items that can be completed in a single iteration. Technical stories are work the team needs to perform but unlike user stories do not have a direct user value counterpart. The hierarchical nature of the backlog facilitates the comprehension of the project's scope and supports the progressive refinement of the items identified, their estimation and the collective assignment to milestones. The structure proposed is compatible with the definition of backlog posited nowadays by most practitioners and tools, e.g. SAFe (epics, capabilities, features, stories), Jira (initiatives, epics, stories), Azure (epics, features, stories), Rubin (epics, themes, stories).

Since the backlog forms the basis for planning, it cannot be open ended in the sense of a backlog in a traditional agile project. Balancing predictability with progressive refinement requires the creation of planning aggregates for which a budgetary allowance will be made, in the understanding that when the time comes and they are defined, either we will circumscribe our level of ambition to the available budget, or the plan will need to be revisited.

A project whose final outcome is not well defined could be scoped in terms of learning activities such as running a design sprint and planning packages that have a definite purpose, e.g. Release 1, Release 2, etc., and budget, but whose exact content has not yet been decided.

The second step in the process is the definition of milestones. Milestones are chosen to signal the attainment of a major achievement, the delivery of key components or assemblies, the completion of important process steps or to mark a commitment made to the team, e.g., a customer makes proprietary equipment or technology required by the project available to the team. Notice that in the diagram there are arrows back and forth between steps 1 and 2. This is so because although the product backlog will normally inform the choice of milestones, sometimes the establishment of a particular milestone might result in the creation of new backlog items that must be incorporated to it or leads to its rearrangement.

In step 3, we document the dependencies existing between milestones by means of the Milestone Dependency Diagram. Notice the diagram contains no dates, except for those associated with hard milestones. This is to permit the consideration of different

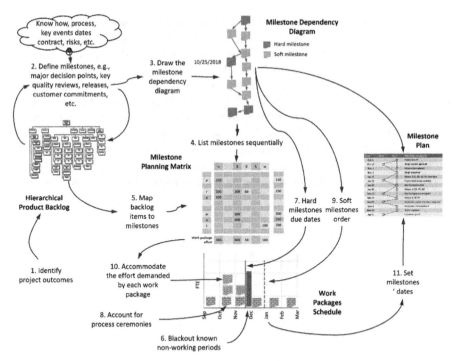

Fig. 3. Visual Milestone Planning Method

staffing and timing strategies later in the process. The process for the creation of the Milestone Dependency Diagram starts with the writing of each identified milestone name on a sticky note[1] and its quick ordering, according to their most obvious sequence of completion, followed by a discussion of specific dependencies, the connecting of the corresponding milestones, and, if necessary, the reordering of the original sequence. The dependencies between milestones are finish-to-finish, since these are more obvious than the most common finish-to-start and give a lot of flexibility on when to start working on a work package. A simple example of a finish-to-finish dependency is that between coding and testing. One could start writing test cases before coding begins, but one cannot finish it until the coding is done. In the fourth step, each cell in the header row of the Milestone Planning Matrix is populated with the name of the milestones. Although not strictly required by the process, listing them chronologically from left to right greatly contributes to the matrix readability and ease of work.

---

[1] Although it is possible to do this using digital tools, it is recommended at least initially to do it this way because VMP promotes involvement and commitment, through the reification of the planning constructs: work packages, milestones and schedules employed in the planning process and their direct manipulation by the team members who collectively create the plan.

In step 5, backlog items are associated with the milestones they help realize via the body of the Milestone Planning Matrix. See Fig. 5. The association is informed by the milestone definition, for example, a "Release 1" milestone would be associated with all backlog items included in the said release. The association is done by labeling a row in the planning matrix with the name of the top-most backlog item whose descendants all contribute to the same milestone and recording the effort required by it at the intersection of the row with the column corresponding to the milestone with which the item is being associated. A milestone can have multiple backlog items associated with it. In most cases, backlog items would be associated with a single milestone in its entirety; there are, however, a circumstances like planning packages or integrative efforts where it is convenient to allocate fractions of the total effort required by the item to multiple milestones.

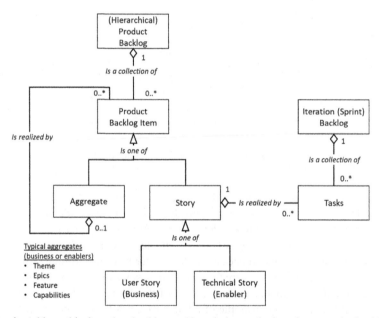

Fig. 4. A hierarchical product backlog and its relation to the iteration or sprint backlog

In step 6, the team will black out known non-working periods such as the holidays, training, and mandatory vacations, since in principle, there would be no work carried out during that time.

In step 7, the team will mark all the hard milestones in the work packages scheduling canvas. Hard milestones will act as anchor points for the plan.

In steps 8, 9 and 10, the team iteratively builds the Work Packages Schedule, see Fig. 6, by posting sticky notes on an empty space in the work package scheduling canvas, starting first with the work corresponding to the process ceremonies, following with the work corresponding to the hard milestones and finally with that of the soft milestones. Since the planning involves the physical positioning of sticky notes on the canvas, there must be a correspondence between the work hours represented by each note and the canvas' physical dimensions. If for example, we choose a $3'' \times 3''$ sticky note to represent 40 h of work, each three inches on the time axis of the canvas will correspond to a week and three inches in the resources axis will correspond to a full time equivalent (FTE) resource. Had we chosen a lower granularity, e.g., a sticky note to represent 150 h of work, which would be useful in the case of a larger project, each three inches on the time axis would correspond to a month instead of a week. One could rip off sticky notes to express fractions of effort or time, but this should be hardly necessary given the resolution of the plan.

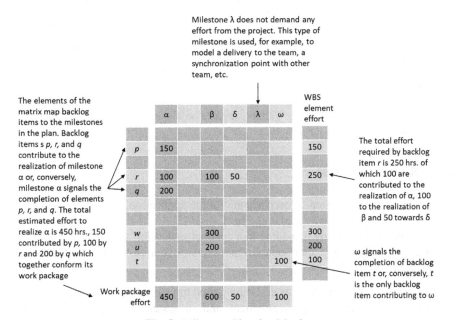

Fig. 5. Milestone Planning Matrix

In step 11, the plan is completed by sprucing the milestone sequence diagram, assigning due dates to the soft milestones, adding responsibility information, and integrating all of them in a common document. The approximate due date for each soft milestone is found by looking in the Work Packages Schedule for the date aligned with the right edge of the time box associated with the milestone. Hard milestones have, by definition, a set date.

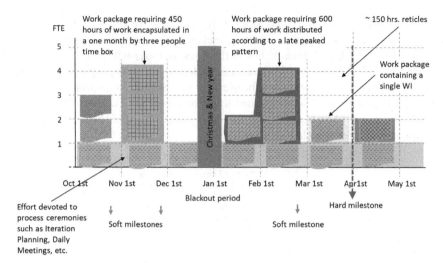

Fig. 6. Iterative construction of the Work Packages Schedule using sticky notes to represent the effort required to realize each milestone

5 Detailed Example

This section provides a step-by-step account of the application of the process in Fig. 3 to the creation of the milestone plan in Fig. 1.

Imagine your company is bidding in a contract to develop an ecommerce site for a small book publisher and after some discussion with your customer you sketched the following notes:

1. Customer wants to include a beta testing period to validate the site design.
2. Customer will not accept deployment until a system wide acceptance test is satisfactorily completed.
3. Customer sign-off will follow satisfactory deployment of the system.
4. Customer would like to have at least three software releases: one to collect users' feedback via beta testing, another one to confirm the progress of the system towards the launch date and the final one to complete the system with minimum risk to the launch date.
5. In the first release she would like to include the following user stories: Category List (CL), Book Details (BD), Add to Cart (AC), Check-Out (CO) and the Data Base epic
6. In the second release, the Category Book List (CBL), Remove from Cart (RC) and Shipping Method (SM)
7. The content of the third release is not known at this time, but the customer would like to reserve a significant number of hours to incorporate the feedback resulting from beta testing and introduce other user stories that might emerge during development
8. The customer is preparing to launch its business around the beginning of May of next year so she would like the system to be ready at least one month before that.

For its part, your company:

9. Cannot start the project until the end of September and has only four developers to work on the project.
10. To minimize the risk of rework, it does not plan to start programming until the infrastructure is selected and the user interface and information architecture design are well underway.

5.1 Step 1

Based on the requirements above and its professional knowledge the development team created the backlog shown in Fig. 7 describing their understanding of the project's scope of work and the estimated effort required for its execution. The required software capabilities were grouped into four epics: Browsing, Buying and Data Base to increase the readability of the backlog as the team felt a grouping based on Releases would have hindered the comprehension of system functionality. UX design, Infrastructure Selection, Beta and Acceptance testing are technical stories that could have been made part of the Website Software deliverable, but which the team chose to put at the first level of the backlog to highlight its understanding of the customer wishes. After some discussion about how many hours to reserve for the final release, the team decided to allocate 450 h since this was compatible with the team's resource availability, the customer schedule and provided ample time to incorporate feedback and complete a few, yet undiscovered, features.

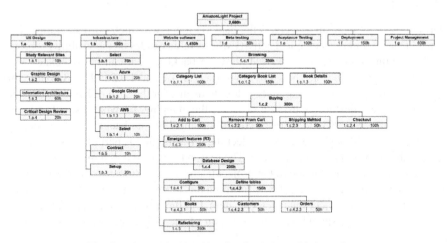

Fig. 7. Hierarchical backlog for the AmazonLight project

5.2 Step 2

After obtaining concurrence for the backlog from the sponsor, the team started choosing relevant milestones producing the list in Table 1. Beware the solution is not unequivocal.

While there are self-evident milestones like project kick-off, software releases and the customer request for a beta test, others are created by the team based on its best judgment as to what is important and what is not. The completion criteria associated with each milestone defines its meaning and helps identify which backlog items should be mapped onto them. The milestones are organized in what seems like the most logical sequence to make the list easier to understand and search for.

5.3 Step 3

The team constructs the Milestone Dependency Diagram by organizing the milestones identified in the previous step in what seems like the most logical sequence, and then by connecting them using finish-to-finish dependencies. Notice that the dependency diagram says nothing about when the work for it ought to start. We will address this in step 10.

5.4 Step 4

In this step, the team reads the Milestone Dependency Diagram in its most natural sounding order, writing the milestones names from left to right as headers of the MPM. If two milestones have a similar due date, it doesn't matter which one is listed first, since the sole purpose of the ordering is to increase the matrix' readability.

5.5 Step 5

During this step, the team associates the backlog items with their corresponding milestones. This is a rather mechanical activity whose value resides on the visibility it brings to the planning process. As discussed above, a backlog item can be associated with more than one milestone as shown by rows 1.a, 1.d, 1.e and 1.c.5 in Fig. 8. While this technique relieves us from creating backlog items just for the sake of having each item map to a single milestone, abusing it obscures the mapping, for what it should be used sparingly. Milestone "Cloud Infrastructure Available" has no backlog item associated with it, because although the work to select the infrastructure is part of the scope of the project, the effort to provision it, is not. The reason to include it as a milestone is that it represents a commitment made to the project team by the customer so it could beta test the system and to signal that a delay in fulfilling this promise could affect its completion date. In the case of project management, item 1.g, the effort was not allocated to any milestone to be later spread over the life-span of the project according to a uniform profile.

Table 1. Potential milestones for the AmazonLight project

Milestone	Rationale (from notes above)	Hard date	Completion criteria
Project kick-off	9	October this year	Development team assembled, meeting with project sponsor concluded
Design concept approved	10		Information architecture and UI designed and approved by sponsor
Infrastructure selected	10		Cloud provider selected. Consider AWS, Azure, Google Cloud and 2 others
Design completed	Proposed by team		Feedback from sponsor incorporated into design
Cloud infrastructure available	Proposed by team		Cloud production environment available
Release 1: CL, BD, AC, CO, Data Base	4, 5		Indicated functionality is ready and tested at 90% coverage and working in production configuration. No broken menus or links
Beta testing launched	1		Release 1 software made available to beta users. User behavior hypotheses defined. Website instrumentation working
Release 2: CBL, RC,SM	4, 6		Indicated functionality is ready and tested at 90% coverage and working in production configuration
Beta testing results reviewed	1		All insights arising from the beta testing disposed

(continued)

Table 1. (*continued*)

Milestone	Rationale (from notes above)	Hard date	Completion criteria
Release 3: Emergent features	7		Reserved effort to implement changes suggested by the beta testing and unknown features
Acceptance testing procedure approved	2		Acceptance test suite approved by sponsor. Includes at least one positive, one negative and one invalid test case for each functionality
Acceptance test completed	2		All acceptance test passed with no objection from sponsor
System deployed	8	April next year	All functionality running in production environment, operators trained. System must run for at least 15 consecutive days without a fault attributable to software
Customer sign-off	3		Customer accepts ownership of the software
Project closed	8	May next year	Project postmortem executed; all records archived

5.6 Step 6

The team marks the Christmas and New Year weeks as a non-working period.

5.7 Step 7

Beside its start and end, the project contains only one hard milestone, the "System Deployed" milestone set for the beginning of April. As by definition, a successful plan must satisfy its hard milestones, we start by marking them on the Work Package Schedule canvas as they would constrain how the work could be organized.

5.8   Steps 8, 9 & 10

The goal of these steps is to establish a window of opportunity in which the work stated by each work package must be executed. To do this, the team will label or somehow tag as many sticky notes as needed to cover the effort required by each work package and accommodate them in an appropriate empty space on the Work Package Schedule canvas. The tagging is important to identify which work corresponds to what, so that is possible to rearrange it if necessary. The team starts by accommodating the effort corresponding to all cross-cutting work packages, then that corresponding to the work packages connected to hard milestones and finally those corresponding to the rest of the work packages in the order dictated by the milestones' dependencies. If necessary, the team might intersperse buffers to protect milestones deemed critical.

Figure 2 shows a stylized version of a possible plan for the AmazonLight project. Notice that due to the holiday period, extending from late December to early January the effort for the Release 1 work package was spread over two months by splitting the sticky notes.

As shown by the figure, with the constraints put on the available resources – three developers and a project manager – it was not possible to deploy the system by April as the customer wanted, so after negotiations it was decided to move the milestone to the beginning of May. Other alternatives could have been to incorporate more resources, reorganize the work, e.g. relax the condition of not doing development work before the design concept has been approved, or renegotiate the scope.

5.9   Step 11

In Step 11, the milestone plan is completed by reading from the Work Package Schedule the approximate date in which the work associated with each milestone will be completed and assigning it as the due date for the milestone.

6   Summary

In this paper, we explained how the VMP method introduced in [7] can be used in an agile context. The method is based on the manipulation of reified constructs such as work packages and milestones in a collective practice, which promotes shared understanding and buy-in into the plan. The VMP method has evolved over three years of classroom and consulting experience and has been put into practice in mid-sized capstone projects, 2,500 to 5,000 person-hours long, and at two industrial organizations. It has also been evaluated for usability using the Process and Practice Usability Model [15].

Although further experience and assessments are required, its initial evaluation and observations point in the direction of the method's ease of use and its value in organizing a project.

WBS Code	AmazonLight Project	Total Effort	Project kick-off	Design concept approved	Infrastructure selected	Cloud infrastructure available	Design completed	Release 1: CL, BD, AC, CO, Data Base	Beta testing launched	Release 2: CBL, RC, SM	Beta testing results reviewed	Release 3	ATP approved	ATP completed	System deployed	Customer sign-off	Project closed
1.a	UX Design	150		140			10										
1.b	Infrastructure	100			100												
1.c.1.1	Category List	100						100									
1.c.1.2	Category Book List	150								150							
1.c.1.3	Book Details	100						100									
1.c.2.1	Add to Cart	100						100									
1.c.2.2	Remove From Cart	50								50							
1.c.2.3	Shipping Mehtod	50								50							
1.c.2.4	Checkout	100						100									
1.c.3	Emergent features (R3)	250										250					
1.c.4	Database Design	200						200									
1.d	Beta testing	50							40		10						
1.e	Aceptance Testing	100											50	50			
1.f	Deployment	150													150		
1.c.5	Refactoring	350						150		100		100					
1.g	Project Management	600															
	Work Packages	2600	0	140	100	0	10	750	40	350	10	350	50	50	150	0	0

Fig. 8. Milestone Planning Matrix for the AmazonLight project

References

1. Cohn, M.: Agile Estimating and Planning. Prentice-Hall, Upper Saddle River (2006)
2. Cockburn, A.: Crystal Clear a Human-Powered Methodology for Small Teams. Addison Wesley, Upper Saddle River (2004)
3. Highsmith, J.: Agile Project Management, 2nd edn. Addison-Wesley, Upper Saddle River (2010)
4. Brechner, E.: Agile Project Management with Kanban (2006)
5. Andersen, E.: Warning: activity planning is hazardous to your project's health!. Int. J. Project Manag., 89–94 (1996)
6. Andersen, E., Grude, K., Haug, T.: Goal Directed Project Management, 4th. Kogan Page, London (2009)
7. Miranda, E.: Milestone planning: a participatory and visual approach. J. Mod. Project Manag. 7(2) (2019)
8. Kuhrmann, M.: Hybrid software development approaches in practice: a European perspective. IEEE Softw. 36(4) (2019)

9. Miranda, E.: Milestone driven agile execution. In: Balancing Agile and Disciplined Engineering and Management Approaches for IT Services and Software Products. IGI Global (2021)
10. Miranda, E.: Bridging the gap between agility and planning. PM World J. **11** (2020)
11. Fontdevila, D., Genero, M., Oliveros, A.: Towards a usability model for software development process and practice. In: Product-Focused Software Process Improvement. PROFES 2017 (2017)

Quantum as a Service Architecture for Security in a Smart City

Vita Santa Barletta[1], Danilo Caivano[1], Alfred Lako[2], and Anibrata Pal[1(✉)]

[1] University of Bari Aldo Moro, Bari, Italy
{vita.barletta,danilo.caivano,anibrata.pal}@uniba.it
[2] Polytechnic University of Tirana, Tirana, Albania
alfred.lako@fin.edu.al

Abstract. Smart Cities are becoming a reality now with ample interest and investment from both government and private entities. As the number of Smart Cities increases, so does the sheer size and variety of data, the major part of which comes from Internet of Things (IoT) sensors embedded in devices. Millions of intelligent devices may be vulnerable to cyberattacks or threats, potentially harming one or more connected devices or exposing sensitive data. Therefore, Smart Cities have Intelligent Operations Centers (IOC), using different machine learning (ML) algorithms to monitor the data and take necessary actions to protect or contain any security incident. The advent of Quantum Computing (QC) has led to many initiatives for using QC in various applications of a Smart City but using Quantum Computing as a service is not yet fully contemplated in this context. In this work, we propose an architecture for Smart City security using Quantum as a Service (QaaS) for analyzing and classifying Smart City data. The proposed architecture uses two different Quantum Classifiers, implemented in the D-Wave Leap Quantum Cloud (QBoost) and IBM Quantum Services (Variational Quantum Classifier), for real-time classification of data and displays security incidents on a conveniently designed dashboard for further actions by the Security Operations Center (SOC) specialist. Further experiments have shown that D-Wave Leap Quantum Cloud-based QBoost performed the best among the quantum classifiers both regarding quality and time.

Keywords: Quantum Computing · Quantum as a service · Smart City · Software Engineering

1 Introduction

Smart Cities are not a vision of the future anymore. As large cities line up on their missions to convert into Smart Cities, they are adopting cutting-edge technologies like Smart Internet of Things (IoT) Devices, Artificial Intelligence (AI) and Machine Learning (ML), Cloud Computing Services, Machine-to-Machine Communications, and Mesh Networks. The mission statement of a Smart City is advancement in the six action fields, 'smart government', 'smart economy', 'smart environment', 'smart living', 'smart mobility', and 'smart people' [6,30].

J. M. Fernandes et al. (Eds.): QUATIC 2023, CCIS 1871, pp. 76–89, 2023.
https://doi.org/10.1007/978-3-031-43703-8_6

Various cities across the world are already on their way to the development and implementation of smart technology. Some cities like Barcelona, Dubai, London, Singapore, Tokyo, and Hong Kong are already striding ahead in their journey towards their evolution into Smart Cities[1].

A smart city has more services, since the intelligence of a city is implemented through the deployment of devices, sensors, and infrastructures that connect objects and people through services in various areas [6]. Therefore, the sheer size and complexity of the data are enormous, and a large part of that comes from IoT devices. Smart City IoT data are vulnerable to cyber attacks like DoS, DDoS, Password, Backdoor, and Ransomware. Thus, we need a secure and solid data collection, processing, and data anonymization system in place to cater to the security and privacy needs of a Smart City [5,11].

To handle growing Smart City data analysis and classification, various Intelligent Operations Centers (IOC) have been proposed. IBM IOC is one of the most popular IOCs [8,37], automatically alerting the conflicts between city agencies, using reporting and monitoring to optimize planned and unplanned operations, and adapting the system based on the acquired information. Apart from optimizing planned and unplanned city-wide operations, conflict resolution or adaptation of existing systems, IOCs also enforce, much required, security and privacy controls for data protection [4,8,17].

Security Operations Center, or SOC, is a specialized IOC responsible for protecting an organization against cyber attacks. The assets of the organization are monitored around the clock by security experts or SOC analysts using various tools to generate detailed reports or action plans. SIEM, or Security Information and Event Management system, is an essential tool for SOC analysts to detect, protect, remediate, or prevent further attacks using ML-based and Fuzzy Logic-based algorithms [12,20].

But the advent of Quantum Computing (QC) has opened avenues for a newer paradigm of computational science and, along with it, the application of the same in different aspects. QC claims to offer exponentially faster processing speeds and the capability of solving problems that were thought to be unsolvable until now [14,35]. Although the application of QC is limited mostly to the research community, it is envisioned that, quite soon, QC may be omnipresent. Therefore, owning to the promises of QC, in this paper, we propose a Quantum as a Service (QaaS) based architecture for detecting security incidents which can be easily coupled with systems like SOC and/or SIEM. The proposed architecture exploits the power of QC by using Quantum Machine Learning (QML) algorithms available in Quantum Cloud Services (QCS) to perform decision-making or classification tasks.

The rest of the paper is organized as follows: Sect. 2 discusses the relevant literature. Section 3 describes the proposed methodology before moving on to the experiments in Sect. 4. Section 5 presents the results and related discussion. Finally, Sect. 6 presents the concluding remarks and future directions.

---

[1] https://www.twi-global.com/technical-knowledge/faqs/what-is-a-smart-city.

2   Related Works

Smart City's Security and Privacy concerns call for the implementation of up-to-date data protection. The area of Smart City is quite mature and consists of a lot of quality research on Smart City Cybersecurity. The prominent solutions propose novel AI or ML-based information classification systems, Intelligent Operations Centers (IOCs), or Security Information and Event Management (SIEM) systems. In [17], the authors propose a Splunk[2] SIEM for smart cities that collects and forwards event logs generated by smart devices to a SOC. A more holistic approach has been suggested by the author in [36], where the best practices, both physical and digital, are deemed extremely important. A case study on IBM's IOC [37] proposes a thorough analysis of the operational system to centralize different city departments and agencies for required decision-making. In [32], the authors used different machine learning algorithms like Logistic Regression (LR), Support Vector Machine (SVM), Decision Tree (DT), Random Forest (RF), Artificial Neural Network (ANN), and K-Nearest Neighbors (KNN) to classify Smart City data. Also, in a couple of studies on Smart City Network [2] and IoT Traffic data [15], the authors implemented Support Vector Machine (SVM), Random Forest (RF), K-Nearest Neighbors (KNN), and Decision Tree (DT), and a two-level novel deep learning based multi-class classification algorithms. A cybersecurity risk management for Smart City infrastructure based on object typing, data mining, and quantitative risk assessment infrastructure using ANN was proposed by the authors in [19]. The resulting system automatically, unambiguously, and reasonably assess the cyber risks for various objects.

In the past couple of decades, Quantum Computing, and more specifically Quantum Machine Learning (QML), has been an important topic of research for implementing solutions in optimization, classification, or clustering algorithms in Quantum Computers (QC) [7]. IBM[3] came up with the first-ever quantum computer with five qubits in May 2016. Currently, the recent most experimental quantum computer is working with more than 400 superconducting transmon qubits[4]. The superconducting transmon qubits used to build the IBM quantum computers are not natural qubits but are made from superconducting materials like niobium and aluminium by patterning them on a silicon substrate and are formed by isolating two energy levels out of many to form an approximate qubit. These are stored in dilution refrigerators at 15 mK (millikelvin) in a dilution refrigerator at the IBM Headquarters in New York, USA. IBM quantum computing is available over the cloud with limited capabilities and is accessible through a token-based API. IBM's Qiskit Machine Learning provides an interface for quantum machine learning, which includes Quantum Kernels and Quantum Neural Networks for classification and regression. The FidelityQuantumKernel class computes kernel matrices for datasets and can be used with Quantum Support Vector Classifiers/Regressors [33]. It also supports existing classical kernel-based algorithms. Qiskit Machine Learning defines a generic neu-

---

[2] https://www.splunk.com/.
[3] https://www.ibm.com.
[4] https://quantum-computing.ibm.com/services/resources.

ral network interface implemented by EstimatorQNN and SamplerQNN. The former combines parametrized quantum circuits with observables, while the latter translates bitstring quasi-probabilities to desired outputs. Training is supported through learning algorithms like NeuralNetworkClassifier/Regressor [13], with Variational Quantum Classifier/Regressor [16,21] providing convenient implementations using feature maps and ansatz construction.

VQC (Variational Quantum Classifier) is a quantum machine learning algorithm. It uses a parameterized quantum circuit and classical optimization to train the circuit's parameters. The circuit encodes input data, and the optimized parameters determine the classification decision, making VQC capable of solving binary classification tasks.

Quantum Annealing is an optimization process for finding the global minimum of a given objective function over a given set of candidate solutions that returns low-energy solutions. D-Wave[5] specializes in quantum annealing and provides quantum computers based on this approach [34]. D-Wave quantum computers, consisting of Quantum annealing processors, utilize qubits existing in superposition states of 0 and 1. During the quantum annealing process [18], the qubits collapse from typical quantum superposition states into 0 or 1 (classical states), with their probabilities controlled by biases and entanglement with couplers. Biases set the external magnetic field, favoring a specific state, while couplers link qubits to influence their behavior. This entanglement introduces correlations and allows qubits to collectively represent multiple states. By programming biases and couplings, the energy landscape of the problem can be defined, which allows the D-Wave quantum computer to find the minimum energy state. QBoost [27–29] is a quantum annealing-based QML algorithm, which is constructed as a thresholded linear superposition of a set of weak classifiers by minimizing the difference between the observed and labeled predictions. It uses boosting techniques to iteratively train and combine the predictions of these classifiers, ultimately making a final classification decision based on their collective output for binary classification. The problem is formulated as a binary quadratic model and is solved by the D-Wave processors, which is known as quadratic unconstrained binary optimization (QUBO) [28].

Having said that, there are some Quantum initiatives regarding Smart City applications. For example, the Quantum City project[6], established by the University of Calgary, Canada, through a strategic partnership with the Government of Alberta, Canada, and Mphasis[7]. The United Kingdom National Quantum Technologies Program has its own Quantum City program[8], a ten-year £1 billion public and private investment, which targets a seamless transition of quantum technologies from laboratories to practice. Fraunhofer FOKUS[9], on the other hand, is working on "quantum computing as a service" to cater to Smart City application areas.

---

[5] https://cloud.dwavesys.com/leap/.
[6] https://research.ucalgary.ca/quantum-city.
[7] https://www.mphasis.com/home.html.
[8] https://www.quantumcity.org.uk/.
[9] https://www.fokus.fraunhofer.de/en/sqc/quantum_computing.

3 Architecture

The main objectives of this research can be divided into two basic research questions:

- **RQ1: What architecture suits QaaS for Smart City Security?**
- **RQ2: What are the results of exemplary tests on the proposed architecture?**

To answer the first research question, in this paper, we propose a Quantum as a Service (QaaS) architecture for Secure Smart City using Quantum Machine Learning (QML) algorithms for the detection of threats or security incidents (Fig. 1). The existing centralized IOCs mentioned before in Sect. 1 provide a holistic approach to problem-solving in Smart City conflict scenarios. This research proposes an extension of security incident detection in existing systems through a service-based architecture that can potentially improve the existing IOCs or SOCs. In this architecture, the power of QML is exploited in order to accelerate the prediction of security incidents or intrusions, therefore avoiding potential damages or reducing the impact on the connected systems. As a result, this would be an important enhancement in improving the security and privacy concerns of the citizens. The proposed architecture is a Hybrid-Quantum Computing system spanning across classical and quantum computing components. The quantum computational component, or QML algorithms, in this case, are accessed as a service from an external classical component.

The proposed system has a three-layer/tier architecture and is divided into five major parts: (1) Smart City Data Source, (2) Graphical User Interface/ Dashboard, (3) Principal Application, (4) Database, and (5) Quantum Cloud Service. The data source does not entirely belong to the three-tier architecture but constitutes an important part of the proposed system. Although layer and tier have been used interchangeably here, a real-world system should be developed as a three-tier architecture where the presentation, application, and data tiers can be developed in separate infrastructures for added security and modularity. The following subsections discuss the components of the system and the functionality of the proposed architecture.

1. Smart City Data Source. The data source is the smart part of the Smart City (Fig. 1a), where information is exchanged among various interacting components of the Smart City to provide a better life experience for the inhabitants of the city. Data sources are scattered across the city in numerous locations. Although they are physically external to the system, they constitute the system. The data from different sectors of a Smart City are transmitted as CSV (comma-separated value) or other text format files to the application tier. From time to time, the system receives labeled data from different co-operations and organizations, which are used to train the classification models for predicting the incoming real-time data.

2. Graphical User Interface/Dashboard. The proposed system displays the alerts on a Graphical User Interface (GUI), a dashboard (Fig. 1b) in this case,

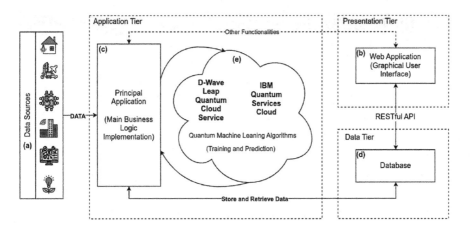

Fig. 1. QaaS Architecture for Smart City Security

showing real-time attacks or security incidents in diverse sectors of the city based on the data received. Incidents related to each of the sectors of the Smart City are shown in separate tabs on the Dashboard in a tabular format. The dashboard is updated in real-time as soon as an incident is registered. It shows all pertinent information on the attack or threat incident encountered. The data is shown in a user-readable format for the security experts to take necessary actions to counter or contain the threat. Each threat or attack is identified by a unique identifier, date, and time of the incident. The dashboard data are loaded from RESTful API (Representational state transfer application programming interface), which fetches data from the database tables. The data from the RESTful API is treated as the data source by the GUI web application. All historic incidents can be reviewed by the security specialist from the dashboard table for reference. Figure 2 shows the sample dashboard developed as a part of the proposed architecture showing real-time threats when the system receives Smart City data. The attack incidents are shown in rows with unique incident IDs and other relevant details like the date and time of the attack, severity if available, category, and type of attack. The dashboard also contains different tabs displaying attack information from different sectors of the Smart City like Mobility, Governance, Economy, Environment, and People. The dashboard was developed using Angular CLI (Version - 15.1.6) and Node.js (Version - 18.14.1).

3. Principal Application. The main application (Fig. 1c) receives incidents in the form of data files from diverse sectors of a Smart City, for example, government, mobility, living, environment, and people. The application implements an Intrusion Detection System pipeline methodology to classify the data for attacks or security incidents, as shown in Fig. 3. According to the IDS methodology, primarily, the data is analyzed and cleaned to remove unwanted fields which do not contribute to the results. Thereafter, appropriate steps are applied to extract the features, and the most important features are selected for further processing. The

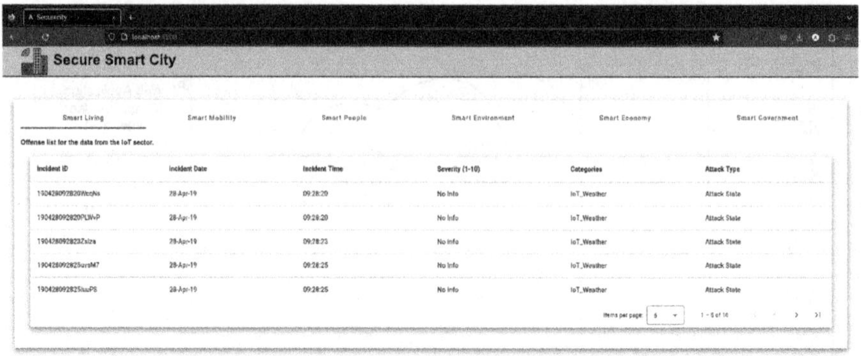

Fig. 2. QaaS Secure Smart City Dashboard

system then trains the machine learning models and validates the same for the prediction phase. During the prediction/testing phase, the test data is processed and classified by the trained ML models. The prediction results can be compared with the existing data to calculate the accuracy, precision, recall, or the F1-score to determine the efficiency of the models.

In the proposed architecture, the training and testing of the data are carried out in D-Wave Leap Quantum Cloud (DLQC)[10] server and IBM Quantum Computing Services Cloud (IBMC)[11]. The application connects to the DLQC instance using a token-based secure native API of the D-Wave system. The principal application invokes the D-Wave python libraries and prepares the data in the specific format as required by QMLs, which in this case is QBoost [27–29] (Quantum Binary Classification algorithm). The main application exploits the IBMC in a similar manner, where it connects to the IBMC instance using a secure token-based API. The Qiskit[12] quantum libraries for QML are invoked for training and prediction phases. After the training and validation phases, the QML models are saved in the local system for further prediction. The system loads the prediction model into the Quantum Cloud during the prediction phase. The main application can predict a single or set of incidents received from the data sources. The incident type prediction is done by the Quantum Cloud, serving the requests from the principal application in order to exploit the QML algorithms to classify between normal or malicious incidents. The main application receives the classification information from the Quantum Cloud through the same token-based API. The attacks, threats, or security incidents the then updated in the database. The proposed system trains the QML models with data from various state-of-the-art or other datasets published from time to time by organizations or institutions. The system saves the best model based on multiple runs. During the real-time prediction phase, the system uses the best model

---

[10] https://cloud.dwavesys.com/leap/.

[11] https://quantum-computing.ibm.com/.

[12] https://qiskit.org/.

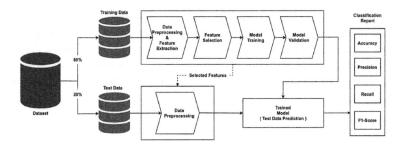

Fig. 3. IDS Pipeline

to carry out predictions. The RESTful API connects to the database instance securely and fetches the specific data from the database tables. The API creates different endpoints for data from different database tables. The data from these tables are converted into JSONs, which are read by the GUI. Python 3.8 was used to design and develop the application and Flask 2.2.2. was used to create the RESTful API for primarily fetching data from the database. The functionality of the API can be further extended to perform functions like POST, PUT, PATCH, and DELETE to perform an update, delete, or other operations in the database based on requirements.

4. Database. The database (DB) (Fig. 1d) comprises the data tier of the system, where all the information from the data sources is stored. Data from each of the sectors, having different features or information, are stored in different DB tables. The RESTful API selects data from each smart city sector incident table of the DB, whereas the main application inserts data into the same table whenever any incident occurs of the respective type. The database was implemented with PostgreSQL 15.2.

5. Quantum Cloud Service. D-Wave Leap Quantum Cloud (DLQC) Service (Fig. 1d), through its native secure API using an encrypted token, allows the D-Wave Leap Quantum Cloud (DLQC)[13] to carry out training and prediction of data. Although DLQC is an external service, it logically belongs to the application tier of the architecture where business decisions are being made. It receives the pre-processed data from the principal application and uses QUBO (Quantum unconstrained binary optimization) algorithms for training and prediction. The DLQC service returns the training or prediction results back to the main application for further processing.

The proposed systems use QBoost [27–29] deployed on the QPU Hybrid Solvers on the Advantage_system5.3 system for the Europe region. The Leap Quantum Cloud service provides quantum hybrid solvers located in different geographical locations. The best solver is selected based on the region and availability. The solver, based on quantum annealing, consists of 5615 working qubits functioning at 16.4 ± 0.1 mK (millikelvin). IBM Quantum Computing Services

---

[13] https://cloud.dwavesys.com/leap/.

Cloud (IBMC) also has been used as an alternative to the DLQC for training and prediction of Smart City data in the proposed architecture. The IBMC receives the pre-processed data from the main application and primarily uses Variational Quantum Classifier (VQC) [21] for training and prediction. IBMC also makes available different Quantum Computers over the cloud for service-based usage.

4 Experiments

To validate the functionality of the proposed architecture, a state-of-the-art publicly available telemetry IoT weather dataset was used, which is a subset of the TON-IoT dataset, [1, 3, 9, 22–26][14]. The Cyber Range and IoT Labs of the School of Engineering and Information Technology (SEIT), UNSW Canberra (ADFA), developed the datasets using realistic and large-scale networks. The attributes of the dataset (Table 1) contain the date and time of the recorded data, respective temperature, atmospheric pressure, and humidity. The data are labeled as 0 and 1 for normal and attack/threat incidents and categorized among various attack categories such as normal, DoS, DDoS, Password, and backdoor attacks.

Table 1. IoT Weather Data Attributes

ID	Feature	Type	Description
1	date	Date	Date of logging IoT telemetry data
2	time	Time	Time of logging IoT telemetry data
3	temperature	Number	Temperature measurements of a weather sensor linked to the network
4	pressure	Number	Pressure readings of weather sensor linked to the network
5	humidity	Number	Humidity readings of weather sensor linked to the network
6	label	Number	Tag normal and attack records, where 0 indicates normal and 1 indicates attack
7	type	Number	Tag attack categories, such as normal, DoS, DDoS, and backdoor attacks

The experiments were carried out on a Ubuntu SMP 20.04 server with 64-bit architecture, AMD Ryzen Threadripper PRO 3975WX CPU with a clocking speed of 4368MHz with 32-Cores and 64 GB of RAM. QBoost-based QML algorithms were carried out on DWave[15] Leap Solvers. Whereas the IBM Qiskit-based QML algorithms were run on Ubuntu SMP with 8 cores CPU of speed 2.1 GHz and 32 GB RAM, the quantum parts were run on the Qiskit backend.

Some features of the dataset, date and time, were removed from the IoT telemetry weather dataset since they did not contribute to the results, and temporal analysis was not carried out in this case. The attack typology feature

---

[14] https://research.unsw.edu.au/projects/toniot-datasets.
[15] https://www.dwavesys.com/.

(Type) was also removed owing to binary classification. Further, there were no NaN or null values in the dataset. As the Temperature, Pressure, and Humidity values were in different measurement units, those were scaled using *MinMaxScaler* [31] into the range of 0 and 1. The TON_IoT dataset contains 650242 records, with 559718 normal records (label 0) and 90524 attack records (label 1). The dataset has only 16.17% attack records, making it unbalanced, which is undesirable as this might lead to biased predictions. To handle data imbalance, it was downsampled using *RandomUnderSampler*[16] library based on the number of records in the minority class so that the train and test data have the same number of normal and attack data. Moreover, all 0 value labels (normal) were converted to −1 to fit QBoost requirements, as it can classify strictly between 1 and −1 only.

Then the processed and scaled data were split into a ratio of 80% and 20% for training and testing, respectively, and consequently were fed to different quantum machine learning classification algorithms. Finally, model accuracy, precision, recall, and F1 scores were calculated to compare the efficiencies of the algorithms in the proposed architecture.

QBoost [27] and VQC [33] were used to validate the proposed architecture. Although the proposal discusses the usage of Quantum as a Service in the context of Smart City Security, for the sake of completeness and fairness, a comparison with Random Forest [10], a state-of-the-art traditional machine learning algorithm, was also carried out. After multiple rounds of testing hyperparameters considered for QBoost are $\langle NUM\_WEAK\_CLASSIFIERS$: [35]$\rangle$, $\langle TREE\_DEPTH$: [3]$\rangle$, $\langle lmd$(lambda): [0.5]$\rangle$, $\langle DW\_PARAMS$: num_reads = [3000], $auto\_scale$ = [$True$], $num\_spin\_$ $reversal\_transforms$ = [10]$\rangle$. For VQC, the hyperparameters considered are $\langle loss$: [$cross\_entropy$]$\rangle$, $\langle optimizer$: [$COBYLA(maxiter$ = 30)]$\rangle$, where the feature map was generated with a ZZFeatureMap using [$reps$ = 1] and the ansatz with RealAmplitudes using [$reps$ = 3]. The hyperparameters for RF are $\langle n\_estimators$: [400]$\rangle$ and $\langle max\_depth$: [30]$\rangle$.

5   Results

In this section, we present the answers to the second research question proposed previously in Sect. 3. Model Accuracy, Precision, Recall, and F1-Score were used to evaluate the machine learning models on the TON_IoT dataset. Additionally, training and testing time performance was measured for each classifier and compared in the purview of the proposed architecture.

Figure 4 shows the quality results of the experiments on the dataset with Random Forest, QBoost, and VQC. Random Forest and QBoost achieved comparable and good classification quality, whereas the performance of VQC was lower. The low performance of VQC can be attributed to the limited number of qubits and noise in current quantum devices. We also have to take into consideration that the IBM quantum computer-based QMLs run on simulators rather

---

[16] https://imbalanced-learn.org/stable/.

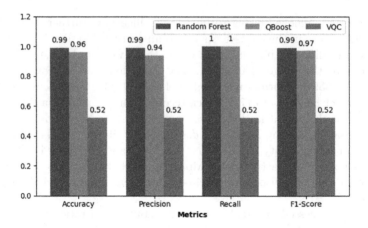

Fig. 4. Quality metrics based comparison of Classifiers

Table 2. Time Performance based comparison of Classifiers (Full Dataset)

Algorithm	Training Time (s)	Prediction Time (s)
QBoost	24.62	0.068
Random Forest	51.7	0.94
VQC	20406.25	179.67

than actual qubits. Although, running any complex algorithm on real qubits would result in very low-quality results owing to the probabilistic and noisy nature of the qubits. Table 2 presents the training and prediction times for the algorithms mentioned above. VQC took almost 5.6 h for training, and about 3 min for prediction, whereas QBoost took 24.6 s and 0.068 s for training and prediction, respectively. On the other hand, Random Forest took 51.7 and 0.94 s on average for training and prediction, respectively.

In this case, QBoost emerged as the best classifier in this domain among other quantum-based classifiers, both with respect to quality and time. The main advantage of using quantum computing services is to exploit the extremely fast running time of quantum algorithms. Although quantum algorithms are not a default choice of training and prediction for classification problems, in many cases, they perform extremely well with respect to time and quality. The general applicability of QBoost should be further investigated for different datasets and features since, being a quantum algorithm, its generalizability has to be specifically studied in different cases before wider application.

6   Conclusion

A Smart City generates data from smart sectors like government, economy, environment, living, mobility, and people. Data is generally captured using IoT sensors which are embedded into different devices. The sensors continuously send the data captured to the Smart City Operations Center. In this paper, we present a Quantum as a Service (QaaS) architecture for Smart City Security that analyzes and classifies Smart City data. We also show that the proposed architecture successfully uses the D-Wave Leap Quantum Cloud and IBM Cloud® to provide the classification of the Smart City incidents. We also compare the QBoost quantum classifier and Variational quantum classifier to present their performance when used in the proposed architecture. Based on the results, we can argue that QaaS architecture with QBoost (D-Wave Leap) can evolve as a viable solution to be investigated further.

Smart City brings in data and constraints from multitudes of sectors and their interconnectivity. Nevertheless, it would be extremely interesting to investigate further with different state-of-the-art datasets like IoT, governance, healthcare, and energy. It would also be interesting to verify the performance of other Quantum Algorithms in this regard, like Quantum Support Vector Machine, Quantum Convolutional Neural Networks, and Quantum Boltzmann Restricted Machines. We are continuing the work on the currently proposed QaaS architecture to integrate it with SOC to empower the security or SOC specialist to make correct decisions and take accurate remedial measures. We are also looking to incorporate security layers in the data transmission between IoT devices and the proposed architecture.

Acknowledgements. This study has been partially supported by the following projects: SSA (Secure Safe Apulia - Regional Security Center, Codice Progetto 6ESURE5) and KEIRETSU (Codice Progetto V9UFIL5) funded by "Regolamento regionale della Puglia per gli aiuti in esenzione n. 17 del 30/09/2014 (BURP n. 139 suppl. del 06/10/2014) TITOLO II CAPO 1 DEL REGOLAMENTO GENERALE "Avviso per la presentazione dei progetti promossi da Grandi Imprese ai sensi dell'articolo 17 del Regolamento"; SERICS (PE00000014) under the MUR National Recovery and Resilience Plan funded by the European Union - NextGenerationEU; PON Ricerca e Innovazione 2014-202 FSE REACT-EU, Azione IV.4 "Dottorati e contratti di ricerca su tematiche dell'innovazione" CUP:H99J21010060001.

References

1. Alsaedi, A., Moustafa, N., Tari, Z., Mahmood, A., Anwar, A.: TON_IoT telemetry dataset: a new generation dataset of IoT and IIoT for data-driven intrusion detection systems. IEEE Access **8**, 165130–165150 (2020). https://doi.org/10.1109/ACCESS.2020.3022862

2. AlZoman, R.M., Alenazi, M.J.F.: A comparative study of traffic classification techniques for smart city networks. Sensors **21**(14), 4677 (2021). https://doi.org/10.3390/s21144677

3. Ashraf, J., et al.: IoTBoT-IDS: a novel statistical learning-enabled botnet detection framework for protecting networks of smart cities. Sustain. Urban Areas **72**, 103041 (2021). https://doi.org/10.1016/j.scs.2021.103041

4. Babar, M., Tariq, M.U., Jan, M.A.: Secure and resilient demand side management engine using machine learning for IoT-enabled smart grid. Sustain. Urban Areas **62**, 102370 (2020). https://doi.org/10.1016/j.scs.2020.102370

5. Barletta, V.S., Buono, P., Caivano, D., Dimauro, G., Pontrelli, A.: An overview on the security technological levels in the Italian smart cities. Proceedings ISSN 1613-0073 (2020). http://ceur-ws.org

6. Barletta, V.S., Buono, P., Caivano, D., Dimauro, G., Pontrelli, A.: Deriving smart city security from the analysis of their technological levels: a case study. In: 2021 IEEE International Conference on Omni-Layer Intelligent Systems (COINS), pp. 1–6 (2021). https://doi.org/10.1109/COINS51742.2021.9524268

7. Barletta, V.S., Caivano, D., De Vincentiis, M., Magrì, A., Piccinno, A.: Quantum optimization for IoT security detection. In: Julián, V., Carneiro, J., Alonso, R.S., Chamoso, P., Novais, P. (eds.) ISAmI 2022, pp. 187–196. Springer, Cham (2023). https://doi.org/10.1007/978-3-031-22356-3_18

8. Bhowmick, A., Francellino, E., Glehn, L., Loredo, R., Nesbitt, P., Yu, S.W.: IBM intelligent operations center for smarter cities administration guide. IBM Corporation, International Technical Support Organization (2012)

9. Booij, T., Chiscop, I., Meeuwissen, E., Moustafa, N., den Hartog, F.: ToN_IoT: the role of heterogeneity and the need for standardization of features and attack types in IoT network intrusion data sets. IEEE Internet Things J. **9**, 485–496 (2021). https://doi.org/10.1109/JIOT.2021.3085194

10. Breiman, L.: Random forests. Mach. Learn. **45**(1), 5–32 (2001)

11. Catalano, C., Afrune, P., Angelelli, M., Maglio, G., Striani, F., Tommasi, F.: Security testing reuse enhancing active cyber defence in public administration. In: ITASEC, pp. 120–132 (2021)

12. Chen, D., Wawrzynski, P., Lv, Z.: Cyber security in smart cities: a review of deep learning-based applications and case studies. Sustain. Urban Areas **66**, 102655 (2021). https://doi.org/10.1016/j.scs.2020.102655

13. Cong, I., Choi, S., Lukin, M.D.: Quantum convolutional neural networks. Nat. Phys. **15**(12), 1273–1278 (2019). https://doi.org/10.1038/s41567-019-0648-8

14. Grover, L.K.: A fast quantum mechanical algorithm for database search. In: STOC 1996: Proceedings of the Twenty-Eighth Annual ACM Symposium on Theory of Computing, pp. 212–219 (1996)

15. Hameed, A., Violos, J., Leivadeas, A.: A deep learning approach for IoT traffic multi-classification in a smart-city scenario. IEEE Access **10**, 21193–21210 (2022)

16. Havlíček, V., et al.: Supervised learning with quantum-enhanced feature spaces. Nature **567**(7747), 209–212 (2019). https://doi.org/10.1038/s41586-019-0980-2

17. Hwoij, A., Khamaiseh, A., Ababneh, M.: SIEM architecture for the internet of things and smart city. In: International Conference on Data Science, E-learning and Information Systems 2021, pp. 147–152. ACM (2021). https://doi.org/10.1145/3460620.3460747

18. Kadowaki, T., Nishimori, H.: Quantum annealing in the transverse ising model. Phys. Rev. E **58**(5), 5355–5363 (1998). https://doi.org/10.1103/PhysRevE.58.5355

19. Kalinin, M., Krundyshev, V., Zegzhda, P.: Cybersecurity risk assessment in smart city infrastructures. Machines **9**(4), 78 (2021)

20. Kurniawan, F., Wibawa, A.P., Susiki, S.M., Hariadi, M.: Makassar smart city operation center priority optimization using fuzzy multi-criteria decision- making. In: International Conference on Electrical Engineering, Computer Science and Informatics (EECSI) (2017)

21. Maheshwari, D., Sierra-Sosa, D., Garcia-Zapirain, B.: Variational quantum classifier for binary classification: real vs synthetic dataset. IEEE Access **10**, 3705–3715 (2022). https://doi.org/10.1109/ACCESS.2021.3139323

22. Moustafa, N.: New generations of internet of things datasets for cybersecurity applications based machine learning: TON_IoT datasets. In: eResearch Australasia Conference, Brisbane, Australia (2019)

23. Moustafa, N.: A systemic IoT-fog-cloud architecture for big-data analytics and cyber security systems: a review of fog computing (2019)

24. Moustafa, N.: A new distributed architecture for evaluating AI-based security systems at the edge: network TON_IoT datasets. Sustain. Urban Areas **72**, 102994 (2021). https://doi.org/10.1016/j.scs.2021.102994

25. Moustafa, N., Ahmed, M., Ahmed, S.: Data analytics-enabled intrusion detection: evaluations of TON_IoT linux datasets (2020)

26. Moustafa, N., Keshk, M., Debie, E., Janicke, H.: Federated TON_IoT windows datasets for evaluating AI-based security applications (2020)

27. Neven, H., Denchev, V., Rose, G., Macready, W.: QBoost: large scale classifier training with adiabatic quantum optimization. J. Mach. Learn. Res. **25**, 333–348 (2012)

28. Neven, H., Denchev, V.S., Rose, G., Macready, W.G.: Training a binary classifier with the quantum adiabatic algorithm (2008)

29. Neven, H., Denchev, V.S., Rose, G., Macready, W.G.: Training a large scale classifier with the quantum adiabatic algorithm (2009)

30. Paiho, S., Tuominen, P., Rökman, J., Ylikerälä, M., Pajula, J., Siikavirta, H.: Opportunities of collected city data for smart cities. IET Smart Cities 4(4), 275–291 (2022). https://doi.org/10.1049/smc2.12044

31. Pedregosa, F., et al.: Scikit-learn: machine learning in Python. J. Mach. Learn. Res. **12**, 2825–2830 (2011)

32. Rashid, M.M., Kamruzzaman, J., Hassan, M.M., Imam, T., Gordon, S.: Cyberattacks detection in IoT-based smart city applications using machine learning techniques. Int. J. Environ. Res. Public Health **17**(24), 9347 (2020). https://doi.org/10.3390/ijerph17249347

33. Rebentrost, P., Mohseni, M., Lloyd, S.: Quantum support vector machine for big data classification. Phys. Rev. Lett. **113**(13), 130503 (2014). https://doi.org/10.1103/PhysRevLett.113.130503

34. Serrano, M.A., et al.: Minimizing incident response time in real-world scenarios using quantum computing. Softw. Qual. J. 1–30 (2023)

35. Shor, P.W.: Polynomial-time algorithms for prime factorization and discrete logarithms on a quantum computer. SIAM J. Comput. **26**(5), 1484–1509 (1997)

36. Toh, C.K.: Security for smart cities. IET Smart Cities 2(2), 95–104 (2020). https://doi.org/10.1049/iet-smc.2020.0001

37. Zhuhadar, L., Thrasher, E., Marklin, S., de Pablos, P.O.: The next wave of innovation-review of smart cities intelligent operation systems. Comput. Hum. Behav. **66**, 273–281 (2023). https://doi.org/10.1016/j.chb.2016.09.030

A Retrospective Analysis of Grey Literature for AI-Supported Test Automation

Filippo Ricca[1]([✉]) [iD], Alessandro Marchetto[2] [iD], and Andrea Stocco[3,4] [iD]

[1] Università degli Studi di Genova, Genoa, Italy
filippo.ricca@unige.it
[2] University of Trento, Trento, Italy
alessandro.marchetto@unitn.it
[3] Technical University of Munich, Munich, Germany
andrea.stocco@tum.de
[4] fortiss GmbH, Munich, Germany
stocco@fortiss.org

Abstract. This paper provides the results of a retrospective analysis conducted on a survey of the grey literature about the perception of practitioners on the integration of artificial intelligence (AI) algorithms into Test Automation (TA) practices.

Our study involved the examination of 231 sources, including blogs, user manuals, and posts. Our primary goals were to: (a) assess the generalizability of existing taxonomies about the usage of AI for TA, (b) investigate and understand the relationships between TA problems and AI-based solutions, and (c) systematically map out the existing AI-based tools that offer AI-enhanced solutions.

Our analysis yielded several interesting results. Firstly, we assessed a high degree of generalization of the existing taxonomies. Secondly, we identified TA problems that can be addressed using AI-enhanced solutions integrated into existing tools. Thirdly, we found that some TA problems require broader solutions that involve multiple software testing phases simultaneously, such as test generation and maintenance. Fourthly, we discovered that certain solutions are being investigated but are not supported by existing AI-based tools. Finally, we observed that there are tools that supports different phases of TA and may have a broader outreach.

Keywords: Test Automation · Artificial Intelligence · Grey Literature

1 Introduction

The adoption of Artificial Intelligence (AI) and Machine Learning (ML) techniques for Test Automation (TA) is attracting the attention of both researchers and practitioners that are recognizing the potential of AI to fill the gap between human and machine-assisted testing activities. In this paper, we refer to such techniques as Artificial Intelligence supported Test Automation (AIsTA). While AIsTA is increasingly being adopted by companies [25], there is still a limited knowledge about the problems it faces, the solutions it proposes, as well as the existing tools and their connection with the software development process.

Several works tried to review the existing works concerning AIsTA [10, 12, 16, 35]. This work is under the umbrella of these secondary studies but it focuses on the grey

J. M. Fernandes et al. (Eds.): QUATIC 2023, CCIS 1871, pp. 90–105, 2023.
https://doi.org/10.1007/978-3-031-43703-8_7

literature [6] to capture the perception of the practitioners about the adoption of AIsTA. To this aim, we first extended the grey literature conducted by Ricca et al. [25] by considering more recent sources (+41%). Secondly, we conducted a retrospective analysis into the whole set of collected data, aiming at capturing the underlying relationships among TA problems, AI-based proposed solutions, and existing tools.

Our analysis revealed that existing taxonomies provide a good degree of generalization, also when considering more recent grey literature sources. Also, we found that some TA problems require solutions that involve several testing phases (e.g., test creation, execution and maintenance), with some tools actually supporting this complex scenario. We believe that our work could help practitioners better comprehend the state of the art and practice in AIsTA, for instance, for selecting the most appropriate tools for their testing purposes of problems. Moreover, our work could help researchers in capturing issues that require more investigation and new research directions.

2   Existing Grey Literature Analysis for AI-Assisted Test Automation

A previous work by Ricca et al. [25] (referred to as previous work, hereafter) presented a study of the grey literature concerning AI/ML-based testing frameworks and tools for Test Automation. The authors analyzed several hundreds web documents from which they retrieved: (a) existing problems about different aspects of the actual automated testing process, (b) solutions based on AI and ML that are used to mitigate such problems and, (c) the list of most popular frameworks and tools available on the market.

The main contribution of the previous work [25] is the construction of two taxonomies of problems and solutions in AIsTA. Moreover, the authors identified the six most-cited AI/ML testing tools that, according to practitioners, can improve the quality of the TA process and the productivity of testers and developers.

In terms of TA problems that are addressed with AI, the taxonomy reports six main categories related to (1) test planning, (2) test design, (3) test authoring, (4) test execution, (5) test closure, and (6) test maintenance [25]. Among the AI-supported solutions to such problems, the taxonomy reports four main categories related to (1) test generation, (2) test oracles, (3) debugging, and (4) test maintenance [25]. Previous work also identified the most popular AIsTA tools, those being Functionize,[1] Applitools,[2] Mabl,[3] Testim,[4] Test.ai,[5] and Appvance.ai.[6] Although being an important first step in understanding this evolving domain, the previous work falls short in providing critical details concerning an examination of the connections between TA problems and investigated solutions and a systematic mapping of AIsTA tools and solutions.

In this work, we first assessed the generalizability of the proposed taxonomy using a set of recent studies not used during its development. After having validated and

---

[1] https://www.functionize.com.
[2] https://applitools.com.
[3] https://www.mabl.com.
[4] https://www.testim.io.
[5] https://www.test.ai.
[6] https://www.appvance.ai.

extended the set of data analyzed by the previous work, aiming at considering more sources, we make a step ahead in collecting and presenting these important relationships based on an analysis of the grey literature. This information can be useful for both practitioners and researchers. Practitioners can determine which solutions to employ based on their specific requirements and challenges, as well as identify the tools that can assist them in implementing the identified solution. At the same time, researchers can focus on areas in which AI is not yet used and that require further investigation.

3   Retrospective Analysis

The objective of our investigation is to gain insights into how practitioners perceive TA problems addressed by AI-enhanced tools, as well as their effectiveness. We focus our retrospective analysis on the grey literature analysis conducted by previous work [25], that we also extended. With this goal in mind, we aim to unravel the connections between existing TA issues and AI-driven solutions, as well as the interplay between current TA tools and these AI-based solutions. We aim to address the following research questions:

RQ$_0$ (Generalizability). *What is the generalizability of the previous taxonomies [25]?*
RQ$_1$ (Problems vs Solutions). *How are TA problems and solutions linked in AIsTA?*
RQ$_2$ (Tools vs Solutions). *How do AIsTA tools and solutions relate to each other?*

RQ$_0$ assesses the degree of generalizability of the existing taxonomies by validating them on a set of studies that we not used during its development. RQ$_1$ investigates the solutions provided by AI-powered test automation designed to address specific TA problems. RQ$_2$ analyzes what solutions can be obtained from AIsTA tools.

3.1   Procedure

Data Extension. Concerning the generalizability of the existing taxonomy (RQ$_0$), we adopted the same experimental procedure outlined in previous work [25], which is composed by four distinct phases: (1) Google/arXiv search, (2) document selection, (3) data extraction, and (4) taxonomy creation. In short, the authors searched a list of possible web documents with a Google-based search to collect as many documents as possible regarding TA conducted with AI/ML solutions (details are available in our replication package [24]). Second, web documents not related to AI/ML-enhanced TA were filtered out adopting some specific inclusion/exclusion criteria. Third, the authors read and analyzed the candidate documents, filling out a form with the information gathered from each source [11]. Finally, following a systematic process [7,8], they created two taxonomies, one for problems and one for solutions, as well as a list of the most adopted AIsTA tools.

By considering the same search strings of the original paper, updated to the years 2022 and 2023, we broadened the investigation of grey literature to include also the most current works released up to February 2023. We followed the same procedure to extract the information from the sources and update the existing taxonomies. A tabular data extraction form was used to keep track of the extracted information [24] (e.g., the list of all the information sources). The authors proceeded with the analysis independently on separate sets of documents, reusing existing labels previously created, should an existing label apply to the document under analysis.

Data Collection. Our pool of data contains the newly collected data and the existing data that were made available in the replication package of the previous work [25]. The extracted information includes: (1) the link of the document, (2) the author(s) of the document, (3) the nature of the document (e.g., blog post, interview transcript, white papers), (4) the data of the document, (5) the TA tool(s), (6) the testing level (e.g., acceptance, unit), (7) the problem addressed, and (8) the solution offered.

Data Preprocessing. We used `Pandas` data-frames [19] to filter the information related to problems addressed and solutions offered (RQ_1) and tools (RQ_2). We discarded the entries for which either the problem, solution, and tool was unspecified or for which it was too generic. On the interesting entries, we counted each pairwise combination of `<problem, solution>` and `<tool, solution>`. Particularly, every source mentioning a problem instance and a solution instance is counted as one connection. From the original pool of 541 pairs, we retained 335 pairs for our analysis (62%).

Data Visualization. We used the `Plotly` library [9] to create different Sankey diagrams [27]. We decided to use Sankey diagrams since they are used to visualize the flow of data from an input set to an output set. The elements of both input and output sets are called *nodes*. Such *nodes* are connected by means of *links*, where each *link* connects an input node to an output node, thus showing that a given relationship exists between input and output. The width of a *link* indicates the absolute values of the matching instances. By using Sankey diagrams in our retrospective analysis, we aim at identifying the connections between TA problems and AI-enhanced solutions, and between the existing AIsTA tools and such solutions, with the goal to surface trends and patterns. For RQ_1, we considered the pairs pertaining to each software development phase separately (e.g., maintenance). It is worthy notice that the Sankey diagrams are built by considering all the collected sources, while the ones shown in this paper focus only on the most evident connections, only for space and readability reason.

3.2 Results

RQ_0 (Generalizability). Table 1 (*Problem*) presents the list of problems in TA that are faced with AI/ML, according to [25], and their occurrences. The table also includes the updated entries and occurrences derived from our extension.

The two most represented sub-categories are *Manual code development* and *Maintenance of test scripts*, two well-known cumbersome activities concerning the development and maintenance of test scripts. More in detail, test development requires both domain knowledge and programming expertise. Domain knowledge is required to identify the test data and test oracle, whereas the programming expertise is required when using script-based testing frameworks to programmatically develop test code (e.g., with Selenium WebDriver [5]). Test maintenance is critical in both mobile and web contexts [3,13], because these kinds of applications are subject to a rapid evolution, thus requiring a non-trivial effort to evolve and maintain existing test code. Other relevant problems are related to *Untested code*, i.e., the inability of automated test suites to test the entire application under test (AUT); *Manual data creation*, i.e., the unavailability of high-quality input data for testing [26]; *Visual analysis*, related to the assessment of

Table 1. Original and Extended Taxonomy (in green) of TA problems and solutions.

Problem	[25]	#	Solution	[25]	#
Test Planning	22	32	**Test Generation**	125	192
Critical paths identification	13	13	Aut. test generation	29	48
Planning what to test	7	9	Aut. generation using machine translation	11	13
Planning long release cycles	2	2	Aut. generation from user behaviour	11	22
Test process management	-	8	Aut. test generation from API calls	6	6
Test Design	8	22	Aut. test generation from mockups	3	3
Programming skills required	5	11	Aut. test generation using crawling	2	11
Domain knowledge required	3	9	Declarative testing	-	2
Test-cases	-	1	Predict faulty-areas	-	4
Programming-skills required	-	1	Aut. data generation	22	22
Test Authoring	109	132	Robust element localization	13	13
Manual code development	52	58	Dynamic user-behaviour properties recognition	8	8
Manual API test development	7	11	Automated exploratory testing	7	10
Manual data creation	19	24	Object recognition engine	6	13
Test object identification	13	13	Mock generation	3	3
Cross-platform testing	10	15	Self-learning	2	3
Costly exploratory testing	5	5	Automated API generation	1	9
Locators for highly dynamic elements	1	1	Page object recognition	1	2
Test code modularity	1	1	**Test Execution**	-	8
Accessibility testing	1	1	Cloud execution	-	2
Adequacy-focus on faulty-areas	-	3	Decoupling test framework from host	-	2
Test Execution	71	103	Smart test execution	-	3
Untested code	29	34	Anomaly detection	-	1
Flakiness	18	22	**Oracle**	38	46
Slow execution time	14	16	Visual testing	38	46
Useless test re-execution	4	7	**Debugging**	62	82
Scalability	2	3	Intelligent test analytics	17	22
Parallelization	2	3	Automated coverage report	14	22
Low user responsiveness	1	1	Noticeable code changes identification	12	13
Slow execution time	14	16	Runtime monitoring	10	11
Platform independence	1	1	Flaky test identification	7	8
Test Closure	47	59	Bad smell identification	1	1
Manual debugging overhead	18	22	Decoupling test framework from host	1	1
Costly result inspection	10	11	Root-cause-analysis	-	1
Visual analysis	19	25	Prediction of failures	-	3
Data-quality	-	1	**Maintenance**	81	141
Test Maintenance	82	102	Self-healing mechanisms	43	43
Manual test code migration	3	3	Self-healing test scripts	24	32
Bug prediction	11	13	Smart locators	19	21
Fragile test script	10	12	Intelligent fault prediction	12	13
Regression faults	2	7	Intelligent selective test re-execution	12	12
Costly visual GUI regression	8	10	Intelligent waiting sync	5	5
Maintenance overhead	48	57	Intelligent test prioritization	4	6
			Aut. identification environment configurations	3	6
			Pattern recognition	1	1
			Remove unnecessary test cases	1	1
			Reduce UI testing	-	1
Unspecified	60	77	Unspecified	91	99
Generic	23	33	Generic	25	30
Total	339	560	Total	422	598

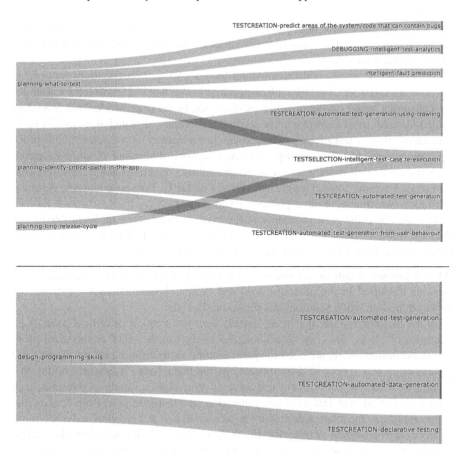

Fig. 1. Problems vs Solutions in the Planning (top) and Design phases (bottom).

the visual correctness of the AUT graphical user interface; *Test scripts Flakiness*, i.e., non-deterministic test scripts that either pass or fail when executed on the same AUT due to environmental factors such as the network traffic [17]); and *Manual debugging overhead*, which concerns the search of the root-cause behind test script failures and breakages.

Table 1 (*Solution*) lists the solutions provided by AI/ML, as presented in [25], as well as the updated entries and occurrences derived from our extension (highlighted in the figure). The most represented category is *Automated test generation*, which includes different sub-categories, such as the usage of machine translation (test cases are described using natural language and the testing framework interprets and translates them in executable test scripts) or crawling [21] (automated AUT model inference at support of test generation). Another relevant category is *Maintenance* of test scripts, often performed with self-healing mechanisms that are able to perform automatic fixes in case of breakage, or via smart locators that are resilient to common breakages causes. Other solutions concern *Debugging* with intelligent test analytics able to reveal the portions of the AUT with high probability of bugs, and *Oracles*, for enabling visual testing, an approach able to automatically check the visual appearance and behavior of a AUT graphical user interface.

The extended version of the taxonomies includes 95 new contributions (out of 231 sources considered, i.e., +41.1% with respect to previous work [25]), which we arranged into categories based on the dimensions described in the prior work. This procedure yielded 419 additional instances to the original taxonomies, of which five new TA problems out of 40 (e.g., test process management, test adequacy on application fault-prone application areas, and data quality), 10 new types of solution out of 44 (e.g., cloud-based test execution, smart test execution, and failure prediction) and 22 new tools out of 71 (e.g., Tricentis Tosca, Google OSS-Fuzz, ChatGPT). For space reasons, we entire list of tools in available in our replication package [24].

Overall, about the generalizability of the existing taxonomies of TA problems and AI-based solutions (RQ_0), we can observe that in our analysis, we have been only partially extended the taxonomies presented by Ricca et al. [25].

RQ_1 **(Problems vs Solutions).** Figure 1 illustrates the relations between problems and solutions identified in the planning (top) and design (bottom) phases. Problems are shown on the left, while solutions are shown on the right.

In the planning phase, the figure depicts the identification of critical paths (e.g., sequences of clicks, links and functionalities to test) in the AUT as the main problem. In the design phase, the need for programming skills required for developing and implementing test scripts is shown instead as the main issue. It is worth noting that deciding on which aspects to focus test automation involves a variety of solutions, such as fault prediction, test analytics, test generation, and test selection. Both Sankey diagrams emphasize the relationship with various automated test creation activities, ranging from crawling-based to behavior-driven development (BDD) solutions. In particular, it is interesting to observe the contribution of crawling (in the planning phase) as a way to identify critical paths in the AUT and that of declarative testing [34] (in the design phase) as a way to separate the design of test cases from their technical implementation. This may be reflective of the separation of testers and developers as two distinct roles in industry.

In Fig. 2, the relationships between problems and solutions in the authoring (top) and execution (bottom) phases are depicted. The primary challenge addressed in the authoring phase is manual code development, which is tackled through various automated test creation activities, including crawling-based and machine-translation-based solutions. Additionally, the generation of automated tests from user behavior and API calls is explored as a potential solution to the problem of manual data creation. Interestingly, the diagram shows that the object identification is a testability problem related to four possible major solutions such as: (i) object recognition engines (i.e., tools that can identity testing elements of the AUT GUI); (ii) exploratory testing (e.g., based on taxonomies of past-discovered bugs); (iii) visual testing (i.e., automated visual checks of the AUT GUI by means of computer vision approaches); and (iv) intelligent fault prediction. Regarding the test execution phase, two primary issues arise, namely test flakiness and identifying portions of code untested. The former can be tackled through various automated techniques such as self-healing test scripts and smart locators or

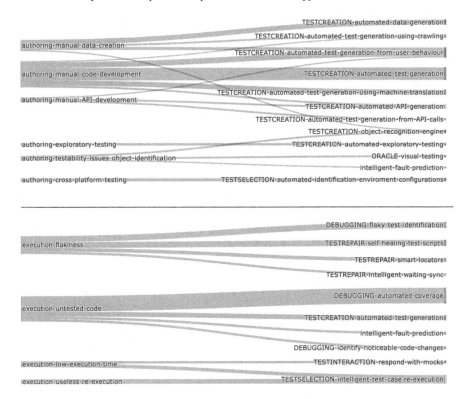

Fig. 2. Problems vs Solutions in the Authoring (top) and Execution phases (bottom).

using intelligent synchronization methods able to insert waiting commands in the right place of the flaky test script and with the right waiting time. The latter involves mainly approaches like coverage analysis, automated test generation and to a minimal extent also fault prediction.

There are two primary concerns related to the closure (top) and maintenance (bottom) phases (Fig. 3). The first concern, which is the visual oracle problem, can be addressed using visual testing solutions. The second concern, which involves the debugging overhead, requires a combination of various automated debugging techniques such as self-healing methods (e.g., to autonomously decide the corrective actions to apply in case of a broken test), automated coverage toolsets, test analytics (e.g., methods for failure analysis), and change impact analysis (e.g., to identify what has been tested). These techniques can also benefit the task of inspecting test results. This Sankey diagram highlights the fact that in some cases there are unique and specific solutions to a problem (e.g., visual oracle problem) while in other cases the problems are more complex (e.g., debugging overhead) and require multiple distinct solutions. Finally, concerning the maintenance phase, the biggest problem is the overhead of maintaining test scripts and the associated cost, which also needs different and multi-faceted solutions. The greatest contribution is given by smart locators and self healing test scripts, being the most cited solutions for this specific problem. Another important problem is that of the fragility of

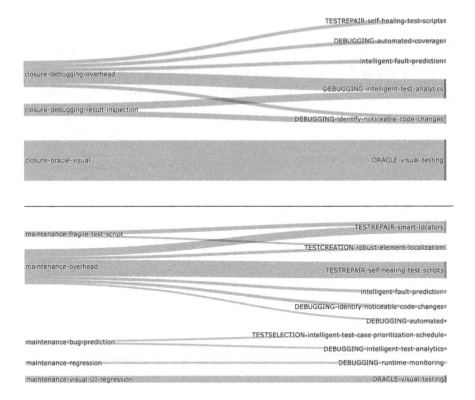

Fig. 3. Problems vs Solutions in the Closure (top) and Maintenance phases (bottom).

test scripts. A test script is fragile if it can no longer identify a web element as the AUT evolves. The proposed solutions, in this case, are the usage of smart locators and robust web element localization.

Overall, about the link between TA problems and AI-based solutions (RQ₁), we can observe that in our analysis, we captured existing links as perceived by practitioners. In particular, we observed that some TA problems require solutions that involves several testing phases and tasks.

RQ₂ (Tools vs Solutions). The relations between tools and solutions are depicted in Fig. 4. The figure highlights three commonly used tools—Applitools, Mabl, and Functionize—each associated with distinct solutions.

Applitools specializes in visual GUI testing (see thicker connection with ORACLE-visual-testing), which involves automating visual testing and creating visual assertions. The creators of Applitools claim that their tool is able to replicate the human vision system to spot functional and visual regressions. Applitools also provides functionality during the debugging phase, allowing developers to identify code changes that have affected the visual appearance of the application. This is helpful for regression testing, to verify that changes to the production code have not caused unintended changes to the GUI. As such, the figure illustrates three primary links for Applitools: visual testing, usage of an object recognition system for test creation, and change impact analysis.

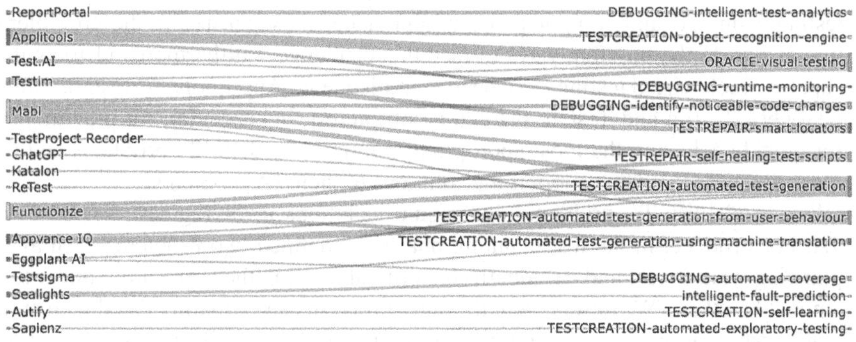

Fig. 4. Tools vs Solutions

Mabl serves as a flexible test automation platform designed for continuous integration and deployment purposes. Its primary function is to facilitate the creation, execution, and maintenance of test scripts. Mabl is associated with a vast range of solutions that include assistance to test generation, automated repair of locators (with a smart element locators strategy), automated visual testing, and debugging. Although the strengths of Mabl are on test creation and maintenance, an important aspect is that of visual testing. Indeed, Mabl is able to identify visual changes in AUT by comparing screenshots from the current test script run to a visual baseline.

Functionize also turns out to be a fairly complete test platform. Functionize performs test script creation using natural language processing (NLP) and user behavior specification. It also offers advanced self-healing maintenance strategies that leverage intelligent element selection. Additionally, Functionize provides intelligent visual differences recognition, allowing developers to quickly identify changes to the user interface that may impact the functionality of the AUT.

In contrast, other tools seem to cater to more specific solutions. For instance, ReportPortal focuses on providing intelligent test analytics, while TestSigma is used for automated test generation with machine translation tools.

Overall, about the link relationship between AI-based solutions and existing tools (RQ$_2$), we can observe that in our analysis, we identified tools that are more flexible and seem to support more solutions in contrast to more specialized tools.

4   Discussion

This section discusses the achieved results in terms of observations and evidences, as well as the open issues and threats to validity affecting our study.

Observations and Evidences. By analyzing the results collected with our retrospective analysis, we derived the following observations.

O1: We can identify TA problems that could be faced by AI-enhanced existing solutions implemented in AI-based tools. For instance, a well-known challenge in GUI testing is the creation of effective oracles [20]. The use of oracles based on visual testing, using AI and computer vision approaches, is suggested in the grey litera-ture as one of the possible ways to face this challenge. Furthermore, 11 tools that support oracle visual testing have been identified, e.g., Applitools, AI testbot, Mabl, Sealights, Testim and Test.ai. **O1** can be of interest, in particular, for practitioners for quickly selecting the most appropriate solutions for their TA problems and the most adequate tools that support the solutions to their TA problems.

O2: We can identify TA problems that require solutions involving several phases of TA. For instance, in the test planning phase, we defined two problems such as (i) planning what to test and (ii) identifying critical paths in the application under test, among the others. We observe that the latter problem can be mainly faced with auto-matic test creation solutions, ranging from crawling the application under test, up to the creation test scripts using user behaviors. The former problem instead can be faced by solutions involving test scripts creation (e.g., automatic test creations solutions, test creation by focusing on application areas that are predicted as more buggy), test selection (e.g., based on fault prediction), test execution (e.g., adoption of intelligent test re-execution strategies), and, finally, test debugging approaches (e.g., adoption of test analytics). **O2** can be of interest, in particular, for researchers that can better highlight as some TA problems are addressed from different perspec-tives, i.e., for some problems, specific ad-hoc solutions can be adequate while, for other problems, more complex solutions need to be studied.

O3: We identified solutions presented in the grey literature that are not supported by existing available tools. However, it is important to keep in mind that the absence of a tool does not necessarily indicate a lack of existing solutions for a particular prob-lem. It could simply mean that the specific tooling solutions were not mentioned in the literature due to the incompleteness of our analysis. For instance, decoupling the test framework from the host environment is referenced, in the grey literature, as one possible solution for facilitating cross-platform testing. However, it seems that this solution is not adequately supported by the existing AI-enhanced tools, that mainly provide approaches that allow the identification of different environ-mental configurations, to face cross-platform testing. Another solution that seems to be not adequately supported by tools concerns the execution of test cases with mock responses: no tools support the construction of mock objects that can be used in TA. Concerning the test selection and optimization, solutions aiming at prioritiz-ing test cases, removing unnecessary test cases and GUI-based testing seem to be not adequately supported by existing AI-enhanced tools. **O3** can be of interest to both professionals and researchers with the aim of developing innovative tools and technologies capable of supporting the identified solutions.

O4: We identified tools that support solutions related to different TA phases while other tools are specific for a given TA phase. For instance, tools such as Applitools, Egg-plantAI, Functionize, Mabl, and Test.ai, are able to support different TA phases, e.g., test creation, maintenance, execution. Conversely, tools such as Katalon, Retest, Sapienz, and Testsigma seem to be more specific, thus mainly supporting a given testing phase, e.g., test creation. **O4** can be of interest for practitioners for selecting the most appropriate tools to use in their business, by taking into account the prob-lems they have to face and also other aspects such as specificity and flexibility of tools.

Open Issues. Our analysis covers three years of grey literature concerning the usage of artificial intelligence for test automation. We do not claim that this work captures all relevant grey literature but we are confident that the included documents cover the most important tools up to February 2023. On the other hand, the grey literature is the one that reacts faster to rapidly evolving technological advancements, e.g., the recent release of large language models (LLMs) to the public. While these tools were only partially included in our analysis, we expect to see wider adoption of LLMs in the context of test automation in the future. Further research is necessary to fully understand the complex relationships between artificial intelligence and test automation. Nonetheless, our analysis provides a valuable starting point for understanding the current state of the practice.

Threats to Validity. Threats to the internal validity concern biases and errors during the selection of documents and classification of the considered items (i.e., problems, solutions, and AI-based test automation tools). In particular, the classification task is very difficult in the context of grey literature because the web documents are often informative and non-technical and the terminology is vague and sometimes ambiguous. We relied on an existing taxonomy of works and on an existing procedure, thus we also inherit the threats of the previous work. Our search may have missed relevant documents that are not captured by the search queries. To minimize classification errors, we followed a systematic and structured procedure with multiple interactions. Each doubt concerning creating a new category or classifying an item was discussed among the authors. Concerning the external validity, we considered only Google/arXiv documents in a specific time frame, and our findings may not generalize to other documents or other search engines and repositories. Concerning reproducibility, all our results, in terms of data, plots and references are available in our replication package [24].

5 Related Work

5.1 Test Automation and AI/ML

In the software testing community, there is an increasing adoption of AI/ML solutions to automate the different phases of testing and to deal with problematic issues (e.g., test-suite maintenance and test case prioritization). Test generation is one of the most relevant areas in which the adoption of AI/ML has been investigated. For instance, Zhang et al. [39] and Walia et al. [37] propose the adoption of Computer vision approaches to automate the GUI test generation, with the goal of reducing the required human effort. Qian et al. [23] adopt an evolved OCR-based technique for localizing GUI elements for test generation. Test maintenance is another well-known testing phase that traditionally requires a huge human effort (e.g., for page object generation [29–31]) and so in which AI/ML techniques can be beneficial. In fact, computer vision approaches [1] have been also widely used for web test migration [14, 15, 28] and test repair [33]. Neural embedding of web pages are used to automated the web page similarity for automated model inference [32]. Code-less functional test automation is investigated by Vos et al. [36] and by Phuc Nguyen et al. [22] for test maintenance. The latter study combines Selenium and a ML technique for reducing the time spent by testers changing and modifying the test code. Among other testing issues, Camara et al. [2] propose an ML-based app-roach for using test code smells as predictors of flaky tests. Mahajan et al. [18] use a computer vision approach for the detection of cross-browser incompatibilities. Feng et al. [4] adopt a computer vision approach for prioritizing test cases for mobile applica-tions. Yadav et al. [38] use ML to check the new code and identify areas of the code in which the test coverage can be increased. Differently from these works, we do not aim at investigating a specific AI/ML technique for TA but rather we aim at going in-depth in the grey literature about TA and AI/ML techniques by realizing a retrospective anal-ysis for capturing the state-of-the-art in terms of TA problems, proposed solutions, and existing tools.

5.2 Secondary Studies

In the literature there are several reviews and surveys in the context of TA via AI/ML. For instance, Trudova et al. [35] report on a systematic literature review (SLR) con-ducted to study the role of AI/ML in TA. The result of the review confirms that most of the literature studies investigate the use of ML and computer vision techniques for reducing manual intervention in software testing and improving both the effectiveness and reusability of test suites. Lima et al. [16] report on a SLR in which they show that fuzzing and regression testing are the most studied types of testing that adopt ML techniques such as, in particular, neural networks. Leger et al. [12] report on a liter-ature review about the adoption of AI in software testing, especially, by focusing on challenges' identification. They show that the most relevant ones are, e.g., the domain knowledge gap problem, the training data availability, the oracle problem, the computa-tional, cost size and quality of the dataset, test case design, and test result interpretation.

More related to the work presented in this paper are the following two papers. Jha et al. [10] present a preliminary SLR about E2E test automation tools by focusing on test-ing phases where AI techniques can be adopted: test script generation, test data genera-tion, test execution, test maintenance, and root cause analysis. They also briefly present existing AI-enhanced tools such as Katalon Studio, Applitools, Testim, TestCraft, Para-soft SOAtest, Mabl, AccelQ, and Functionize.

We believe that our work could help practitioners better comprehend the state-of-the-art of AI/ML for test automation, for instance, select the most appropriate tools for their testing purposes of problems. However, our work could help researchers in capturing issues that could require more investigation and new research directions.

6   Conclusions and Future Work

This paper focuses on the analysis of the grey literature about how practitioners perceive the adoption of AI to improve TA. We presented the results of a retrospective analysis conducted by starting from the data collected by Ricca et al. [25] which was extended with additional sources and analyses.

Our investigation include several interesting results, for instance, about the identi-fication of: (i) TA problems faced by existing AI-enhanced solutions implemented in provided tools; (ii) TA problems that requires solutions involving several TA phases (e.g., test creation, execution and maintenance); (iii) solutions investigated but not supported by existing available tools; and, finally, (iv) tools supporting multiple TA phases.

Future research directions consist in conducting a multi-vocal literature review [6] by integrating the findings gathered from the grey literature with those of the white literature. It would be also interesting to conduct controlled experiments with existing AI-enhanced tools, to quantify the benefits they provide and to validate the observed connections with the TA problems and the investigated solutions.

References

1. Bajammal, M., Stocco, A., Mazinanian, D., Mesbah, A.: A survey on the use of computer vision to improve software engineering tasks. TSE **48**(5), 1722–1742 (2020)
2. Camara, B., Silva, M., Endo, A., Vergilio, S.: On the use of test smells for prediction of flaky tests. In: SAST 2021, pp. 46–54. Association for Computing Machinery (2021)
3. Choudhary, S.R., Zhao, D., Versee, H., Orso, A.: WATER: web application test repair. In: Proceedings of 1st International Workshop on End-to-End Test Script Engineering, ETSE 2011, pp. 24–29. ACM (2011)
4. Feng, Y., Jones, J.A., Chen, Z., Fang, C.: Multi-objective test report prioritization using image understanding. In: Proceedings of 31st IEEE/ACM International Conference on Automated Software Engineering, ASE 2016, pp. 202–213. ACM, New York (2016)
5. García, B., Gallego, M., Gortázar, F., Munoz-Organero, M.: A survey of the selenium ecosystem. Electronics **9**, 1067 (2020)
6. Garousi, V., Felderer, M., Mäntylä, M.V.: Guidelines for including grey literature and conducting multivocal literature reviews in software engineering. IST **106**, 101–121 (2019)
7. Gyimesi, P., et al.: BugJS: a benchmark of javascript bugs. In: Proceedings of 12th IEEE International Conference on Software Testing, Verification and Validation, ICST 2019, p. 12. IEEE (2019)
8. Gyimesi, P., et al.: BugJS: a benchmark and taxonomy of javascript bugs. Softw. Test. Verification Reliab. **31**(4), e1751 (2020)
9. Plotly Inc.: Collaborative data science (2015). https://plot.ly
10. Jha, N., Popli, R.: Artificial intelligence for software testing-perspectives and practices. In: CCICT 2021, pp. 377–382 (2021)
11. Kitchenham, B., Charters, S.: Guidelines for performing systematic literature reviews in software engineering (2007)
12. Leger, G., Barragan, M.J.: Mixed-signal test automation: are we there yet? In: 2018 IEEE International Symposium on Circuits and Systems (ISCAS), pp. 1–5 (2018)
13. Leotta, M., Clerissi, D., Ricca, F., Tonella, P.: Approaches and tools for automated end-to-end web testing. In: Advances in Computers, vol. 101, pp. 193–237 (2016)
14. Leotta, M., Stocco, A., Ricca, F., Tonella, P.: Automated migration of DOM-based to visual web tests. In: Proceedings of 30th Symposium on Applied Computing, SAC 2015, pp. 775–782. ACM (2015)
15. Leotta, M., Stocco, A., Ricca, F., Tonella, P.: PESTO: automated migration of DOM-based web tests towards the visual approach. Softw. Test. Verification Reliab. **28**(4), e1665 (2018)
16. Lima, R., da Cruz, A.M.R., Ribeiro, J.: Artificial intelligence applied to software testing: a literature review. In: 2020 15th Iberian Conference on Information Systems and Technologies (CISTI), pp. 1–6 (2020)
17. Luo, Q., Hariri, F., Eloussi, L., Marinov, D.: An empirical analysis of flaky tests. In: Proceedings of the 22nd ACM SIGSOFT International Symposium on Foundations of Software Engineering, FSE 2014, pp. 643–653. Association for Computing Machinery, New York (2014)

18. Mahajan, S., Halfond, W.G.J.: Detection and localization of HTML presentation failures using computer vision-based techniques. In: Proceedings of 8th IEEE International Conference on Software Testing, Verification and Validation, ICST 2015, pp. 1–10 (2015)
19. McKinney, W., et al.: Data structures for statistical computing in python. In: Proceedings of the 9th Python in Science Conference, Austin, TX, vol. 445, pp. 51–56 (2010)
20. Memon, A., Banerjee, I., Nagarajan, A.: What test oracle should i use for effective GUI testing? In: 18th IEEE International Conference on Automated Software Engineering, 2003 Proceedings, pp. 164–173 (2003)
21. Mesbah, A., van Deursen, A., Lenselink, S.: Crawling ajax-based web applications through dynamic analysis of user interface state changes. ACM Trans. Web 6(1), 1–30 (2012)
22. Phuc Nguyen, D., Maag, S.: Codeless web testing using Selenium and machine learning. In: ICSOFT 2020: 15th International Conference on Software Technologies, ICSOFT 2020, pp. 51–60. ScitePress, Online, France (2020)
23. Qian, J., Ma, Y., Lin, C., Chen, L.: Accelerating OCR-based widget localization for test automation of GUI applications. Association for Computing Machinery (2023)
24. Replication Package (2023). https://github.com/riccaF/quatic2023-replication-package-material/
25. Ricca, F., Marchetto, A., Stocco, A.: AI-based test automation: a grey literature analysis. In: Proceedings of 14th IEEE International Conference on Software Testing, Verification and Validation Workshops, ICSTW 2021. Springer, Cham (2021)
26. Ricca, F., Stocco, A.: Web test automation: insights from the grey literature. In: Bureš, T., et al. (eds.) SOFSEM 2021. LNCS, vol. 12607, pp. 472–485. Springer, Cham (2021). https://doi.org/10.1007/978-3-030-67731-2_35
27. Schmidt, M.: The sankey diagram in energy and material flow management. J. Ind. Ecol. 12(2), 173–185 (2008)
28. Stocco, A., Leotta, M., Ricca, F., Tonella, P.: PESTO: a tool for migrating DOM-based to visual web tests. In: Proceedings of 14th International Working Conference on Source Code Analysis and Manipulation, SCAM 2014, pp. 65–70. IEEE Computer Society (2014)
29. Stocco, A., Leotta, M., Ricca, F., Tonella, P.: Why creating web page objects manually if it can be done automatically? In: Proceedings of 10th International Workshop on Automation of Software Test, AST 2015, pp. 70–74. IEEE/ACM (2015)
30. Stocco, A., Leotta, M., Ricca, F., Tonella, P.: Clustering-aided page object generation for web testing. In: Bozzon, A., Cudre-Maroux, P., Pautasso, C. (eds.) ICWE 2016. LNCS, vol. 9671, pp. 132–151. Springer, Cham (2016). https://doi.org/10.1007/978-3-319-38791-8_8
31. Stocco, A., Leotta, M., Ricca, F., Tonella, P.: APOGEN: automatic page object generator for web testing. Software Qual. J. 25(3), 1007–1039 (2017)
32. Stocco, A., Willi, A., Starace, L.L.L., Biagiola, M., Tonella, P.: Neural embeddings for web testing. arXiv:2306.07400 (2023)
33. Stocco, A., Yandrapally, R., Mesbah, A.: Visual web test repair. In: Proceedings of the 26th ACM Joint European Software Engineering Conference and Symposium on the Foundations of Software Engineering, ESEC/FSE 2018. ACM (2018)
34. Triou, E., Abbas, Z., Kothapalle, S.: Declarative testing: a paradigm for testing software applications. In: 2009 Sixth International Conference on Information Technology: New Generations, pp. 769–773 (2009)
35. Trudova., A., Dolezel., M., Buchalcevova., A.: Artificial intelligence in software test automation: a systematic literature review. In: Proceedings of the ENASE, pp. 181–192. INSTICC, SciTePress (2020)
36. Vos, T.E.J., Aho, P., Pastor Ricos, F., Rodriguez-Valdes, O., Mulders, A.: Testar - scriptless testing through graphical user interface. Softw. Test. Verification Reliab. 31(3), e1771 (2021)

37. Walia, R.: Application of machine learning for GUI test automation. In: 2022 XXVIII International Conference on Information, Communication and Automation Technologies (ICAT), pp. 1–6 (2022)
38. Yadav, V., Botchway, R.K., Senkerik, R., Kominkova, Z.O.: Robot testing from a machine learning perspective. In: 2021 International Conference on Electrical, Computer and Energy Technologies (ICECET), pp. 1–4 (2021)
39. Zhang, C., Cheng, H., Tang, E., Chen, X., Bu, L., Li, X.: Sketch-guided GUI test generation for mobile applications. In: Proceedings of ASE 2017, pp. 38–43 (2017)

Process Improvement Using the Scientific Method
Demonstration in Requirements Engineering

Isabel Lopes Margarido[✉] [iD]

Porto, Portugal
isabel.margarido@fe.up.pt

Abstract. There are several methods successfully used for Process Improvement. In EQualPI (a framework to Evaluate the Quality of Implementation of Process Improvements) our main concerns are the performance in terms of efficiency and effectiveness of the outcomes of a process, this being more relevant than only considering compliance. Additionally, we believe that a Process Improvement method must be repeatable, reliable and unbiased. Given that the Scientific Method is used to create new knowledge, applying such method to Process Improvement can greatly contribute to more rigorous and less prone to bias results. In this paper we present our definition of the Scientific Method applied to Process Improvement, which we have based on and validated through a quasi-experiment with two groups of graduate students and undergraduates. The output of our process improvement was later adopted by an organisation. Our method is tailorable and with our quasi-experiment we showed that the Scientific Method in Process Improvement can be applied to smaller and lower maturity organisations.

Keywords: Process Improvement · Scientific Method · Requirements Engineering · Continuous Improvement · Unbiased Research · Organisations

1 Introduction

Organisations cannot rely on the same processes forever, they cannot be stagnated in time as otherwise, in this fast paced changing world, they may fail to fulfil their purposes. Consequently, as changes occur, new knowledge integrates the company through workers, technologies and research, their processes must be adapted. The *as is* process must be gathered in order to understand where improvement opportunities lie, documented in the *to be*, object of an experiment, and the obtained data objectively analysed. When positive changes are identified, they must be documented and communicated using a Change Management approach in order to ensure that changes are introduced smoothly, and stakeholders are engaged and informed. Workers with different roles must be involved

---

I. Lopes Margarido—Independent Researcher.

J. M. Fernandes et al. (Eds.): QUATIC 2023, CCIS 1871, pp. 106–120, 2023.
https://doi.org/10.1007/978-3-031-43703-8_8

in the changes definition. Therefore, people are more prone to adhere to the process and potential resistance points are addressed, creating an environment that embraces continuous process improvement. Furthermore, as defended by Watts Humphrey and claimed in [10], processes are defined by the people using them, we not only agree but also share the opinion expressed in [13], that as processes are used by people they change. For that reason we also recommend process adjustment after deployment.

There are several continuous improvement methods and process improvement frameworks documented in the literature, such as: Shewhart Cycle PDSA (Plan, Do, Study, Act) - derived from the more known PDCA cycle (Plan, Do, Check, Act), Deming's wheel [15], Juran's Quality Improvement Process [8], Six Sigma [7] and the IDEAL model (Initiating, Diagnosing, Establishing, Acting and Learning) [14].

Although, these methods are widely used with success in industry, some additional structure and recommendations could greatly benefit the Continuous Process Improvement area. Providing the set of tools used in Science to ensure the required information about a process is gathered, will allow experimentation before adopting a new process, and procedures can be documented in a manner that allows the experiment to be repeated. Such steps are found in the Scientific Method, used to generate new knowledge and prove or refute theories. We argue that including that method in Process Improvement can significantly aid those working in such an important area for organisations.

The remainder of this paper is organised as follows: Sect. 2 reviews existing continuous process improvement methods; in Sect. 3 we present the quasi-experiment that we conducted [11] and the adoption of the results of that process improvement in industry. Section 4 is where we propose and detail our Process Improvement method that includes steps of the Scientific Method. We discuss our research in Sect. 5. Our conclusions and proposed future research work are in Sect. 6.

2 Continuous Process Improvement

In this section we present some of the better known Continuous Process Improvement methods. The benefit attributed to the use of the scientific method was already tackled by Shewhart [15]. The authors carried out an analysis of the evolution of integrating the Scientific Method into the Science of Improvement. In 1939, Shewhart turned his 3 steps product improvement cycle (Specification, Production, Inspection) into a cycle, claiming "It may be helpful to think of the three steps in the mass production process as steps in the scientific method." Therefore, the following terms are equivalent: *specification <=> making a hypothesis, production <=> testing the hypothesis* and *inspection <=> carrying out an experiment.* In this paper we go further, not only taking into consideration the scientific method process mapped in [5] but also other details covered in this section and our own professional experience.

Shewhart's improvement cycle was extended with a 4th step in 1950 by Deming, who later coined it "Shewhart cycle for learning and improvement" [15].

That step was "redesign through marketing research" and the method got known by the PDSA acronym, representing the following steps (Fig. 1):

1. Plan: plan a change or a test, aimed at improvement;
2. Do: carry out the change or test;
3. Study: analyse results to gather lessons learnt or understand what went wrong;
4. Act: adopt the change or abandon it or, alternatively, run through the cycle again.

Fig. 1. Shewhart cycle for learning and improvement: Plan, Do, Study, Act [15]

Juran's Quality Improvement Process [8] is defined as a continuous process established in the organisation, coupled to a governance model and intended to last through the organisation lifetime, and involves the definition of a plan, and specific and upper management roles. The author considered the relevance given to new developments was inherently given greater emphasis and structure than the necessity of reducing "chronic waste", and with less attention to quality. The details of organising and forming a quality council are thus described, as well as those of preparing improvement projects that would include criteria and roles needed in the improvement project team. We summarise the steps:

- Awareness: have proof of the need;
- Determine the potential return on investment;
- Select processes and project to implement;
- Diagnosis journey: understand the symptoms;
- Formulate theories to identify the causes and select the ones to be tested, do retrospective analysis and check lessons learnt;
- Remedial Journey: choose remedies to remove the causes;
- Establish controls to hold the gains;
- Institutionalise the process improvement.

Six Sigma was used in Motorola to reduce defects. After being published, it was adopted by many others [7]. It includes a method to define new processes, named DMADV (Define, Measure, Analyse, Design and Verify) and the approach for improving while eliminating defects, DMAIC (Fig. 2) meaning:

- Define: the problem, its impact and potential benefits;

- Measure: identify the relevant measurable characteristics of the process, service or product, define the current baseline and set the improvement goal;
- Analyse: identify the process variables causing the defects/inefficiencies;
- Improve: establish acceptable values for those variables and improve the process to perform within the limits of variation;
- Control: continue measuring the new process to ensure the process variables have the expected behaviour and achieve the established improvement goal.

Fig. 2. Six Sigma's DMAIC: Define, Measure, Analyse, Improve, Control [7]

The IDEAL model is a continuous process improvement framework published by the Software Engineering Institute (SEI) [14] consisting of five phases and their respective activities (Fig. 3):

- Initiating – after a stimulus for the improvement. This phase includes activities to characterise the identified need and to start a project: set context, build sponsorship and charter infrastructure;
- Diagnosing – understanding the current state (*as is*) and defining what the desired future state (*to be*) is. Includes the activities to characterise current and desired states, set priorities and develop approach;
- Establishing – definition of the plan on how to achieve the desired state and test and improve the solution to implement. Includes the activities to plan actions and create, pilot test, refine and implement solution;
- Learning – analyse what was done, understand if the goals were achieved, learn from the experience and prepare for future improvement. Includes the activities to analyse and validate and propose future actions.

We have defined an 8 steps Process Improvement method considering part of some of the prior models, the Scientific Method, a quasi-experiment and our professional knowledge.

3   Basis Upon Which we Define our Process Improvement Method

Our research begun with conducting an improvement using the scientific method. We posed two research questions: R1) Is it possible to have a good classification list specific for requirements defects? R2) Will that list help find more requirements defects? To answer R1 we conducted a quasi-experiment[1] with Requirements Reviews and R2 was answered after the adoption of its results by a CMMI Level 5 organisation.

---

[1] In this paper, after indicating we did a quasi-experiment we may use experiment and quasi-experiment to designate it.

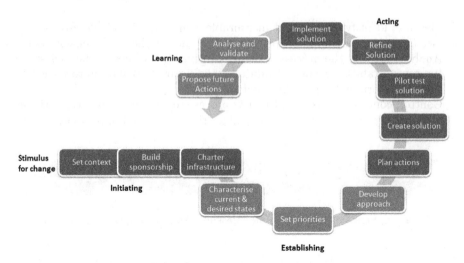

Fig. 3. IDEAL model: Initiating, Diagnosing, Acting, Learning [6]

3.1 A Quasi-experiment with Requirements Reviews

The quasi-experiment that we conducted was a Process Improvement to the *Review Requirements* process, following the scientific method. Our research [11] is summarised in Table 1.

In our experiment we compiled all defects classifiers found in the literature review that we conducted at the time, and removed several of them according to the criteria that we have set, ending-up with 9 classifiers for the type of defect attribute, to which we tried to give a clear and meaningful definition. After refining it for the second group experiment we had the following classifiers: 1) Missing or Incomplete; 2) Incorrect Information; 3) Inconsistent; 4) Ambiguous or Unclear; 5) Misplaced; 6)Infeasible or Non-verifiable; 7) Redundant or Duplicate; 8) Typo or Formatting; 9) Not Relevant or Extraneous. We summarise both groups quasi-experiments in Table 2.

We can conclude that the experiments are not comparable due to the different environments, circumstances and groups. Furthermore, we had no control group to ensure a comparison of using or not the classifiers; it would not even be possible, because we identified the defects in the SRS to focus on gathering a good taxonomy.

Table 1. Summary of information of the validation of the Process Improvement using the Scientific Method

Label	Description
Motivation	Requirements defects are on the top causes of software failures and factors impacting software maintainability [3]. However, in 2011 there was no defect classification specific to requirements defects. To ensure the quality of the defect classification that we created we did an experiment.
Method	Do a literature review to define a classification of defects adequate for use in requirements reviews. Conduct experiments with graduate students and undergraduates. Analyse the data of the first experiment to refine the classification of defect types.
Results	Gathered a classification for type of defect, specific for requirements, now in used in at least one organisation. Defined the steps to be considered when doing Process Improvement

Table 2. Experiment conditions of each group

Experiment Information	Group 1	Group 2
Education	Graduates	Undergraduates
Experience	Perform the review of a Software Requirements Specification (SRS) document	Perform the review of an SRS document.
Subjects	19	5
Introduction	We did a presentation of the scope and instructions about the experiment	The teacher gave them the introduction.
When	During a class to clarify doubts about the final project	Presented before the exam to be performed after the exam.
Preparation time	3 min to read the classifiers list (no individual record)	Average of 3 min to read (2 of them skipped the reading and were the ones who spent more time doing the classification).
Experiment duration	40 min to do the classification (no individual record)	13 min on average doing the classification

3.2 Adoption by an Organisation

Even though we could not fully test the process improvement and progressively deploy and control its results, the requirements defect classification that we have created was introduced in an organisation in 2013 as part of an improvement initiative. They considered that the use of the new requirements taxonomy more successfully characterised requirements defect types when compared to using the Orthogonal Defect Classification (ODC), where all requirements defects were labelled as *Documentation*. Therefore, they adopted our Requirements Defects Types taxonomy and extended the classification to have a *Not Applicable* (N/A) and two types related with the document itself, respectively *Not Requirements - Content* and *Not Requirements - Typos or Formatting*. The classification results were used to do a Pareto chart to evaluate which requirements defect types contributed to 70% of the requirements defects: Ambiguous or Unclear (25%), Typo or Formatting (17%), Incorrect Information (16%) and Missing or Incomplete (12%) (Fig. 4).

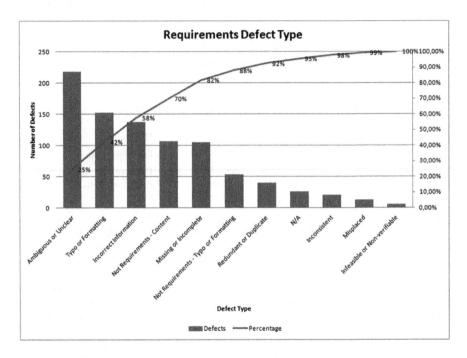

Fig. 4. Percentage of defects found in requirements reviews by type

The analysis results were inputs of a Causal Analysis and Resolution (CAR) project: used to define solutions to address the problems in the origin of these types of defects, and to prevent them in future reviews. The metric we recommended that should be monitored to improve the *Requirements Review* process was the *number of requirements defects only found on posterior phases of the development cycle*. However, the organisation was interested in measuring other aspects of requirements reviews and introduced several other improvements that cannot be isolated in their effect from that of using the taxonomy. Nonetheless, they indicated that the number of defects found in requirements was considerably higher than before introducing the taxonomy, showing an improvement.

The organisation used the defects classification scheme to support two of the goals mentioned in *Step 2*, and to [2]: 1) Identify those requirements defects which were more frequent and had higher impact; 2) Analyse the root cause of requirements defects. We agree with Card [1,11], a defect taxonomy should support the specific analysis interests of the organisation that is going to use it, namely in the implementation of defect causal analysis.

With this section's results we validated EQualPI's Process Improvement steps, following the Scientific Method. The experiment with students followed *Steps 1 to 7*. Even though we could not validate *Step 8 - Progressively deploy and control*, the output of our improvement was adopted by an organisation, lending recognition to its value and de facto satisfying this last step. Furthermore, together, the results also validated the two research questions that we posed.

4   Process Improvement Method

Doing Process Improvement involves steps that are common, regardless what the organisation intends to change, but each improvement or step also has its particularities. There are several methodologies, some of which we mentioned in this paper, that can be used to deal with this and it is not our intention to provide a new one. Explaining how Process Improvement shall be carried out in individual cases is not within the scope of this paper.

However, in the experiment we conducted we followed the Scientific Method (see Fig. 5), which is rigorous and well suited to render Process Improvement repeatable and unbiased results. Our approach also contributes to increase the accuracy, and control when conducting a Process Improvement. We will stick to the steps that were followed in that Process Improvement experiment, and highlight important elements to consider while carrying it out, particularly to complement improvement steps with the Scientific Method.

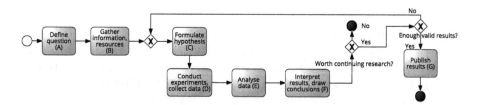

Fig. 5. Representation of the scientific method (adapted from [5])

4.1   Scientific Method in Process Improvement

Process Improvement is a continuous activity of organisations, so there will always be future opportunities to restart the procedure. In the next paragraphs we detail the steps followed in applying the Scientific Method in Process Improvement depicted in Fig. 6.

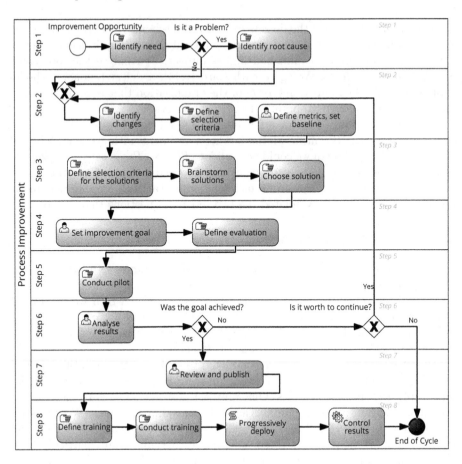

Fig. 6. Scientific Method in Process Improvement

Step 1 - Identify a need and characterise the current process
   The first step of process improvement is the identification of a need, e.g. an
organisation may want to achieve a business goal that cannot be attained
using the current organisation setting, or the organisation may be facing a
problem that needs to be solved, as it is affecting the success of their business.
   – In our experiment the *need* was to reduce the number of defects from
     the requirements phase, only detected in posterior phases of the software
     development cycle.
When the need exists it is necessary to find the reason why it cannot be
fulfilled in the current setting, the root cause of the problem or to identify
which processes can be changed to achieve a goal.
   – The target process area was Requirements Management, more specifically
     the process *Review Requirements*.

- The process improvement aimed to detect defects more effectively in requirement reviews, hence, we gathered a defect classification taxonomy, specific for requirements.

It is important to be able to measure improvements [9], otherwise one cannot determine if they were beneficial or nefarious. It is necessary to determine the performance indicators that need to be monitored and create a baseline of those indicators. When EQualPI is used to monitor a Process Improvement that task is facilitated because it is even possible to detect its effect in other processes by in turn monitoring some of their indicators.

The baseline provides the state of the current process, *as is*, including the indicators values in that state. At this stage the improvement is characterised in terms of what the *need* and the *goal* to achieve are.

Step 2 - Identify and define improvement

It is necessary to determine the changes to implement, following established selection criteria: what methods will be used and what metrics can be chosen to monitor impact of the changes. If the case is to solve a problem whose origin is unknown, one must select an adequate set of metrics to monitor and analyse it in order to determine the root cause of the problem and help define a solution to it. For control, the baseline of the chosen metrics is set.

- If we could pilot our improvement in an organisation, we would want to understand the number of defects that were detected in posterior development phases that were caused by requirements defects. Therefore, the metrics to monitor would be the *defects per phase originated in the requirements phase*. The organisation that adopted the classifiers list did not monitor exactly those metrics, but did focus on finding a higher number of defects in the Requirements phase.

Step 3 - Determine selection criteria and select improvement methods accordingly (This step is specific to what we did to design our improvement, and may only be applicable on similar ones.)

- In our experiment we assembled a classifiers list, by reviewing the literature to find what defects classifications were used and which ones were specific/more adequate to classify requirements defects. Another aspect considered was whether there were recommendations on how to correctly define a classification list or not, and used the quality properties of a good classification scheme [4] as a reference.

Step 4 - Set improvement goals and how to validate them

Organisations have to ensure that improvements are not only effective but also efficient and must guarantee Return on Investment (ROI).

- If our improvement was to be done in an organisation it would be necessary to analyse the costs of requirements reviews and of fixing defects in posterior phases, such as development, validation and maintenance. The current costs and the goal costs to be achieved would also have to be documented. A simulator could be used to predict the ROI of the improvement, where cost of training personnel, ramp-up time and updating tools would also need to be considered.

- In an organisation setting, to test our process improvement, the final number of defects per phase originated in the Requirements phase would have to be reduced to consider the improvement successful.

- The goals of our experiment were to ensure that the classification list was useful to classify requirements defects; people would understand the list, and they would do an uniform classification without confounding classifiers.

- We validated the classifiers list by measuring the level of concordance of individuals when classifying the same defect. Formalising the hypothesis H, when reviewing requirements specifications:
  H_0 - all subjects use the same value to classify the type of a defect.
  H_1 - not all subjects use the same value to classify the type of a defect.

- We performed a Cochran test, which is binomial, considering that when the subjects chose the most used classifier they answered as the *majority (1)* and when they used any other classifier, they chose *other (0)*. The Fleiss' kappa was used to measure the level of agreement between subjects to classify the same defect.

In any improvement that involves classification, a similar experiment design can be used. In some cases, one way of evaluating adherence to a process is doing a survey. We also like to (correctly) perform individual interviews.

Step 5 - Pilot the process improvement

To pilot a Process Improvement it is necessary to select projects, that are representative of the population, to use the improvement, and to include a control group that will use the current practices. The people using the *to be* process need to receive training. The criteria to select pilots can vary, but here are a couple of examples: 1) Projects with good effort and cost margins, to ensure the team has time to follow new practices without compromising the project's successful completion. 2) Projects of short duration, to get results faster, in case the improvement does not require a given project size.

- In our experiment the subjects were instructed on how to execute the process, i.e. how to do the assigned task, and we included a table with the definition of each defect type, followed by an example of how to use it.

Step 6 - Analyse pilot results

Analyse the results of the pilot to verify: 1) If the improvement actually occurs. 2) What is the impact on the indicators of the process and on the indicators of other processes that may be impacted as well. So, several ones may have to be monitored to understand whether the improvement needs refinement and a new experiment should be executed. 3) If it is necessary to repeat steps 2, 3, 4 and 5.

– We did a second experiment (group 2) because we realised that the results obtained with the first classification list were not satisfactory. So, we followed the lessons learnt to refine the Requirements Type Classification list.

Step 7 - Prepare final version
(When applicable)
The final process must be documented and training material prepared so the users can learn the new process. In our case, as in others, this step may also include updating existing tools, add tool tips to help people remember definitions, and update Help with definitions and examples. New tools or changes to existing ones should be tested in pilot projects, to validate them and ensure that they are ready to be used in practice. It is crucial to ensure everyone has a common understanding or if refinement is needed.

Step 8 - Progressively deploy and control
Do the progressive deployment as indicated in the Setup phase of EQualPI [12], while controlling the indicators in parallel, progressively train all teams.

5   Discussion

To analyse the execution of the Process Improvement steps using the Scientific Method more objectively, we mapped the activities of each step and identified them as mandatory or not. Per mandatory activity there is a maximum score of 2, when the activity is successfully performed, and 0, if it was not executed. In case of partially conducting the activity the score given is 1. We summarise the evaluation in Table 3. The total score if all mandatory activities are executed is 36. Evaluating the steps we executed while conducting the experiments with the students we sum a total score of 25, having performed ~70% of the mandatory activities. If we consider in addition the data of the implementation of the process improvement results by an organisation, the score increases to 33, having performed ~92% of the mandatory activities. We can also see that the a set of steps and involved activities can be found in the analysed related work.

5.1   Process Improvement Steps

We did not fully validate *Step 1 - Identify a need and characterise the current process* because we did not use an indicator of the current state of the process, the *"as is"*, before starting the improvement. Ideally, to be able to measure the effect of the improvement we would have the number of requirements defects detected in requirements reviews vs those detected in posterior phases, before introducing the improvement. That baseline would allow us to measure the effect of the improvement by increasing the number of defects detected in the requirements phase, and getting a reduction of those defects in the next phases of the projects.

Table 3. Evaluation of the improvement steps we executed

Improvement steps and respective activities	SM	Act	Man	Exe	Score
Step 1 - Identify a need and characterise the current process	**A**	4			
Identify need			Yes	Yes	2
Root causes/Process to improve			Yes	Yes	2
Step 2 - Identify and define improvement	**B**	6			
Determine changes to implement			Yes	Yes	2
Selection criteria			Yes	Yes	2
Define metrics to monitor and set baseline			Yes	Par	1
Step 3 - Determine selection criteria and select improvement methods accordingly	**B**	6			
Define selection criteria for the solutions			Yes	Yes	2
Brainstorm solutions			Yes	Yes	2
Select solution to implement according with the criteria			Yes	Yes	2
Step 4 - Set improvement goals and how to validate them		4			
Set target goal	**C**		Yes	Par	1
Define methods to analyse and determine if the goal was achieved			Yes	Yes	2
Step 5 - Pilot the process improvement	**D**	2			
Conduct pilot of the improvement with a group of subjects representative of the population			Yes	Par	1
When needed/possible have a control group not subject to the improvement			No	No	
Step 6 - Analyse pilot results		4			
Analyse pilot results	**E**		Yes	Yes	2
Determine if the goal was achieved	**F**		Yes	Yes	2
If needed repeat steps 2 to 5			No	Yes	
Step 7 - Prepare final version		2			
Publish the final version of the improvement	**G**		Yes	Yes	2
Step 8 - Progressively deploy and control		8			
Define training process			Yes	Yes	2
Conduct training			Yes	Yes	2
Gradually deploy to other subjects			Yes	Yes	2
Control the improvement variables to ensure there are no deviations from the goal			Yes	Yes	2
Total		36			33

Note: Going back to Fig. 5 we added the letters attributed to each activity of the Scientific Method to collumn SM. Only the mandatory (Man) activities of a step receive a score: Yes = 2, Partially (Par) = 1 and No = 0. Act indicates the maximum score of the activities of a given step, Exe means Executed.

All other steps could be adapted to the improvement, although we would rather have validated *Step 4 - Set improvement goals and how to validate them* with more quantitative goals related to reducing the number of defects in subsequent phases of the development process, rather than just getting a good level of agreement using the classification scheme. Considering the goal of showing that a list of defects types specific for requirements defects is more appropriate than those that are non-specific, the experiment should have been done with a control group that would use for example ODC to classify the defects, as indicated in *Step 5 - Pilot the process improvement.*

Regarding *Step 8 - Progressively deploy and control* we could not directly validate it, as it would require following the deployment in the organisation that adopted it and measure the effects of using it. Nonetheless, one of the quantitative goals we would set if we conducted the experiment in the organisation ourselves, namely to reduce the number of defects in subsequent phases, was achieved, since the organisation did find a higher number of defects in requirements reviews than before introducing the improvement, when they were using the ODC classification. Additionally, the organisation also used the defects classification to analyse and address the most common defect types and further improve the requirements process to prevent them, serving one of the purposes of implementing it: to be able to analyse and correct the causes of those defects.

6   Conclusion

Of the 8 Process Improvement Steps in EQualPI we validated 7 and 2 were only partially validated as we could not define the metrics to monitor as indicated in *Step 2 - Identify and define improvement.* The group of subjects used to test the improvement may not be representative of the population as required in the first activity of *Step 5 - Pilot the process improvement*; it depends if they are already working as practitioners, even though they may represent some at the beginning of their career and some who have already been working in the field.

The Process Improvement procedure is focused on organisations. For that reason we consider it would be easier to follow those steps in an organisation. Nonetheless, we were able to complete almost all steps in the academic setting, showing that the process can be used, and is useful, for its purpose. While Juran's quality improvement and DMAIC put emphasis in determining the root causes of defects and eliminating them, reducing "chronic waste" [8], the improvement steps in EQualPI are more in alignment with implementing an improvement not just focused on reducing defects but also on having better ways of doing the work, in line with IDEAL, DMADV and PDSA, which in the end eliminates processes inefficiencies and ineffectiveness as well. The benefits of following the Process Improvement using the Scientific Method, that we describe in this paper, are getting more accurate results by having a pre-validation; benefiting of the Scientific Method for rigour, diminishing bias and having details that allow repeatability; and have extra-cautions for more successful Change Management and deployment.

As future research we will conduct an experiment regarding use of the Scientific Method for Process Improvement in industry.

References

1. Card, D.: Defect analysis: basic techniques for management and learning. Adv. Comput. **65**, 259–295 (2005). https://doi.org/10.1016/s0065-2458(05)65006-1
2. Card, D.N.: Learning from our mistakes with defect causal analysis. IEEE Softw. **15**(1), 56–63 (1998). https://doi.org/10.1109/52.646883

3. Chen, J.C., Huang, S.J.: An empirical analysis of the impact of software development problem factors on software maintainability. J. Syst. Softw. **82**(6), 981–992 (2009). https://doi.org/10.1016/j.jss.2008.12.036

4. Freimut, B., Denger, C., Ketterer, M.: An industrial case study of implementing and validating defect classification for process improvement and quality management. In: Proceedings of the 11th IEEE International Software Metrics Symposium, p. 19. IEEE Computer Society (2005). https://doi.org/10.1109/METRICS.2005.10

5. Goulão, M.C.P.A.: Component-Based Software Engineering: a Quantitative Approach. Doctoral, Universidade Nova de Lisboa, Faculdade de Ciências e Tecnologia (2008)

6. Gremba, J., Myers, C.: The ideal model: a practical guide for improvement. SEI Bridge **1**(3), 1–6 (1997)

7. Hahn, G.J., Hill, W.J., Hoerl, R.W., Zingraph, S.A.: The impact of six sigma improvement - a glimpse into the future of statistics. Am. Stat. **53**(3), 208–215 (1999). https://doi.org/10.2307/2686099

8. Juran, J.M., Godfrey, A.B.: Juran's Quality Handbook. McGraw-Hill, New York (1998)

9. Kitchenham, B.: Software Metrics: Measurement for Software Process Improvement. Blackwell Publishers Inc., Hoboken (1996)

10. Korsaa, M., et al.: The people aspects in modern process improvement management approaches. J. Process Evol. Process **25**(4), 381–391 (2013). https://doi.org/10.1002/smr.570

11. Lopes Margarido, I., Faria, J.P., Vieira, M., Vidal, R.M.: Classification of defect types in requirements specifications: literature review, proposal and assessment. In: Proceedings of the 6th Iberian Conference on Information Systems and Technologies (CISTI), Chaves, Portugal, pp. 555–561. IEEE (2011)

12. Lopes Margarido, I.: EQualPI: a Framework to Evaluate the Quality of the Implementation of the CMMI Practices. Doctoral, Faculdade de Engenharia da Universidade do Porto (2016)

13. Malinova, M., Gross, S., Mendling, J.: A study into the contingencies of process improvement methods. Inf. Syst. **104**, 101880 (2022). https://doi.org/10.1016/j.is.2021.101880

14. McFeeley, B.: IDEAL^{SM}: a user's guide for software process improvement. Technical report, CMU/SEI-96-HB-001, CMU/SEI (1996). https://doi.org/10.21236/ada305472

15. Moen, R., Norman, C.: Evolution of the PDCA cycle. In: Proceedings of the 7th ANQ Congress. Asian Network for Quality, Tokyo, Japan (2009)

Logs Based Verification Tool of Serious Game for Autistic Children

Arini Nur Rohmah[1] and Nelly Condori-Fernandez[2]([✉])

[1] Lappeenranta-Lahti University of Technology LUT, Lappeenranta, Finland
arini.nur.rohmah@student.lut.fi
[2] Centro Singular de Investigación en Tecnoloxías Intelixentes, CITIUS,
University of Santiago de Compostela, Santiago, Spain
n.condori.fernandez@usc.es

Abstract. Serious games are referred to as entertaining tools with a purpose of education. The correct implementation of serious games is very important to ensure a high level of adoption of the competencies by the game users, which can be even more challenging if we target autistic children. Understanding the actual needs of Children with Autism Spectrum Disorder (ASD) and supporting their learning activity through serious games can be a burden. This paper presents the architecture of logs based Verification tool, named GVT, to identify potential scenes of the serious game that might be causing any negative emotion on the autistic children. GVT architecture follows a client sever model, which enables to merge the game logs with the emotional data logs. The data analysis and visualization, carried out at the server side, should provide relevant information to support developers to enhance the quality of serious games for autistic people.

Keywords: Verification tool · Serious game · Inclusive game · Game logs · Stress · Autistic Children

1 Introduction

Lack of stress management is a common trait for children with Autism Spectrum Disorder (ASD) [16]. The traits which contribute to their aggressive behaviours include easily getting bored, having a temper tantrum, and meltdowns [11,16]. Those aggression highly happen when the children doing a learning activity especially at school or home [7]. Maintaining emotional stability is the key approach to effectively prevent aggressive behavior in children with autism [2].

One of the best attempts to engage children with ASD in a fun learning activity is by utilizing serious games (SG) [15]. However, stress level of children with mental disorder may be influenced by SG. Therefore, to mitigate the occurrence happens when children with ASD play SG, it will be beneficial if there is a tool to verify and analyze the SG for autistic children by considering those aspects.

© The Author(s), under exclusive license to Springer Nature Switzerland AG 2023
J. M. Fernandes et al. (Eds.): QUATIC 2023, CCIS 1871, pp. 121–129, 2023.
https://doi.org/10.1007/978-3-031-43703-8_9

Various guidelines, case studies, and tools have been developed to evaluate, validate, and analyze game design elements, aiming to enhance player satisfaction. However, there is limited development of a verification tool (VT) to assess game feasibility and maintain targeted players emotional stability. Creating a VT for this purpose can assist game developers in identifying potential stress triggers for autistic players and guide them to design more stressless games.

This paper proposes a prototype game verification tool (GVT) to enhance the design of SG for autistic children. The GVT helps game developers analyze elements that may cause high stress levels by integrating game player logs and emotion logs. The current prototype uses synthetic data for emotion logs, but the final version will connect with a mobile emotion detector app through Bluetooth. Players will wear a wearable emotion detector (ED) that generates data through the mobile app. By connecting the GVT with the mobile device via Bluetooth, it can analyze the data similar to the proposed prototype.

The paper is structured as follows: Sect. 2 maps related findings based on cost and stakeholder involvement. Section 3 describes the proposed GVT architecture and data analysis process. Section 4 covers the development process. Finally, Sect. 4 concludes the paper, addressing limitations and providing recommendations.

2   Related Work

Several verification and validation (V&V) methods have been proposed to assist game developers for developing more inclusive games. In this section, we present some of those previous approaches used to assess or verify game components. Our analysis was carried out based on two criteria: end-user involvement and cost. Figure 1 shows a mapping of these previous works in games V&V.

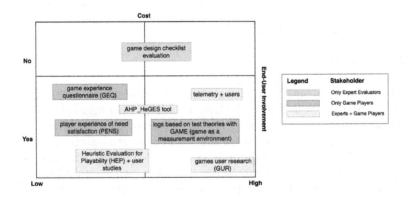

Fig. 1. Mapped evaluation techniques

Identifying and validating game design elements can be done according to what the game is targeted for. For example, the research done by Razali N. E.

M. et al [12] focuses on the validation of serious game elements in the context of climate change. The validation method does not require the end-user involvement, instead, it needs experts in climate change topic to validate the game design using a *game criteria checklist*. It is considered relative costly due to the number of experts required. According to the authors, the validation process might take more than two weeks.

Another validation approach is based on questionnaires. Jsselsteijn et al. proposed a *Game Experience Questionnaire* (GEQ), which consists of: (i) core questionnaire (ii) social presence module and (iii) post-game module [5, 6]. Moreover, a scoring guideline was also proposed to facilitate how to evaluate the questionnaire result. Considering that the duration to do the analysis using this method is according to how many participants (which when there is a small number of participant, the duration will be short) and there is no expert or expensive equipment needed, the method is considered low cost. Another common-used game validation method using questionnaire is *Player Experience of Need Satisfaction* (PENS) proposed by Ryan et al. [6, 13]. PENS has been created as an elaboration theory of self-determination theory (SDT) [13]. SDT itself discusses factors related to motivation (either to undermine or facilitate it). Since this method does not need much resource and the number of participant as well as the duration are not fixed, it is also considered low cost.

Heuristic Evaluation for Playability (HEP) is a method proposed by H. Desurvire et al. [3]. HEP needs several evaluators to inspect the game based on player logs. The method also requires the involvement of game players to which they have to fill satisfaction questionnaire. Even though the method was stated to be cheap, fast, and easy [3], we consider that gathering evaluators in one place may be challenging. Thus, we mapped the cost of HEP is in middle-low. H. M. Omar et al. developed an AHP_HeGES (Analytic Hierarchy Process Based Holistic Online Evaluation System for Educational Computer Game) tool [10]. AHP_HeGES combines two evaluation techniques: Playability Heuristic for Educational Game (PHEG) and Playability Assessment for Educational Computer Game (PAEG) [10]. AHP_HeGES is an online tool for educational computer game experts' evaluators in which addressing the challenge faced by HEP (to gather evaluators in one place). By online tool, evaluators are not required to be in the same place. The evaluation process of AHP_HeGES focus on formative evaluation. The cost of using AHP_HeGES tool is considered in the middle range since it requires the maintenance of the tool and the database system to save the PHEG module from expert evaluators.

Takahiro Miura et al. in their research proposed a method called GAME (*Game As a Measurement Environment*) [8]. This method is for evaluating both game content and interface based on test theories (i.e., classical test theory and item response theory). This method aims for effectively evaluating inclusive games. It is considered relatively costly, since it requires a high number of participants and time. For example, according to the evaluation carried out by the authors using GAME, it took more than two months to gain a total of 388 participants [8].

Games User Research (GUR) technique was proposed by Lennart E. Nacke [9]. The technique is used to optimize the user experience in games and virtual entertainment products. Physiological evaluation is aimed to be a standard tool in GUR. Considering that the targets are for academic and industrial applications, it was stated that currently the physiological evaluation methods used for GUR require expensive equipment which is used primarily in a laboratory setting [9]. With that point, the cost to apply GUR is the highest compared to other mapped techniques. On the other hand, *telemetry and users* analytics technique focuses in two aspects of game analytics: game telemetry and game metrics. This analytic technique was raised by Anders Drachen et al [4]. Overall, the technique collects over a distance data which is valuable for game development or game research to be transformed into metrics to which then being analyzed. As there are eight total steps to be done, in which the data processing and analytic part are considered complicated, the cost to operate this technique is considered high as well [4].

In accordance to our findings, the most closest research is GUR. However, physiological responses evaluation in GUR requires these following equipment: Electromyography (EMG), Electrodermal Activity (EDA) and Galvanic Skin Response (GSR), Cardiovascular Measures, and Electroencephalography (EEG) in which those are considered obtrusive for mental disorder children especially children with ASD. Meanwhile, considering that our research focuses in analyzing game elements to maintain players stress level, we need to diminish using equipment that may trigger high stress level for players when carrying the testing and evaluation process. Doing so, our technique only entails a simple wearable stress detector for players to use. Hence, our technique is reconnoitred as unobtrusive for autistic players.

Previous techniques primarily target general games and involve end-users in the verification and validation (V&V) process. However, those approaches do not address the limitations of children with mental disorders, making the V&V process less inclusive. On the other hand, a simple V&V tool can be beneficial in terms of cost and time, supporting not only industrial applications but also small start-ups or individual game developers interested in creating serious games for autistic children to validate their games.

Taken that into account, GVT has been developed to be a simple but beneficial low-cost serious games verification tool for autistic children. The next section will discuss about the proposed GVT architecture and the required player logs.

3   GVT Architecture

The current GVT architecture uses a client-server model. Figure 2 shows how a GVT server shares resources to analyze the data gathered from a network, where the game to be verified and the GVT desktop are hosted.

GVT desktop app is composed of **GVT configurator** module, which allows to (i) set local host IP address, (ii) get game path, and (iii) choose emotion detector (ED) device. Module (ii) and (iii) require **GVT user** to input

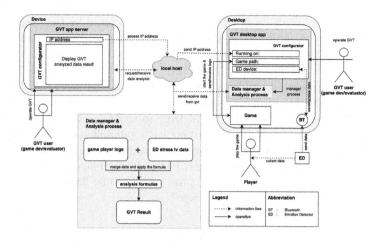

Fig. 2. GVT architecture

and choose Game path and the ED device respectively to initialize the GVT. When the GVT desktop app is initialized, it will directly start the **Game** inside the chosen path to be verified. The **Data manager** starts monitoring the player logs and the player's emotion logs (stress level values) is collected by **ED** via Bluetooth (**BT**) during the game playing. Since we are still in the development process of GVT, instead of using a real ED, the emotion logs of ED for the prototype was generated by synthetic data. The synthetic data range value is based on range generated by a device from a research done by Suni-Lopez et al. in [14]. The value is in a 5 points range, which 1 represents absent of stress (relaxed) while the presence of stress starts from point 4 (with the highest level correspond to 5). The data is then going through **Analysis process** to be analyzed. From other **Device**, GVT user can operate the **GVT app server**. GVT user is required to operate it in order to display the result from Data manager & Analysis process accordingly.

GVT is required to have usable characteristic for GVT users which is including to have the following quality properties: appropriateness, recognizability, learnability, and operability along with availability and maintainability.

3.1 Data Manager and Analysis Process

GVT entails game player logs and emotion logs. Author proposed that there is minimum requirement for the player logs. The **player logs** preferably is in json format with minimum having these following variables: (i) time: yyyy-MM-dd HH:mm:ss, (ii) scene: scene_name, (iii) asset: asset_name, (iv) events: click/drag/drop, (v) task: success/fail.

Player logs time variable should represent the time for every triggered events. Scene should indicate chapters of the game which are composed of assets, tasks, and events. Meanwhile, asset is property that construct the game (for example:

button, image, etc.). Task presents game challenge to fulfill by the player, while events are how the player finish the task using external input (for example mouse manipulation).

In addition, as GVT requires to present valuable data analysis for game developers, data generated by player logs must be examined with the formula as shown in Table 1. From player logs and emotion logs, GVT can deliver new data: "time spent", "time accumulation", "total time in scene", and "average stress in scene". In order to provide game developers with valuable data analysis, Game Verification Tool (GVT) necessitates the examination of data generated by player logs using the formula outlined in Table 1. By analyzing player logs and emotion logs, GVT can yield new data such as "time spent", "time accumulation", "total time in scene", and "average stress in scene".

Table 1. Formula

Value	Formula
time spent	ts E0 = $(tE1 - tE0)$
time accumulation	ta En = $\Sigma((tE1 - tE0) + (tE2 - tE1) + (...) + (tEn + 1 - tEn))$
total time in scene	tScene = $\Sigma(tsE1 + tsE + .. + tsEn)$
Avg Stress in Scene	$\Sigma((sE1s * tsE1s) + (sE2s * tsE2s) + ... + (sEns * tsEns))/\Sigma(tsE1s + tsE2s + tsEns))$

Time spent is the duration between the current and next event in the game. It is calculated by subtracting the current event time from the next event time. **Time accumulation** represents the total duration from the first event to the current event. It is calculated by subtracting the previous event time from the current event time and adding the result to the accumulated time. **Total time in scene** is the overall duration spent in a specific scene. It is calculated by summing the time spent on each activity within that scene. **Average stress in scene** represents the average stress level in a particular scene. It is calculated by multiplying the stress level by the time spent in each activity within the scene, and dividing it by the total time in the scene.

By utilizing game logs in conjunction with this formula, developers can distinguish the specific scenes that induce a high average stress level. As scenes consist of assets, events, and tasks, these details provide insight into which elements need improvement in order to make the scene less stressful. In order to test our first GVT prototype, we used a modified existing serious game, called Gemas [1]. Initially, Gemas was a static game for autistic children based on kinect which could not generate player logs. Gemas was then modified into a desktop game which can generate player logs.

4   Conclusions

This research aims to propose a novel solution using emotion logs and game logs to verify serious games for autistic children. To this aim, we analyzed previous V&V approaches based on user involvement (players and experts/non-experts) and estimated cost. Previous approaches primarily focus on player satisfaction, involving game players in the V&V process through questionnaires about their game experience. However, these approaches are not tailored to autistic children, as they are not the target audience. The questionnaire design does not consider the specific needs of children with ASD. Our investigation revealed that the GUR technique closely aligns with our approach, however, physiological measurements may be obtrusive for children with mental disorders, particularly those with ASD. In response to this, we propose an unobtrusive V&V technique specifically designed for them. The insights from this study can assist game developers in creating more inclusive serious games for children with ASD.

GVT aims to evaluate game elements to maintain autistic players stress level. In the end of the research, we expect a fully integration between GVT and emotion detector (ED), built by Suni-Lopez et al. [14]. We are planning to carry out a pilot study to test and evaluate the prototype with end-users who for now are non-autistic children, but later on it would be with actual autistic people. Moreover, we plan also to involve external serious games developers for testing the usability of GVT tool, by focusing on the report of analyzed GVT results.

Limitations: GVT is designed as a straightforward game analysis tool, relying on game player logs and an ED (Emotion Detector). However, certain serious games for autistic children lack player logs, limiting GVT's ability to analyze them. Another challenge is that GVT is currently limited to desktop games (since it is considered that having bigger media can help children with ASD to be more focus), while there are valuable serious mobile games that also require analysis. Further research is needed to see in which extent our script, that was implemented to generate logs for Gemas, could be reused in other games.

Recommendations: There is a space that can be improved in our research work. To fill that space, we recommend a further development of our GVT for not only consider autistic players stress level in particular, but also an extended range of emotions (for instance: happy, anxiety, shock, mad, and etc.) which thus will open a possibility to integrate GVT with other future wearable ED devices. Furthermore, as stated in the Limitations section, our GVT requires game player logs in which generated externally from the games. Addressing that, it will be promising if GVT can generate game player logs automatically internally so that GVT can evaluate both games with and without player logs. Additionally, being able to evaluate serious mobile games for autistic children using GVT will also recommend for a future research.

Acknowledgements. This project is supported by the Spanish Ministry of Science and Innovation. Grant PID2021-123152OB-C21 funded by MCIN/AEI/ 10.13039/501100011033, and by the Erasmus Mundus Joint Master Degree program SE4GD-619839.

References

1. Al Irsyadi, F.Y., Rohmah, A.N.: Game edukasi bagi anak autis bertema anggota keluarga berbasis kinect xbox 360. [serious game for autistic children based on kinect xbox 360 to study family members]. Simetris: Jurnal Teknik Mesin Elektro dan Ilmu Komputer **8**(2), 739–746 (2017)
2. Berkovits, L., Eisenhower, A., Blacher, J.: Emotion regulation in young children with autism spectrum disorders. J. Autism Dev. Disord. **47**(1), 68–79 (2016). https://doi.org/10.1007/s10803-016-2922-2
3. Desurvire, H., Caplan, M., Toth, J.A.: Using heuristics to evaluate the playability of games. In: CHI 2004 Extended Abstracts on Human Factors in Computing Systems, pp. 1509–1512 (2004)
4. Drachen, A., El-Nasr, M., Canossa, A.: Game analytics - the basics. In: Game Analytics Maximizing the Value of Player Data, pp. 13–40 (2013). https://doi. org/10.1007/978-1-4471-4769-5_2
5. IJsselsteijn, W., de Kort, Y., Poels, K.: The Game Experience Questionnaire. Technische Universiteit Eindhoven (2013)
6. Johnson, D., Gardner, M.J., Perry, R.: Validation of two game experience scales: the player experience of need satisfaction (PENS) and game experience questionnaire (GEQ). Int. J. Hum. Comput. Stud. **118**, 38–46 (2018)
7. Machalicek, W., O'Reilly, M.F., Beretvas, N., Sigafoos, J., Lancioni, G.E.: A review of interventions to reduce challenging behavior in school settings for students with autism spectrum disorders. Res. Autism Spectr. Disord. **1**(3), 229–246 (2007). https://doi.org/10.1016/j.rasd.2006.10.005
8. Miura, T., et al.: Game: game as a measurement environment: scheme to evaluate interfaces and game contents based on test theories. Proc. ACM Interact. Mob. Wearable Ubiquitous Technol. **4**(4) (2020). https://doi.org/10.1145/3432702
9. Nacke, L.E.: Games user research and physiological game evaluation. In: Game User Experience Evaluation, pp. 63–86 (2015)
10. Omar, H.M., Ibrahim, R., Jaafar, A.: Methodology to evaluate interface of educational computer game. In: 2011 International Conference on Pattern Analysis and Intelligence Robotics, vol. 2, pp. 228–232. IEEE (2011)
11. Overskeid, G.: Power and autistic traits. Front. Psychol. **7** (2016). https://doi.org/ 10.3389/fpsyg.2016.01290
12. Razali, N.E.M., Ramli, R.Z., Mohamed, H., Mat Zin, N.A., Rosdi, F., Mat Diah, N.: Identifying and validating game design elements in serious game guideline for climate change. Heliyon **8**(1), e08773 (2022). https://doi.org/10.1016/j.heliyon.2022. e08773
13. Ryan, R.M., Rigby, C.S., Przybylski, A.: The motivational pull of video games: a self-determination theory approach. Motiv. Emot. **30**, 344–360 (2006)
14. Suni Lopez, F., Condori-Fernandez, N., Catala, A.: Towards real-time automatic stress detection for office workplaces. In: Lossio-Ventura, J.A., Muñante, D., Alatrista-Salas, H. (eds.) SIMBig 2018. CCIS, vol. 898, pp. 273–288. Springer, Cham (2019). https://doi.org/10.1007/978-3-030-11680-4_27

15. Tsikinas, S., Xinogalos, S.: Studying the effects of computer serious games on people with intellectual disabilities or autism spectrum disorder: a systematic literature review. J. Comput. Assist. Learn. **35**(1), 61–73 (2018). https://doi.org/10.1111/jcal.12311

16. White, S.W., Oswald, D., Ollendick, T., Scahill, L.: Anxiety in children and adolescents with autism spectrum disorders. Clin. Psychol. Rev. **29**(3), 216–229 (2009). https://doi.org/10.1016/j.cpr.2009.01.003

Beyond Dashboards: Operationalising a Measurement Framework for Agile Teams

Gijsbert C. Boon[✉], Christoph J. Stettina, Joost Visser, and Yassin El-Baz

Leiden Institute of Advanced Computer Science, Leiden University, Niels Bohrweg 1, 2333 CA Leiden, The Netherlands
g.c.boon@liacs.leidenuniv.nl

Abstract. *Context:* Abundant literature is available on metrics that can support Agile teams in improving their way of working and performance. However, little knowledge is available on how to operationalise metrics successfully.

Objective: Our objective is to understand the challenges and benefits of selecting measures and introducing these via dashboards in supporting Agile teams in their improvement ambitions.

Method: We report on Action Research in a large international organisation where metrics dashboards are introduced to Agile teams with varying levels of Agile maturity and diverse purposes. We observed dashboard usage and assessed actionability through surveys and interviews.

Results: Our key observations are: (1) Metrics support Agile teams in improving performance with higher gains by teams with lower Agile maturity; (2) Collecting and sharing qualitative survey data interactively during Agile rituals is highly effective; (3) Measurement data quality is a key factor influencing actionability.

Conclusions: Metric dashboards support organisations and Agile teams in their improvement ambitions. Optimal results are achieved by selecting *just enough* metrics based on actionability. Dashboards should be differentiated based on Agile maturity and customised to the needs of teams. Important factors for actionability are the interactive collection of qualitative measures and data quality. Data quality proves to be two-faced: measurement improves adherence to processes and data maintenance while on the other hand, a lack of trust in the numbers impedes the use of measurements.

Keywords: Agile transformation · Metrics · Dashboard · Performance Measurement · Actionability

1 Introduction

Organisations implementing Agile frameworks, like Scrum or SAFe [32], typically apply metrics as part of their continuous improvement cycles and daily work to help teams with dashboards to reflect and improve. However, while many metrics

© The Author(s), under exclusive license to Springer Nature Switzerland AG 2023
J. M. Fernandes et al. (Eds.): QUATIC 2023, CCIS 1871, pp. 130–146, 2023.
https://doi.org/10.1007/978-3-031-43703-8_10

have been discussed in empirical studies, the adoption process, selection of the right measurements and contextual factors are generally less well described [30].

To leverage the most value, it is crucial to understand the bigger picture of how a metric dashboard contributes to the improvement of the work of Agile teams and what the challenges are in selecting the right measurements and adopting these dashboards.

To understand factors like the *actionability* of metrics (i.e. the capacity of a metric to, proactively, raise awareness and take appropriate actions), and improve learning of teams and their alignment with stakeholders, we conducted an Action Research project, captured in the following research question:

RQ *What are the challenges and benefits of operationalising a measurement framework to help Agile teams improve?*

In Sect. 2 we describe the theoretical background on (operationalising) performance measurement in the context of Agile transformations and identify relevant gaps. Section 3 presents our action research approach to addressing the RQ. We share our learnings and recommendations in Sect. 4.

2   Theoretical Background

In this section we describe key elements related to the measurement of software development and the benefits and limitations of performance measurement and management in the context of Agile transformations.

Ample research has been published on measurement in specific areas such as software [21], processes [30], and maturity [10,13]. To broaden the scope to a more holistic concept of *performance*, literature has suggested three starting points for understanding this performance in an Agile context (cf. [19]): (1) strategic business objectives [16,18], (2) stakeholder needs [24,25], and (3) Agile principles [28]. We will now provide an overview of these perspectives and their respective backgrounds.

Perspective of *Business Objectives*. The Balanced Scorecard (BSC) model, developed by Kaplan and Norton [16] in the early 1990s, is one of the best-known approaches to determining performance objectives and measuring business performance. The aim of the model was *to align business activities to the vision and strategy of the business, improve internal and external communications, and monitor business performance against strategic goals* [16]. By using four perspectives (1) financial, (2) customer, (3) internal business processes, and (4) learning and growth, it offers a holistic approach *for motivating and measuring business unit performance*. We observe several potential weaknesses in the Agile context: (1) BSC mentions measuring business *unit* performance, not explicitly on other constructs e.g., processes, teams or people, which are obviously at the heart of Agile considering the Agile Manifesto [3]. (2) As noted by many (e.g., [20,24,27]), you might want to consider a broader group of stakeholders and therefore achieve an even more holistic and long-term approach. (3) Khurum et al. [18] created the

Software Value Map (SVM) building on Kaplan and Nortons BSC perspectives to project the BSC into the realm of software development. Alahyari et al. [1] projected this Value Map in an Agile software development context, concluding customer value as the most prioritised perspective, while innovation and learning and financial value received almost no priority. However, Korpivaara et al. [19] stated that financial performance objectives are also relevant for scaled Agile organisations. (4) We may conclude there is no shared opinion on the priorities of measurements.

Perspective of *Stakeholder Needs*. A broader stakeholder-driven approach attempts to optimise the needs and objectives of *all* stakeholder groups, including internal (e.g., the development team itself) as well as external stakeholders (e.g., customers, suppliers, partners, users). While not all stakeholder groups may be equally relevant in all contexts, Oza and Korkala [29] suggest that a stakeholder-driven approach balances different viewpoints and therefore provides a comprehensive foundation for performance metrics collection strategy. The term *stakeholder* in this paper is used in alignment with Mendelow's definition: *stakeholders of an organisation are those who depend on the organisation for the realisation of some of their goals, and in turn, the organisation depends on them in some way for the full realisation of its goals* [26] as opposed to a more narrow definition of stakeholders primary referring to customers or users, often used in practitioner context and in the aforementioned BSC-framework. List et al. [24] highlight the importance of *ownership* of this stakeholder-driven measurement: a stakeholder group invested in the performance of a metric, combined with the ability to impact it, will be more likely to yield results. Several challenges are relevant as raised by Ram et al. [30] on the operationalisation of metrics: (1) data availability, (2) supported by work processes (integration in these processes), and (3) actionability.

Perspective of Agile Transformations and Principles. Instead of applying general performance measurement approaches in an Agile context, other studies suggest that performance dimensions for Agile organisations can be derived from the Agile Manifesto and its accompanying principles [9,17,28,31,32]. Olszewska et al. [28] introduce a model containing eight quantitative metrics based on four areas: *Responsiveness, Throughput, Workflow distribution* and *Quality*. An international survey performed by Stettina et al. [33] compared the survey results to previous results of Laanti et al. [23], Olszewska et al. [28] and SAFe [32]. Next to this, including the context of Agile maturity, differentiation of organisational layers and additional measurements of *Employee satisfaction and engagement* as stakeholders into their framework. A case study of a large-scale Agile transformation of a financial services organisation supported by backlog data measurements is described by Boon and Stettina [4]. In these studies, the concept of deriving performance benefits is broadened to the way organisations follow Agile principles, which corresponds to Agile maturity [19]. Fontana et al. [10] state that 'Agile maturity means fostering more subjective capabilities, such as collaboration, communication, commitment, care, sharing and self-organisation' and present a framework [11] in which *ambidexterity* plays an important role; being adaptive, *explore* what practices work balanced with the process of *exploitation*, associated with its implementation aspect; execution and seeking efficiency. Improvement is guided by acting on the outcomes instead of following prescribed practices. Metrics geared towards principles are often based on software development activities and in that respect focused on internal delivery efficiency instead of externally generated outcomes. Few studies have shed light on how Agile organisations combine and prioritise internally oriented metrics based on Agile principles with those that measure external outcomes [19].

Kupiainen et al. [21] conducted a systematic literature review to identify the motivations and use of metrics within the context of Agile software development, concluding that there was a lack of empirical studies in an industrial context. This conclusion is supported by Ram et al. [30], researching the rationale and operational challenges of metrics in Agile software development.

With this overview of perspectives we identify the following research gaps:

1. Literature describes a need for selecting, prioritising and balancing the right metrics in measuring progress towards business goals and improving performance. However, empirical studies are scarce and sometimes contradictory;
2. The scope of stakeholder needs might be broadened beyond customers and feedback should be used for continuous improvement, i.e. the ability to act upon the results, expected in Agile contexts. Stakeholder-driven measurement is well documented, however, the questions raised to operationalise metrics seem unanswered.

In summary, we derive two main points of interest in using metrics for agile teams: (1) how one selects and prioritises the right measurements, and (2) how to operationalise these metrics to become effective for agile teams. In other words, do teams actually use the measurements to improve? We will reflect on these aspects in section *Learnings and discussion*.

3   Action Research

We applied Action Research (AR), a methodology to create knowledge through executing organisational change via a collaboration between researchers and practitioners [12]. AR is executed in four stages (see Fig. 1): diagnosing the current state, planning intervention actions, executing these actions, and reflecting on the results.

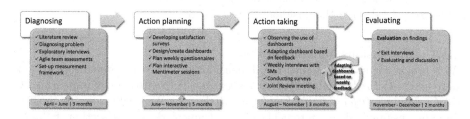

Fig. 1. Overview timelines, stages, and activities of Action Research

We applied the five principles of Canonical AR [8] as follows: (1) Researcher-client agreement: the research was executed as part of a formal thesis assignment of the fourth author, hosted by the case organisation, and supervised by the other authors. (2) Cyclical process model: We adopted the process model of Diagnosing, Action Planning, Action Taking, Evaluating and Specifying Learning. One full cycle was completed. (3) Theory principle: The theoretical ambition is to understand the selection and operationalisation of measurements in Agile teams. (4) Change through action: the action researcher actively participated throughout the entire project. (5) Learning through reflection: surveys and interviews have been conducted to gather feedback.

The case organisation is a multinational global food corporation based in the USA with offices in the Netherlands. Several introductory conversations were held with key stakeholders e.g., the EMEA Lead Project Management Office (PMO) and an Agile coach. Seven agile teams were selected to participate, with an average team size of eight persons, ranging from four to thirteen members. Teams have been selected based on the fact they were Agile teams, open to participating, and their scopes were diverse (e.g., customer-facing, back-end).

3.1   Diagnosing

The case organisation introduced the Scrum framework some years ago; some teams longer than others (see Table 1). The initial question was to determine the right set of metrics to help improve teams. For this, a diverse and broad set of potential metrics was gathered. However, the way forward in selecting, assessing actionability measurements and potential benefits or challenges of introducing a measurement framework was unclear to management. In consultation with stakeholders and sponsors, the researchers proposed to conduct an AR project to iteratively explore which measurements and visualisations are most useful or actionable in the given organisational context using a metric dashboard.

To examine the current situation, exploratory interviews were held with the aforementioned stakeholders. The objective was to introduce, design and experiment with a performance measurement framework by means of a dashboard integrated into the Agile way of working for seven participating teams. In order to understand the context of these participating teams their Agile maturity was assessed with a questionnaire of eleven questions to gain an understanding of the way teams worked and to reflect on the influence of maturity on their use and need for measurements. We used the Agile maturity model of Laanti [22].

Below, we describe our initial selection of measurement (Sect. 3.1.1), the surveys (Sect. 3.1.2), and the dashboard (Sect. 3.1.3).

3.1.1   Dimensions and Categories

As a pragmatic starting point, the dimensions proposed by Stettina et al. [33] were used: (1) *Productivity*, (2) *Responsiveness*, (3) *Quality*, (4) *Workflow health*, (5) *Customer satisfaction*, (6) *Employee satisfaction*. We briefly describe the first four dimensions and measurements of this framework in this section, followed by a section elaborating on the last two survey measurements. Table 2 presents a complete list of the dimensions and (examples of) measurements. An example of a dashboard is shown in Fig. 2.

- *Productivity* this metric was not incorporated as management feared it could be perceived as micro-managing and therefore negatively influence the acceptance of the dashboard by teams;
- *Quality* we limited the scope of this category to statistics data on bugs;
- *Workflow health* e.g., `velocity, effort planned past 5 sprints` and *Workflow health current sprint* e.g., `items with no estimates`;
- *Responsiveness* e.g., `average cycle time, lead time`.

3.1.2 Satisfaction Surveys

Employee Satisfaction Surveys. It is evident that the inclusion of measurements conveying happiness of team members (i.e. employees) as key stakeholders (in terms of e.g., morale or satisfaction) might be relevant. Multiple measurement models focus on Employee satisfaction and have been evaluated by authors, however, the Minnesota Employee Satisfaction Questionnaire (MSQ) [34] was selected since it is considered the most pragmatic and is well-known. In consultation with stakeholders it was compacted, to ensure a high response rate, while keeping the essential parts. The MSQ categories used for questions are *Collaboration, Autonomy, Accomplishment feeling, Ability,* and *Stress-levels.* Agile teams varied in using Mentimeter (interactive, online) and Microsoft Forms (via email forms) as alternative survey tools within retrospectives (see Table 1 with team descriptives e.g., survey medium chosen, frequency of use and response rate).

Customer Satisfaction Surveys. Regarding Customer satisfaction, abundant models and questionnaires are available as well e.g., Net Promoter Score (NPS), and Customer Satisfaction Score (CSAT). The American Customer Satisfaction Index (ACSI) framework [2] has been selected by the researchers. Next to the fact that ACSI is amongst the most cited frameworks, the described *antecedents* are generic enough for use in the customer satisfaction context by all teams. This led to six questions based on each of the four antecedents: *Customer loyalty, Perceived Quality, Perceived Value, Expectations (i.e., Overall, Communication and Predictability)*. We limit our motivation for these models and their satisfaction measures respecting the scope of this paper.

3.1.3 PowerBI Dashboard

The set-up and design of PowerBI dashboards were executed in close cooperation with participating teams and the team's data was connected: (1) the Azure DevOps backlog, (2) Employee satisfaction survey results, and (3) Customer satisfaction survey results. Measurements were selected that fit within the dimensions of the framework and their availability. To avoid overwhelming team members with many metrics and visualisations, the sponsors challenged the design to fit into a *single* page. Via multiple design iterations together with teams, this ambition aligns with the recommendation of e.g. Hartmann & Dymond [14] of using a small set of metrics.

Table 1. Descriptives on participating teams: maturity, former use of metrics, # years active as a team, survey medium, interval to assess employee satisfaction and response.

Team	Agile Maturity (Laanti model)	# metrics already used before research	# years ago started	Employee satisfaction frequency	Employee satisfaction medium	Employee satisfaction response
A	Novice/Fluent	none	1.5	Monthly	MS Forms	low
B	Fluent/Advanced	4	3	Sprint	Mentimeter	high
C	Fluent/Advanced	5	1	Sprint	Mentimeter	high
D	Advanced	none	3	Monthly	MS Forms	low
E	Beginner	none	n.a	Monthly	MS Forms	low
F	Novice/Fluent	3	1	Sprint	Mentimeter	high
G	Fluent	1	2	Monthly	MS Forms	low

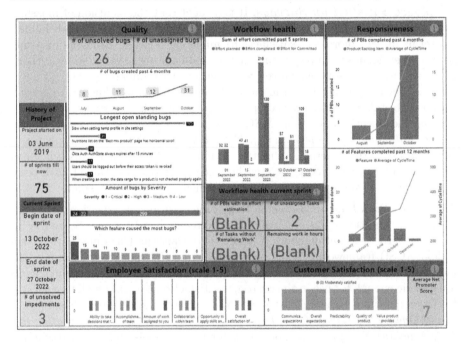

Fig. 2. Example of a PowerBI dashboard. Categories of Quality, Workflow Health, Responsiveness, Employee and Customer Satisfaction accompanied by custom information for teams. Categories and visualisation are similar for all team dashboards.

3.2 Action Planning

We planned several ways to collect findings: (1) Exploratory interviews, (2) Weekly meetings, (3) Interactive plenary meetings, (4) PowerBI dashboards, (5) Microsoft Forms and Mentimeter surveys, and (6) Exit interviews.

Semi-structured exploratory interviews were conducted with Scrum Masters and Product Owners. Questions were determined in consultation with the sponsor and other researchers, and their objective was twofold. First, as an introduction of the researcher and to manage expectations regarding the context, scope and approach of this AR. The second objective was to collect relevant background on team composition, deepen the researcher's knowledge of their Agile mindset, products and purposes, and understand their (customer-)stakeholder context. For all participating Agile teams, custom dashboards (see Sect. 3.1.3) were created with a selection of measurement dimensions described in the following sections.

An overview of the AR stages was presented in Fig. 1; the next section will elaborate on the content of the activities executed during these stages.

3.3   Action Taking

The action taking phase using the dashboards spanned over eleven weeks and was executed by the action researcher. During this time period, the action researcher was available for teams to observe, support teams and customise dashboards.

Weekly Interviews with Scrum Masters. Starting from the beginning of the action taking phase, the researcher updated the log starting the key question "Have you opened and used the dashboard this week?". However, to improve the understanding of actionability, after three weeks, the researcher focused on inquiring on *what concrete actions* had been taken by the team based on dashboard measures. Other questions zoomed in on presented metrics, the clarity of the dashboard presentation, change requests, and ideas for alternative metrics.

Employee Satisfaction Surveys. Teams using the Microsoft Forms tool were surveyed via email; the Scrum Master stimulated responses in their meetings and known communication channels. With the teams using the interactive Mentimeter survey, the researcher conducted the survey during the team's retrospectives with identical questions (results stayed hidden until all participants responded, to avoid influencing other team members).

Customer Satisfaction Surveys. The Microsoft Forms tool was used for Customer satisfaction surveys. A link was periodically sent via e-mail to customer stakeholders. The results of the Customer satisfaction surveys were added to the dashboard. Because of the lower frequency of these surveys, conclusions on their response rate changes are indeterminate.

Joint Demo & Review Session. In addition to the weekly individual interviews, a plenary meeting was planned in week 7 to share findings and report on the research progress. The group of attendees consisted of Scrum Masters, Product Owners, Agile coaches, stakeholders from PMO and the leadership team. During this session, an interactive Mentimeter survey was held to gather feedback and suggestions for improvement: (1) what participants liked so far in this measurement research, (2) what they missed and, (3) how likely they would recommend the dashboard/metrics approach to colleagues, similar to a Net Promoter Score query.

Logbook. During the action-taking phase, a detailed logbook was kept for each team registering notes on the weekly team interviews and additional observations of the participating researcher during the team meetings such as stand-up and retrospective meetings.

3.4   Evaluating

In this section we present our main observations and feedback from the weekly interviews, a plenary feedback session and exit interviews, followed by sections on benefits, challenges and discussion on the results.

3.4.1   Observations

We start by describing our main observations on usefulness, frequency of use, key factors influencing actionability and potential improvements to the research.

Do Teams Perceive the Metric Dashboards (Approach) as Useful? As part of weekly updates, we monitored closely whether teams used the dashboard and how they perceived its usefulness (cf. [7]). As part of the plenary exit meeting, we validated the (positive) feedback by asking *would you recommend this dashboard/metrics approach to other colleagues?*. Rated 7.5 on a 10-point scale.

How Often do Teams Use the Dashboards? More importantly, are teams using the metrics dashboard in their ambitions to improve their work, and, if so, how often? Teams reported in both their weekly updates and exit interviews using it *once or twice per sprint* as a common and desired frequency, either as part of rituals with the whole team and stakeholders present (e.g., planning, review, retrospective) and used by Scrum Masters individually to obtain insights in the team's activities.

What are the Factors Influencing Usability and Actionability? We report on three of the most important factors according to our findings:

(1) Agile Maturity: While all participating Agile teams experienced some benefits in using the dashboard, teams with lower Agile maturity reported to benefit more from the dashboard than teams with a higher level of Agile maturity to support their work. Teams with a lower level of Agile maturity experienced benefits using the dashboard to support their data maintenance and adherence to Agile processes. As an anecdotal example, the use of health metrics reminded teams to correctly assign effort estimations to user stories and to distribute unsolved bugs among team members. Teams with higher Agile maturity were less driven by metrics to guide them in their Agile work. Instead, potential improvements such as 'trusting each other to get the job done' was reported as more relevant, but could not be supported by metrics.

(2) Timing and right occasion: Not all metrics are relevant *all* the time. Some metrics might be more useful at the beginning of the sprint (e.g., the use of health metrics to check the hygiene of the backlog), while other metrics are useful during the sprint (e.g., cycle time to understand if items are lagging or impediments

arise), or metrics that are most useful at the end of a sprint (e.g., velocity in retrospect to learn how much work can be done at a sustainable pace). Other metrics add value to quarterly/yearly meetings (e.g., financial data) or release schedules (e.g., customer satisfaction).

(3) Selecting the right measurement dimensions: Some dimensions resulted in more actions than other categories as reported by Scrum Masters and their teams. We share these observations and summarise these in Table 2:

Quality Dimension. One team reported the category *Quality* as most useful and actionable. Another team stated to have been intensively using the metric `longest open bugs` in the *Quality* category.

Workflow Health Dimension. One team used the category *Workflow health current sprint* to manage their administrative process to improve data quality. Two teams explicitly confirmed this category proved actionable to mature their way of working.

Customer and Employee Satisfaction Surveys. Overall Scrum Masters emphasised the usefulness and actionability of these dimensions because quantifying customer satisfaction adds value and reported survey results could help them in their dialogue with other stakeholders to shed light on the question *what value is our team delivering?* Scrum Masters using the interactive Mentimeter tool during retrospective rituals reported the outcomes quantified their 'gut feelings'. Teams using Microsoft Forms for employee satisfaction showed a decreasing response rate as opposed to teams using Mentimeter (see Table 1). In contrast, two Scrum Masters stated that teams should already be aware of Employee and Customer satisfaction, so these two categories were less interesting in their opinion. Low to no actionability was observed or reported by Scrum Masters or team members when data on *employee satisfaction* was only visible on the dashboard presenting historical data.

With regard to the dimension of *Responsiveness*, it was unclear whether actionability was low caused by its looking back-nature (e.g., how many features/user stories were completed and what was their cycle time) or the perception of the Scrum Masters that Responsiveness metric data quality was not on par.

What are Potential Improvements of Metric Dashboards and Their Adoption? Participants have been asked to share their thoughts on potential improvements and missing elements regarding the dashboards. The majority of feedback concerned adding other metrics, followed by requests for (minor) changes in functionality and more emphasis on support and adoption management: (1) Other metrics 42% (e.g., focus on metrics that convey outcome & delivered value); (2) Functionality 25% (e.g., drill down functionality); (3) Adoption, support and change management 25% (e.g., more attention to adoption during the introduction and continuing support for dashboards afterwards). In summary, our key takeaways are (1) consider adding (or swapping with current) metrics on outcome c.q. value as a follow-up ambition; (2) pay close attention

Table 2. Measurement dimensions, measurements and observations on actionability.

Dimensions	Included	Measurement examples	Actionability remarks
Productivity	No	n.a.	not included
Responsiveness	Yes	lead time cycle time # user stories (PBIs) completed (period) # features completed (period)	mixed findings, data quality plays role trusting measurements
Quality	Yes	longest open bugs # unsolved bugs # unassigned bugs # bugs by severity # bugs created past 4 months Which feature caused most bugs	Positive on actionability e.g., actions taken on longest open bugs
Workflow health	Yes	Velocity Effort Planned past 5 sprints Effort completed, committed Current sprint: No estimates Current sprint: unassigned tasks Current sprint: tasks without remaining work	Positive on actionability. Improves data quality and adherence to processes
Customer satisfaction	Yes	Customer loyalty: how likely would you recommend this development team to your peers? (10-point scale) Perceived Quality: How satisfied are you with the quality of the product? (5-point Likert) Perceived Value: How satisfied are you with the value the product provides to you? (5-point Likert scales)	Mixed observations on actionability.
Employee satisfaction	Yes	How satisfied are you with the collaboration within the team? Autonomy: How satisfied are you with the ability as a team to take decisions that lead to better results? Accomplishment: How proud are you of the accomplishments as a team? Stress-level: How satisfied are you with the amount of work that was assigned to you? Ability: How satisfied are you with the opportunity to apply your skills (5-point Likert scales)	Mixed observations, Interactive measurement better on actionability and response rate

to the introduction and adoption, the continuous iterative improvement and support of dashboards. We reflect on the two observed topics *data quality* and the *interactive use* of measurements in our Learnings and discussion section. We continue with a summary of the benefits and challenges.

3.4.2 Benefits

The Potential of Transparency that Measurements Offer. The introduction of dashboards made Agile team processes more transparent, especially beneficiary for teams with a lower Agile maturity. The dashboard with Agile metrics motivated Scrum Masters and teams to reflect on the results, improve the quality of their backlogs, and discover ways to improve as a team and in their Agile way of working. The introduction of measurement dashboards was overall perceived as positive. Scrum Masters remarked that some information shared via the dashboard could not be queried or found otherwise as easily. The dashboard made them aware of potential impediments they needed to act on.

The Potential of Interaction Provided by Measuring. Dashboards supported Scrum Masters in their dialogue with team members with regard to their work and (sprint) backlog. Visualising and sharing metrics sparked relevant conversations. Scrum Masters were able to use dashboards to support decisions or requests to the team. The Mentimeter tool was used as an interactive part of retrospectives by some teams and reported on more productive dialogues, contributing to the purpose of retrospectives. Our findings showed that results of Employee and Customer satisfaction surveys both triggered relevant discussions since the outcomes quantified sentiments.

3.4.3   Challenges

One of the main challenges in introducing a dashboard containing Agile metrics was data quality. This caused some metrics to be perceived as not useful or actionable by the Scrum Masters and their teams. The cycle time metric, as an example, becomes useless when items are not registered timely. On the other hand, dashboards were used by teams to improve data quality e.g., workflow health was used effectively to identify unassigned issues.

A second challenge was adoption or implementation management. Scrum Masters and their teams needed to integrate the use of metrics with the use of their dashboard in existing working processes and routines.

The third challenge is to balance creating a default dashboard catering to the needs of most Agile teams versus accommodating the specific demands and preferences. Each team might use the tool in a different way, which translates into changing the dashboard to accommodate their way of working. On the other hand, one does not want to spend a lot of time customising the dashboard template for each team impeding maintainability and decreasing the ease of adding new measurements or improvements via a default dashboard. A balance needs to be found and evaluated to optimise the use (effectiveness) and efficiency.

The fourth challenge is that both Customer and Employee satisfaction rely on qualitative input from surveys. As observed, potential downsides are the response rate, their subjective nature and in that respect potential data quality issues.

4   Learnings and Discussion

The AR methodology was used to address our research question. Introducing and supporting metric dashboards were our means to the objective of getting a better understanding of both how to operationalise a metrics framework and the way metrics may support Agile teams in their improvement ambitions. We learned from the observed challenges and benefits that three aspects are important: (1) the benefit of an interactive collection of qualitative measurements like Customer and Employee satisfaction, (2) emphasise the importance of adaptation and customisation to (team) needs and maturity, and (3) the role of measurement data quality.

(1) Interactive collection and sharing of qualitative data. Measures related to stakeholders are of special interest for our research since stakeholder-driven

measurements (e.g., Customer and Employee satisfaction) are identified as key perspectives for performance measurement [19]. Customer satisfaction is often referred to as the highest priority in performance objectives [30]. An Agile mindset focuses on customer collaboration and (people) interactions, through the values of the Manifesto [3]. However, Agile methodologies do not explicitly prescribe specific metrics on Customer or Employee satisfaction. We reported ambiguity in the findings. On the one hand, both satisfaction metrics stimulated dialogues with teams and stakeholders and confirmed sentiments. On the other hand, only a limited number of actions have been reported based on these measurements and therefore some teams suggested that these metrics should not have the highest priority to be included in the dashboards. Our take on this ambiguity is that the metrics become more actionable when they are interactive, on the other hand, the interactive aspect of metrics makes them less interesting to display on the dashboard. We suggest when using qualitative dimensions like employee/team member satisfaction to conduct these interactively as an integral part of team rituals to ensure engagement, improve dialogue with stakeholders, and thereby actionability.

(2) Adoption management and customising. We recommend organising a well-guided introduction. Nudging teams using the dashboard and embedding using metrics in their day-to-day rituals are fundamental. Furthermore, continuous technical support and support from management are reported as crucial. Customising the framework to fit the maturity and the needs of the teams iteratively proved a success factor for the use(fullness) of dashboards and should be weighed against maintainability and efficiency aspects. Teams use only a limited set of metrics effectively, guided by actionability, so the focus should be on *just enough* metrics. Our point of departure was a basic set of measurement dimensions inspired by Stettina et al. [33], excluding the *Productivity* dimension, herewith avoiding potential discussions on the micro-management perception. It proved productive to *just start* with this set, avoiding being immersed in lengthy discussions, and incrementally optimising this selection of right measurements. We suggest that *right* measurements in this context are *actionable* measurements.

(3) Measurement Data quality. During the project data quality and the efficiency of the collection of data proved a prerequisite for the use of metrics. There are two sides to this story. As an example, the dimension *Workflow health* helped teams to improve data quality. Especially, teams with *lower* maturity benefited from using the dashboards to improve the quality of (following) the process and data. A measurement like *Workflow health* enhances the actionability of the measurement framework in general. On the other hand, teams stopped using metrics (e.g., `lead` or `cycle time`) when they did not trust the numbers. It is therefore important to understand these dynamics as part of the selection process.

4.1   Limitations and Threats to Validity

Our research was limited to seven teams to ensure a thorough dialogue with team members. However, it is potentially difficult to generalise findings due to this focus. Since the teams had different levels of Agile maturity and teams worked on diverse products, we argue this threat to validity is partly mitigated. The reliability of the observations was impacted by the fact that two of the seven participating Agile teams could not or did not leverage the value from the dashboards as much as was expected; one team was nearing the end of their project, and another team was *on hold* for some weeks. Two additional remarks on team selection; Firstly, we did not observe differences in results due to the team size. Secondly, we introduced a potential bias by selecting teams that were willing to participate. It would improve validity to further assess the impact of these decisions.

Additionally, there are specific threats to (participatory) action research. Even though there is no shared agreement on this topic, we mention known threats relevant to this study. Checkland & Holwell [5] state that action researchers must ensure reproducible research, mitigated by our effort in logging our observations carefully. Herr & Anderson [15] state that because of its participatory nature, it is important to remain aware of the political factor, as the researcher may be indirectly influenced or biased by office politics. Since the seven participating product teams were responsible for different products, the mutual influence was limited and most interactions with the researcher and team were in separate meetings. Furthermore, the role of the sponsors of this AR was not steering but limited to providing feedback on some occasions. Finally, Coughlan & Coghlan [6] state that a principal threat to the validity of this methodology is the researcher's potential lack of neutrality. This threat has been mitigated by the factual and neutral formulations in logbooks and regular mutual feedback moments with other authors (not operationally involved). Finally, the ambition of this research was to study how measurement may support improving the way of working of teams, not to measure the improvement in performance. For this reason, we can not draw conclusions on the direct relation between performance and metrics.

5   Conclusions

The objective of this Action Research study was to investigate the benefits and challenges of operationalising a performance measurement dashboard to support Agile teams in achieving their improvement ambitions. The measurement dimensions framework as proposed by Stettina et al. [33] was used as the starting point for designing dashboards and team rituals for seven teams over a period of nine months.

The study shows that differentiating dashboards based on Agile team maturity supports actionability. Additionally, data quality affects actionability in two ways: (1) low data quality impedes the use of measurements by a lack of trusting the numbers, and (2) transparency improves adherence to processes and data maintenance and therefore stimulates action taking. Another finding is that qualitative measures (i.e. stakeholder dimensions) become more actionable when used in an interactive and shared format. In selecting and prioritising *just enough* metrics, we learned that *actionability* should be a key criterion; adding judgement power to criteria like perceived usefulness (cf. [7]). We conclude that the success of the use of dashboards depends on the guidance, integration in new (or existing) work processes and (continuous) adaptation to the team's needs.

The contributions of this study are twofold: (1) it provides empirical evidence of the encountered benefits and challenges when operationalising a measurement framework, and (2) to practitioners, it demonstrates how the Agile teams in this study achieved optimal results by selecting just enough metrics while focusing on actionability, data quality and team maturity.

References

1. Alahyari, H., Svensson, R.B., Gorschek, T.: A study of value in agile software development organizations. J. Syst. Softw. **125**, 271–288 (2017)
2. Anderson, E.W., Fornell, C., Lehmann, D.R.: Customer satisfaction, market share, and profitability: findings from Sweden. J. Mark. **58**, 53–66 (1994)
3. van Bennekum, A., Beck, K., Schwaber, K., Fowler, M., Sutherland, J., et al.: Agile manifesto (2001). https://agilemanifesto.org/
4. Boon, G.C., Stettina, C.J.: A case for data-driven agile transformations: can longitudinal backlog data help guide organizational improvement journeys? In: Stray, V., Stol, K.J., Paasivaara, M., Kruchten, P. (eds.) XP 2022. LNBIP, vol. 445, pp. 114–130. Springer, Cham (2022). https://doi.org/10.1007/978-3-031-08169-9_8
5. Checkland, P., Holwell, S.: Action research: its nature and validity. Syst. Pract. Action Res. **11**, 9–21 (1998)
6. Coughlan, P., Coghlan, D.: Action research for operations management. Int. J. Oper. Prod. Manag. **22**(2), 220–240 (2002)
7. Davis, F.D.: Perceived usefulness, perceived ease of use, and user acceptance of information technology. MIS Q. **13**(3), 319 (1989)
8. Davison, R., Martinsons, M.G., Kock, N.: Principles of canonical action research. Inf. Syst. J. **14**(1), 65–86 (2004)
9. Dubinsky, Y., Talby, D., Hazzan, O., Keren, A.: Agile metrics at the Israeli air force. In: Agile Development Conference (ADC 2005). IEEE Computer Society (2005)
10. Fontana, R.M., Fontana, I.M., da Rosa Garbuio, P.A., Reinehr, S., Malucelli, A.: Processes versus people: how should agile software development maturity be defined? J. Syst. Softw. **97**, 140–155 (2014)
11. Fontana, R.M., Wojciechowski, J., Montaño, R.R., Marczak, S., Reinehr, S., Malucelli, A.: A countrywide descriptive survey of agile software development in brazil. In: Stray, V., Stol, K.J., Paasivaara, M., Kruchten, P. (eds.) XP 2022. LNBI, vol. 445, pp. 185–202. Springer, Cham (2022). https://doi.org/10.1007/978-3-031-08169-9_12
12. Greenwood, D.J.: Introduction to Action Research. Sage Publications, Thousand Oaks (2007)
13. Gren, L., Torkar, R., Feldt, R.: The prospects of a quantitative measurement of agility: a validation study on an agile maturity model. J. Syst. Softw. **107**, 38–49 (2015)

14. Hartmann, D., Dymond, R.: Appropriate agile measurement: using metrics and diagnostics to deliver business value. In: AGILE 2006. IEEE (2006)
15. Herr, K.G., Anderson, G.: The action research dissertation: a guide for students and faculty. In: The Action Research Dissertation: A Guide for Students and Faculty (2005)
16. Kaplan, R.S., Norton, D.P.: The balanced scorecard-measures that drive performance (1992)
17. Kersten, M.: Project to Product: How to Survive and Thrive in the Age of Digital Disruption with the Flow Framework. IT Revolution Press, Portland (2018)
18. Khurum, M., Gorschek, T., Wilson, M.: The software value map - an exhaustive collection of value aspects for the development of software intensive products. J. Softw. Evol. Process **25**(7), 711–741 (2013)
19. Korpivaara, I., Tuunanen, T., Seppänen, V.: Performance measurement in scaled agile organizations. In: Proceedings of the Annual Hawaii International Conference on System Sciences. Hawaii International Conference on System Sciences (2021)
20. Kueng, P.: Process performance measurement system: a tool to support process-based organizations. Total Qual. Manag. **11**(1), 67–85 (2000)
21. Kupiainen, E., Mäntylä, M.V., Itkonen, J.: Using metrics in agile and lean software development – a systematic literature review of industrial studies. Inf. Softw. Technol. **62**, 143–163 (2015)
22. Laanti, M.: Implementing program model with agile principles in a large software development organization. In: Proceedings of the International Computer Software and Applications Conference, COMPSAC 2008, pp. 1383–1391. IEEE CS, Washington, DC (2008)
23. Laanti, M., Salo, O., Abrahamsson, P.: Agile methods rapidly replacing traditional methods at Nokia: a survey of opinions on agile transformation. Inf. Softw. Technol. **53**(3), 276–290 (2011)
24. List, B., Bruckner, R., Kapaun, J.: Holistic software process performance measurement: from the stakeholders' perspective. In: 16th International Workshop on Database and Expert Systems Applications (DEXA 2005). IEEE (2005)
25. Mahnic, V., Vrana, I.: Using stakeholder-driven process performance measurement for monitoring the performance of a scrum-based software development process. Elektrotehniski Vestnik/Electrotech. Rev. **74**, 241–247 (2007)
26. Mendelow, A.L.: Information systems for organizational effectiveness-the use of the stakeholder approach. In: Information Systems for Organizational Effectiveness-the Use of the Stakeholder Approach (1984)
27. Neely, A., Adams, C., Crowe, P.: The performance prism in practice. Meas. Bus. Excell. **5**(2), 6–13 (2001)
28. Olszewska, M., Heidenberg, J., Weijola, M., Mikkonen, K., Porres, I.: Quantitatively measuring a large-scale agile transformation. J. Syst. Softw. **117**, 258–273 (2016)
29. Oza, N., Korkala, M.: Lessons learned in implementing agile software development metrics. In: UKAIS (2012)
30. Ram, P., Rodríguez, P., Oivo, M.: Software process measurement and related challenges in agile software development: a multiple case study. In: International Conference on Product Focused Software Process Improvement (2018)
31. Russo, D.: The agile success model. ACM Trans. Softw. Eng. Methodol. **30**(4), 1–46 (2021)
32. SAFe®: Scaled Agile Framework (2021). https://www.scaledagileframework.com/

33. Stettina, C.J., van Els, V., Croonenberg, J., Visser, J.: The impact of agile transformations on organizational performance: a survey of teams, programs and portfo-
lios. In: Gregory, P., Lassenius, C., Wang, X., Kruchten, P. (eds.) XP 2021. LNBIP,
vol. 419, pp. 86–102. Springer, Cham (2021). https://doi.org/10.1007/978-3-030-
78098-2_6
34. Weiss, D.J., Dawis, R.V., England, G.W.: Manual for the minnesota satisfaction
questionnaire. Minnesota studies in vocational rehabilitation (1967)

Exploring Data Analysis and Visualization Techniques for Project Tracking: Insights from the ITC

André Barrocas[1], Alberto Rodrigues da Silva[2(✉)], and João Saraiva[3]

[1] Instituto Superior Técnico, Universidade de Lisboa, Lisbon, Portugal
andre.barrocas@tecnico.ulisboa.pt
[2] INESC-ID, Instituto Superior Técnico, Universidade de Lisboa, Lisbon, Portugal
alberto.silva@tecnico.ulisboa.pt
[3] DefineScope, Setúba, Portugal
joao.saraiva@definescope.com

Abstract. Data analysis has emerged as a cornerstone in facilitating informed decision-making across myriad fields, in particular in software development and project management. This integrative practice proves instrumental in enhancing operational efficiency, cutting expenditures, mitigating potential risks, and delivering superior results, all while sustaining structured organization and robust control. This paper presents ITC, a synergistic platform architected to streamline multi-organizational and multi-workspace collaboration for project management and technical documentation. ITC serves as a powerful tool, equipping users with the capability to swiftly establish and manage workspaces and documentation, thereby fostering the derivation of invaluable insights pivotal to both technical and business-oriented decisions. ITC boasts a plethora of features, from support for a diverse range of technologies and languages, synchronization of data, and customizable templates to reusable libraries and task automation, including data extraction, validation, and document automation. This paper also delves into the predictive analytics aspect of the ITC platform. It demonstrates how ITC harnesses predictive data models, such as Random Forest Regression, to anticipate project outcomes and risks, enhancing decision-making in project management. This feature plays a critical role in the strategic allocation of resources, optimizing project timelines, and promoting overall project success. In an effort to substantiate the efficacy and usability of ITC, we have also incorporated the results and feedback garnered from a comprehensive user assessment conducted in 2022. The feedback suggests promising potential for the platform's application, setting the stage for further development and refinement. The insights provided in this paper not only underline the successful implementation of the ITC platform but also shed light on the transformative impact of predictive analytics in information systems.

Keywords: Data Analytics · Machine Learning · Project Management

J. M. Fernandes et al. (Eds.): QUATIC 2023, CCIS 1871, pp. 147–162, 2023.
https://doi.org/10.1007/978-3-031-43703-8_11

1 Introduction

IT organizations seek to satisfy customer needs and stay competitive, often leaning on project management practices for improved performance control. The absence of effective project management practices can lead to substantial losses due to communication gaps, poor planning, or disregard for requirements engineering practices, compromising product quality and customer satisfaction [1–3]. To counteract these challenges, solutions have been proposed, such as the introduction of Domain-Specific Languages (DSL) from the ITLingo research project. These languages, which include Requirement Specification Language (RSL), Project Specification Language (PSL), and Test Specification Language (TSL), were developed specifically for the efficient specification of project requirements, plans, and tests, respectively [1–3].

Support during software development processes is critical to mitigate risks and uncertainties, manage costs, and ensure deadline compliance [4]. Given that organizations generate daily data, the role of data analysis and visualization becomes critical to comprehend current and historical project performance.

Machine learning techniques, fed with past project data, can predict potential future issues and suggest preventive measures [5]. These tools aid in work planning and information dissemination among stakeholders, reducing process inconsistencies [6].

Our proposed approach addresses these issues by providing mechanisms to guide software development processes. This involves investigating collaborative platforms and cloud tools to manage organizations and workspaces in line with agile processes. To evaluate this approach, we use tests focusing on learnability and usability.

The paper will discuss core theoretical and technological concepts, including data analysis, machine learning, visualization aspects, and project management theory. We will also detail our proposed solution, its architecture, requirements, and technological aspects, before evaluating and testing the ITC platform.

2 Background

We introduce and discuss general concepts underlying this research, namely on data analysis and agile project management aspects.

2.1 Data Analysis and Visualization

Data analysis is integral across various domains, in particular helping businesses maximize their potential through data mining [9]. In project management, statistical techniques and artificial intelligence, particularly neural networks, aid in predicting project performance and making complex decisions [10, 11].

Organizations generate vast amounts of data, and data visualization provides a comprehensive means of summarizing this data. It facilitates communication, reduces misinterpretation, and offers insights by visually representing data through tools like dashboards and charts [12–14].

Statistical techniques, namely descriptive and inferential statistics, summarize the characteristics of a dataset and make informed predictions about a population parameter, respectively. They enable a deeper understanding of data, thereby enhancing decision-making capabilities [15].

2.1.1 Data Types

To report, analyze, and interpret data, as well as to understand and apply the findings, it is essential to have a basic understanding of data and variables. The combination of the data types that compose the dataset influences the choice of the data visualization to be implemented. At the highest level, data can be classified into two general categories: quantitative and qualitative.

Quantitative data is countable or measurable, while qualitative data is usually interpretation-based, descriptive, and not easily measured [15]. Quantitative data can be continuous and discrete (ratio) data. Continuous data are measured, have a constant sequence, or exist in a continuous range. This data type can be meaningfully divided into smaller or finer increments. Height, weight, temperature, and length are all examples of continuous data. Ratio data, considered another form of continuous data, have the same properties as interval data but the distinguishing property of ratio data is that it has a true definition of an absolute zero point.

Qualitative data can be classified as nominal or ordinal. Nominal data (also called categorical data) represent types of data that may be divided into groups (e.g., race, sex). This data type can be classified as dichotomous (two categories) or polytomous (more than two categories). Ordinal data is data in which the values follow a natural order, while discrete data can be counted (e.g., age, educational level). Nominal data can only be classified, while ordinal data can be classified and ordered [15].

2.1.2 Data Visualization Techniques

Data visualization techniques are pivotal to effectively presenting findings from specific datasets and understanding trends, patterns, and relationships among data elements. The choice of visualization type, such as Bar Charts, Line Charts, Pie Charts, Scatter Plots, and Histograms, is dictated by the specific needs and nature of the data [14].

Bar charts, a commonly used technique, excel in comparing quantities across different categories, facilitating understanding of data trends. Line charts are excellent for tracking changes over time, connecting individual numeric data points to illustrate sequences of values. Pie charts serve to represent parts of a whole, ideal for showing relative proportions or percentages, although it's recommended to limit pie wedges to six for clarity. Scatter plots help examine relationships between variables, with the capacity to highlight trends, concentrations, and outliers. Histograms are suitable for analyzing data distribution across groups and presenting continuous numerical data [14].

In addition, project-specific visualizations like Gantt Charts, Burn-up charts, and Burn-down charts play key roles in project management. Gantt charts provide a holistic view of tasks, deadlines, milestones, and resource planning, supporting informed decision-making. Burn-down charts depict remaining work and facilitate predicting completion likelihood over time [16]. Conversely, Burn-up charts represent the project's progress and work done over time, serving as an intuitive figure of the project's status [16].

2.1.3 Random Forest Algorithm

Random Forest is a robust machine learning algorithm that forms the core of the predictive analytics models in ITC. It is a type of ensemble learning method, developed by Leo Breiman, which operates by constructing multiple decision trees and outputting the class that is the mode of the classes for classification, or the mean prediction of the individual trees for regression [29].

The algorithm provides a strong balance between accuracy and interpretability. It manages to handle a large number of inputs, effectively dealing with missing values and maintaining accuracy when a large proportion of the data is missing [30].

In the context of ITC, Random Forest was chosen for its reliability and versatility. This algorithm is adequate for predicting project success due to the complexity of the datasets and the non-linear relationships of the domain specification languages (DSLs). The decision trees within a Random Forest can be understood as individual "rules" contributing to the final decision, providing insights into the significant factors influencing project predictions. This combination of accurate predictive capability and interpretability allows for more informed decision-making in project management [31].

2.2 Agile Project Management

Project Management (PM) is a set of practices crucial for maintaining control of project aspects like scope, quality, schedule, budget, resources, and risk to align with project objectives [2]. Notable international PM frameworks include the PMBOK Guide, ISO 21500, IPMA ICB, and PM2 [17–20].

Traditional PM follows a "waterfall" model where the project plan is fixed from the beginning [22]. However, this approach struggles with the uncertainty and need for change in contemporary IT projects [23]. Agile methods, such as Scrum and Kanban, which focus on adaptability, communication, and collaboration, are often more suitable for these projects [23–25].

Scrum defines roles (Product Owner, Scrum Master, Development Team) and uses short iterations or sprints for better control and risk reduction [23]. Kanban, less prescriptive, limits work-in-progress for efficiency and is based on the Just-in-Time premise [25]. Both methods contribute to enhanced project performance, improved customer satisfaction, and quicker product delivery [8].

3 ITC Overview

The ITC is an advanced multi-organization and multi-workspace platform designed to collate, manage, and analyze project-related data, transforming them into actionable insights for strategic business decision-making. Key to this tool is its user-friendly interface and intuitive management of workspaces and technical documentation. It incorporates standard features of agile project management tools and draws inspiration from emerging collaborative solutions such as cloud-based Integrated Development Environments (IDEs), to provide a conducive environment for quality and swift software development.

ITC stands out for its compatibility with various technologies and languages explored in prior research projects. For instance, it integrates seamlessly with predefined project data templates like the PSL and RSL Excel Templates, thereby streamlining data synchronization. It also has robust automation capabilities, from automatic text extraction to document automation, empowering users to effortlessly manage and utilize their stored organizational and project data.

The platform further bolsters data analytics through its built-in dashboards, presenting critical project data in an easily digestible format. A crucial aspect is its predictive analytics models, designed to monitor project costs, enhance project productivity, and aid managers in informed decision-making.

ITC's architecture has been designed to seamlessly integrate with an online IDE, enabling users to directly access, modify, and deploy software development artifacts stored in the platform's database. This integration would bolster the software development and deployment process within each workspace's scope.

ITC employs a client-server-style architecture, comprising a front end accessible through a web browser, a back-end server, and a relational database. The architecture utilizes PostgreSQL for database implementation and employs the Django application framework [27], supplemented with JavaScript libraries like Chart.js for dashboard development. The platform is also mobile-responsive, ensuring usability across various device sizes.

This introduction presents an overview of the main elements of ITC, focusing on users and roles, organizations, workspaces, agile processes, file management, data import, document automation, notifications, data analysis, and project prediction, with a spotlight on its robust data science and analytics capabilities.

Users and Roles. Users may have different roles, determining the permissions to access the platform's pages, access certain information, and perform system actions that guarantee the access and management of the information. User roles may be changed easily at the platform, organization, and workspace levels, and the users' information may be searched, filtered, and sorted. User roles also can be chosen when some invitation is sent to be part of one specific organization or workspace.

Organizations. ITC allows users to store, search and visualize several organizations' information. To better structure teams and facilitate collaborative work is possible to create several workspaces inside each organization space, named as "organization". Each organization may store files, namely libraries and templates (e.g., PSL Excel Template, RSL Excel Template), that may be used and filled with projects' data at the workspace level. The system stores and processes projects' data to provide intuitive statistics about organizations, intending to present and track their performance, such as: to analyze and compare budgets between project costs, to track projects to aid in business decisions. During the registration process, the user who registers in the system can create a new organization, thus becoming the organization manager of that organization. After the creation, the user has immediate access and control over it. A user can be added or invited to be a member of an organization that already exists in the platform. In this case, the organization manager of that organization needs to accept the access request to that organization. At any moment, a user with an organization manager role may access the list of the organization users from this organization, invite a new one or change user roles. Each organization provides statistics to analyze its data, namely on the analytics page and on its main page. It is possible to edit information related to the organization's name, organization activity type, or country on the settings page.

Workspaces. Workspaces are created in the scope of an organization. The main workspaces' properties are: project management process, status, project benefits, success criteria, general costs, and schedule information. These properties can be defined manually or automatically imported from files uploaded on the platform. Users can manage documents, the product backlog, and sprint backlogs. A workspace is a helpful space to support collaborative project management and contains several pages with several features. The system allows the storage of files (e.g., PSL Excel files) filled with project data. This data can be automatically imported from these files and consequently saving time. The users may select or merge the relevant data stored in these Excel files (e.g., related to the product backlog, sprint backlog items, project costs) and choose what they want to import into the database. This feature is particularly useful to promote better collaboration between teams or stakeholders since they may share dispersed files. ITC provides visual insights such as statistics and intuitive dashboards to analyze workspace data, that may be imported or not. Users may generate project management reports by using the data stored in the database in the scope of each workspace.

Agile Processes. ITC supports Scrum and Kanban agile processes, allowing users to manage product backlog, sprint backlog, and Kanban board. It enables storing associated data, like files, images, and effort for each task.

In Scrum, users access the Sprint Backlog and Sprint History pages for managing sprints and tasks, including a search function for sprint history and statistics. Sprint creation requires specifying relevant information such as name, schedule, and stakeholders. This data can be imported from Excel or entered manually. The system detects whether a task ID already exists in the database from the imported data and updates or creates information accordingly. For manual creation, all task details must be provided. ITC also enables the creation of tasks by importing items from the product backlog, assigning unique task IDs and defining different types of effort for each task.

In the Kanban process, the Sprint Backlog and Sprint History pages are replaced by the Kanban page that shows the Kanban board and task creation function. Like in Scrum, Kanban data can be imported from Excel or DSLs, generating the charts automatically.

Files Management. ITC supports the storage of multiple files, promoting the reusability and integration with ITLingo templates (e.g., PSL Excel Template). ITLingo libraries contain reusable specifications (e.g., defined in PSL or RSL languages), which can be used to create new specific specifications. ITC supports reusing these templates, importing data, and saving time by using these data in the scope of each organization and respective workspaces.

ITC ensures that users can access the same documents' versions that stakeholders may share. ITC allows selecting and merging data from these Excel files, allowing to select the content that the user may need (e.g., stakeholders, use cases, open issues, product backlog items).

Data Import. The stakeholders involved in each software project constantly generate data in organizations, including information related to requirements, bugs, budget, risks, and effort. When multiple stakeholders work simultaneously, there are problems with versions, data consistency, outdated information, and erroneous data. ITC system allows import specific data from Excel files (namely based on PSL Excel templates) to speed processes, adding new information or updating existing data stored on the database. Furthermore, it is possible to partially select specific information from these Excel files and synchronize it with the information in the database. ITC avoids duplicate information, detecting duplicated IDs of data elements stored in these Excel files. Hence, the ITC updates the information on the database if the ID already exists in the specific workspace, not duplicating data, otherwise will create the data on the database. It is possible to select a specific PSL Excel worksheet(s) to be imported, namely: (1) all the project data (several worksheets) or only, (2) product backlog items, (3) sprint backlog or kanban tasks, and (4) project stakeholders.

Document Automation. Document automation allows to generates documents or reports containing text, tables, and figures about a specific topic [3]. ITC provides a report automation system that uses the data stored in the database to generate different reports. This feature is handy and saves time once the production of these technical artifacts can be a very monotonous and repetitive activity. Standard project management reports must follow certain practices or contain certain types of information. Some of them are identified in PMBOK [17]. Bragança carried out a study to understand what are the common reports in project management [26]. During his research, he designed the functionality to generate automatic reports in the PSL Excel template. The document templates collected and produced by Bragança were adapted to be used in ITC.

Notifications. ITC includes a notification system to share relevant information and events that happen in the scope of organizations and projects. That notification system enables real-time notifications allowing directly read messages from the notification bar. Important information is automatically sent, namely invites to members of organizations or of specific workspaces. Also, accepting or rejecting the invite directly on the notification message is possible. Besides that, the system informs when one invite is accepted or rejected and when the project's planned end date is approaching. Invites to be member of organizations or workspaces are made even if a person does not have yet an account on the platform. In these cases, an email is sent to invite the user to register in the system. Depending on the invitation type, the invite to be member of a specific organization or workspace is made at the organization or workspace level. Supposing the user's email is already registered on the system, one invitation notification shall be sent, and it shall be possible to accept or reject the invite.

Data Analysis. ITC supports the analysis of project-related data by summarizing and centralizing information. ITC helps to make more informed correct decisions with less uncertainty. The user explores the data through interaction with charts and obtain a summary of the characteristics and statistics of the organizations' and projects' data. ITC supports dashboards at the organization and workspace levels to track progress, working hours, outcomes, and other relevant information. ITC includes (i) an organization main page that summarizes the organization's data and (ii) an organization analytics page that analyzes the data at a detailed level. The data analysis mechanisms in the scope of each organization can be summarized as the following: (1) Compare organizational productivity changes over time, namely work completed over time, (2) track completed work per workspace, (3) analyze workspaces' status, (4) compare users involved per workspace, (5) analyze workspaces' costs, namely to better understand how to use the available budget, comparing planned cost and the current cost among workspaces. Figure 1 presents the ITC organization analytics page.

Project Prediction. The system is designed to effectively manage and predict project outcomes. It begins by integrating multiple data sources, including project details and domain specifications, to create a unified project dataset. This rich dataset feeds into a machine learning model, in this case, a Random Forest Regressor, which is trained to predict project success based on multiple variables like project scope, budget, duration, team members, and complexity. The predictive functionality is multifold. It aids in resource allocation, suggesting which projects deserve more budget and time considering their potential success. It supports risk management by identifying projects that are predicted to have less than 50% success, thus aiding in early risk identification and mitigation. It also aids in project planning by predicting project duration and in performance evaluation by estimating project success. The system also leverages its predictive analytics for project prioritization. It ranks projects based on their predicted success and provides a list of top-priority projects. This allows stakeholders to allocate resources and attention to projects that are more likely to succeed. The results are presented in dashboards and reports to support informed decision-making for effective project management.

Figure 2 presents the ITC workspace analytics page.

4 Evaluation

ITC was evaluated in the scope of an user assessment with independent researchers, teachers, and students, mainly to test its collaborative and data analytics features. This user assessment was based on a fictitious organization and a fictitious project discussed in an MSc-level Information Systems Project Management course. In this study, the robustness of the machine learning algorithm deployed in the ITC system was thoroughly assessed using standard evaluation metrics such as the Root Mean Square Error (RMSE) and the R-Squared values. The model yielded an impressively low RMSE value of 0.16, indicating a low degree of error, and a high R-Squared value of 0.89, demonstrating that a significant proportion of the variance in our dependent variable was accurately predicted from the independent variables. These results underscore the machine learning model's strong predictive capabilities and its practical value in managing and forecasting project outcomes.

4.1 User Assessment

We conducted a user assessment to evaluate the system and receive preliminary feedback from people not directly involved in this research. These tests were helpful to find problems and solve them, and evaluate the usability, some collaborative features, as well as the capacity to understand the data visualization mechanisms provided by ITC, in

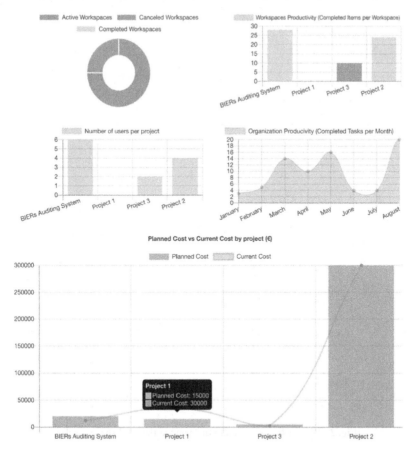

Fig. 1. Screenshot of the analytics page at the organization level.

particular, to test the ability of the users to analyze a fictious organization data and take some conclusions about it. In this evaluation process, we used usability tests with users in individual sessions to interact directly with the platform. Finally, we elaborated a questionary for the users to gather vital feedback to guarantee that the system meets the user's needs and analyze the obtained results.

The tests phase was performed between June and August of 2022. The questionary was answered by a group of 21 participants with ages ranging from 18 to 60 years old and at least a Bachelor of Science degree, namely 9 with a BSc, 9 with an MSc, and 3 with a Ph.D. degree. Most participants had little professional experience, in particular, 13 participants with less than 1 year, 5 participants between 1 and 5 years, 1 participant between 5 and 10 years, and 2 participants with more than 10 years of experience. By analyzing the users' background, it is possible to understand that most users have previous training in the project management field. In particular, 14 of the participants have previous training while 7 have no. By comparing the answers, it is possible to

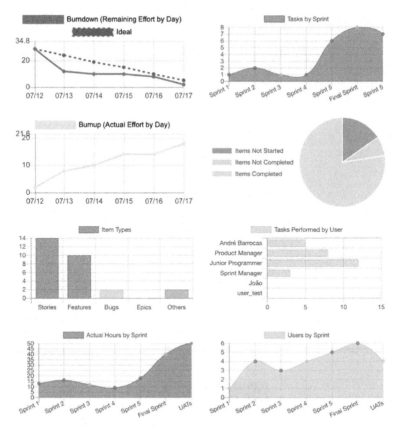

Fig. 2. Screenshot of the analytics page at the workspace level.

understand that most of the users have experience with project management tools while the minority have no experience with these tools.

The user pilot-user test session was conducted under the following conditions: (1) The tests were conducted in a controlled environment without distractions (e.g., office or home environment). (2) Realization of the tasks without previous use and learning of the system. (3) The users were required to have an internet connection and a browser with good JS support. (4) Users were free to think out loud and share ideas. (5) The evaluator didn't interact with the users until the tests are finished (except in case of blocking errors). (6) The session had a maximum of 45 min of duration.

To guide the user assessment test, participants received a script briefly describing the ITC, explaining the goals of the activity, the BIERs' organization, and a fictitious project to be tracked with our system. After contextualizing the users, the steps to be followed to carry out the evaluation tasks were explained.

The user assessment session was divided into two parts: the first part involved testing some of the collaborative features of the platform, while the second involved the ability of users to use the data visualization features, in particular, to understand whether they were able to apprehend the preliminary information that the dashboards intend to transmit.

The first part included tasks 1 to 24 of the script, which involved the registration on the platform, creation of the organization and workspace, and management of the product backlog and sprints. The second part is referent to tasks 25 to 33 of the script. The users were asked to analyze the general statistics related to the BIER organization, its analytics page, the available workspace statistics, and its summarized analytics page, as well as the data analysis and visualization of a stored specific sprint in the historic.

The organization data used for test purposes were mainly imported from excel files, including information related to fictitious projects, to make it possible to compare data at an organization's global level, comparing information among its projects, stakeholders, productivity, effort, and performance.

In the end, participants were asked to fill in a questionnaire to rate the platform, suggest improvements, report errors, and answer the data analysis questions. That questionary was structured into the following sessions:

(1) **Respondent Characterization.** The first three questions (Q1 to Q3) were focused on the general characterization of the participants with the following aspects: age, gender, and academic level.
(2) **User Background Analysis**. Four questions (Q4 to Q7) were directly related to user background analysis, namely related to the years of experience, previous experience in project management subjects, and related tools.
(3) **User Experience Overall Assessment**. Eight questions (Q8 to Q15) focused on test usability and learnability aspects of ITC. We asked the percentage of completed the tasks proposed and asked participants to rate on a 5-Likert scale (i.e., from 1 to 5, 0-completely disagree, 5-completely agree) aspects related to the interface complexity, usability, feature integration, interface inconsistencies, and learnability.
(4) **Data Analysis Questions**. We asked five questions (Q16 to Q20) to evaluate the users' capacity to interpret the dashboards' information. There are a lot of possible aspects to ask related to the dashboards. Still, we focused on testing only two questions related to organization data analytics, two related to workspace data analytics, and one to interpret historic sprint data. We asked about organization productivity, costs, effort, hours of work, and completed items to check if the users understood the charts asking for a concrete answer.
(5) **ITC General Evaluation**: This section has the highest number of questions (Q21 to Q30). In this part of the questionnaire, we asked about aspects related to the usefulness of specific features provided by the platform. We first asked participants to rate in a 5-Likert scale (i.e., from 1 to 5, 0—Do not know, 1-Very Low, 2 -Low, 3-Medium, 4-High, and 5-Very High) how useful the functionalities are to create and manage organizations, workspaces, import project-related data, manage the sprints and tasks, as well as the functionalities to analyze organization's and workspace's statistics, and sprint dashboards. Then, we include an open-ended question for users to provide additional comments (suggestions, problems, or bugs).

4.2 Results Analysis

As mentioned above, the questionary is divided into five sections. The first and second sections were already analyzed previously, describing participant-related aspects, namely the general characterization and background.

Section three analyzed ITC usability and learnability aspects. Responses in this section revealed good interface results. When analyzing the answers, we concluded that 100% of the tasks were completed by the participants. For the remaining questions, we asked participants to rate on a 5-Likert scale (i.e., from 1 to 5, 1-completely disagree, 5-completely agree). Table 1 summarizes the average scores for these questions, based on which we may verify the following findings: Most participants would use the product again. When analyzing the results for the question Q11 - The system is more complex than necessary, we found that although most people disagreed with the question, there were still three people who answered 4, and one who answered 3. The vast majority of people agreed that the system is easy to use and easy to learn, feeling confident when using the product.

Some of the feedback provided by the participants on the open- ended question about the interface and usability aspects was: "The tool is very visual and intuitive, allowing a very interesting analysis of information." and "The platform is very complete and very visual, which I find great. Good job!".

Table 1. User experience overall assessment results.

Questions	Average
I think I would use ITC again	4.43
The ITC is more complex than necessary	1.81
The ITC is easy to use	4.57
The various features of ITC were well integrated	4.62
ITC has inconsistencies	1.52
I suppose most people would quickly learn to use ITC	4.71
I felt very confident using ITC	4.67

(values on a 1–5 scale, 1-completely disagree, 5-completely agree)

Section 4 evaluates the users' capacity to understand the dashboards, as well as the ability to understand the information whose graphics are intended to convey and verify that the data analysis was done correctly, asking for concrete answers. Regarding the first question: Q16 - "Which project has more items solved in this organization?" all participants got it right. In the remaining questions, the vast majority got the answer right. The percentage of correct answers was 95.2% in the question Q17 - "Which project has the current cost higher than planned cost?", 95.2% in the question Q18 - "Which was the remaining effort foreseen in day 12?", 90% in the question Q19 - "Which sprint involved more hours of work?" and 90.5% in the question Q20 - "How many items were completed?".

The participants provided the following feedback on the open- ended question about the data analysis features: "Good monitoring and data analysis tool. You can monitor users and projects (active, canceled, and completed), among other tasks. One note would be to increase the size of the graphs to allow better visibility of the numbers on the scales of the graphs.". The last suggestion was followed, and the numbers of some of the graphs were increased as well as some colors were refined for a better understanding of the values.

Section 5 was very important to detect bugs and system improvements, particularly at the beginning of the testing phase. Users who tested the platform more intensively found a bug in the system that caused a message with no text when no description is provided. Another bug found was related to the drag-and-drop provided by the kanban board. This bug was related to the need to manually refresh the page for the kanban board items to be updated. These bugs were fixed at the beginning of the evaluation phase. Other improvement suggestions were: "I think the description should be an optional field (I ended up placing the name of the task in the description just to fill)" and "It would be interesting to add more integration features with other management tools, for example ". The first suggestion was followed, and task description is no longer a required field. The second suggestion was not implemented because this feature requires extensive work (and shall be considered for future work).

Table 2. ITC usefulness assessment results.

Questions	Average
How do you rate the usefulness of creating and managing organizations?	4.95
How suitable is the platform for creating and managing workspaces?	4.81
How do you rate the usefulness of importing product backlog data?	4.71
How do you rate the usefulness of managing the sprints and the tasks?	4.80
How do you rate the usefulness of the sprint board and its filters?	4.71
How do you rate the usefulness of the organization's data analysis?	4.90
How do you rate the usefulness of the workspace's data analysis?	4.95
How do you rate the usefulness of the sprints' data analysis?	4.95

(values on a 1–5 scale, 1-very low, 5-very high)

In Sect. 5, we also asked about aspects related to the usefulness of specific features provided by the platform. Participants rated, in a 5-Likert scale (i.e., from 1 to 5, 1-Very Low, 2 -Low, 3-Medium, 4-High, and 5-Very High), the usefulness of the functionalities of creating and managing organizations, workspaces, import project- related data, manage the sprints and tasks, as well as the functionalities to analyze organization's and workspace's statistics, and sprint dashboards. Table 2 summarizes the average scores for these supported features based on which we may verify the following findings: All answers were between 4 and 5 (4-High, and 5-Very High) in all questions, with the majority being 5. In question Q23 - How do you rate the usefulness of import product backlog data? there was one person who answered 3 (medium), and the remaining answers were between 4 and 5. With these results, we can conclude that users found all the features they evaluated useful.

Regarding the open-ended questions of Sect. 5, most of the participants did not answer. However, in addition to the feedback, improvements, and bugs that have already been mentioned before, those that answered provided encouraging comments and feedback, such as: "Very good Congratulations!", and "Congratulations on your work!", among the other positive feedback mentioned previously. The analysis of these comments led to the conclusion that this tool is useful and that the work was carried out successfully. To sum up, the results collected and analyzed in all sections had very positive scores. Usability experts like Nielsen and Landauer observed that a group of 5 testers is enough to uncover over 80% of the usability problems [28]. Since our questionnaire focuses on the usability and general evaluation of the ITC, we may conclude that 21 participants are a fair number for an exploratory assessment, allowing us to identify significant flaws in the usability of such proposals. Furthermore, this assessment was also handy for detecting and solving a few bugs.

5 Conclusion

This research led to the creation of ITC, a collaborative platform designed to support a range of software development processes and project management activities. ITC's primary goal is to facilitate effective data management and analysis within organizations. It presents an accessible, user-friendly interface that enables stakeholders to easily navigate and interact with a wealth of project-related information. The key concerns addressed by this system include enhancing organizational performance, promoting synchronized and collaborative work, managing project-related data, fostering collaboration among stakeholders, and translating project performance into decision-making aids. The system's usability and AI capabilities were tested via experiments and user assessments, receiving positive feedback and encouraging results. The performance metrics of the machine learning model integrated into the system, specifically the RMSE and R-Squared values, were found to be 0.16 and 0.89 respectively, indicating its substantial reliability in supporting project management.

Moving forward, some areas for improvement have been identified. Firstly, augmenting ITC's data analysis capabilities could provide greater insights into project costs via predictive models, aiding informed decision-making. There's also room to advance its capacity for predicting project timelines based on past project data. Future research endeavors will be directed towards refining the input variables and tweaking additional hyperparameters to further optimize model accuracy. Secondly, the document automation functionalities could facilitate the inclusion of additional reports on the platform. Lastly, enhancing the integration of ITC with online Integrated Development Environments (IDEs) could provide an all-in-one platform for software development and project management, adding more developer tools and cloud IDE features.

References

1. Patanakul, P., Iewwongcharoen, B., Milosevic, D.: An empirical study on the use of project management tools and techniques across project life-cycle and their impact on project success. J. Gen. Manag. 35(3), 41–66 (2010)
2. el Emam, K., Koru, A.G.: A replicated survey of IT software project failures. IEEE Softw. 25(5), 84–90 (2008)

3. da Silva, R.: ITLingo Research Initiative in 2022," arXiv preprint arXiv:2206.14553 (2022)
4. Nayebi, M., Ruhe, G., Mota, R.C., Mufti, M.: Analytics for software project management - Where are we and where do we go? In: Proceedings - 2015 30th IEEE/ACM International Conference on Automated Software Engineering Workshops, ASEW 2015, March 2016, pp. 18–21 (2016). https://doi.org/10.1109/ASEW.2015.28
5. Kanakaris, N., Karacapilidis, N., Kournetas, G., Lazanas, A.: Combining machine learning and operations research methods to advance the project management practice. In: Operations Research and Enterprise Systems, pp. 135–155 (2020). https://doi.org/10.1007/978-3-030-37584-3_7
6. Novitzká, V., et al.: Informatics 2017 : 2017 IEEE 14th International Scientific Conference on Informatics : Proceedings : 14–16 November 2017, Poprad, Slovakia (2017)
7. Gamito, I., da Silva, A.R.: From rigorous requirements and user interfaces specifications into software business applications. In: International Conference on the Quality of Information and Communications Technology, pp. 459–473 (2020). https://doi.org/10.1007/978-3-030-58793-2_37
8. da Silva, R.: Rigorous specification of use cases with the RSL language. In: International Conference on Information Systems Development'2019, AIS (2019)
9. Smith, A., Gupta, J.N.D.: Neural networks in business: techniques and applications for the operations researcher. Comput. Oper. Res. **27**(11), 1023–1044 (2000). https://doi.org/10.1016/S0305-0548(99)00141-0
10. Wang, Y.-R., Yu, C.-Y., Chan, H.-H.: Predicting construction cost and schedule success using artificial neural networks ensemble and support vector machines classification models. Int. J. Project Manage. **30**(4), 470–478 (2012). https://doi.org/10.1016/j.ijproman.2011.09.002
11. Costantino, F., di Gravio, G., Nonino, F.: Project selection in project portfolio management: an artificial neural network model based on critical success factors. Int. J. Project Manage. **33**(8), 1744–1754 (2015). https://doi.org/10.1016/j.ijproman.2015.07.003
12. Sadiku, M., Shadare, A.E., Musa, S.M., Akujuobi, C.M., Perry, R.: Data visualization. Int. J. Eng. Res. Adv. Technol. (IJERAT) **2**(12), 11–16 (2016)
13. Zheng, G.: Data visualization in business intelligence. In: Global Business Intelligence, Routledge , pp. 67–81 (2017)
14. Hardin, M., Hom, D., Perez, R., Williams, L.: Which chart or graph is right for you? Tell Impactful Stories with Data. Tableau Software (2012)
15. Vetter, T.R.: Fundamentals of research data and variables: the devil is in the details. Anesth. Analg. **125**(4), 1375–1380 (2017)
16. Cabri, A., Griffiths, M.: Earned value and agile reporting. In: AGILE 2006 (AGILE 2006), pp. 6-p (2006)
17. Project Management Institute., A guide to the project management body of knowledge (PMBOK Guide). Project Management Institute (2008)
18. Stellingwerf, R., Zandhuis, A.: ISO 21500 Guidance on project management–A Pocket Guide. Van Haren (2013)
19. Vukomanović, M., Young, M., Huynink, S.: IPMA ICB 4.0—A global standard for project, programme and portfolio management competences. Int. J. Project Manage. **34**(8), 1703–1705 (2016)
20. E. Commission and D.-G. for Informatics, PM2 project management methodology : guide 3.0.1. Publications Office (2021). https://doi.org/10.2799/022317
21. Charvat, J.: Project management methodologies: selecting, implementing, and supporting methodologies and processes for projects (2003)
22. Thesing, T., Feldmann, C., Burchardt, M.: Agile versus waterfall project management: decision model for selecting the appropriate approach to a project. Procedia Comput. Sci. **181**, 746–756 (2021). https://doi.org/10.1016/j.procs.2021.01.227

23. Špundak, M.: Mixed agile/traditional project management methodology–reality or illusion? Procedia-Soc. Behav. Sci. **119**, 939–948 (2014)
24. Beck, K., et al.: Manifesto for agile software development (2001)
25. Alqudah, M., Razali, R.: A comparison of scrum and Kanban for identifying their selection factors. In: 2017 6th International Conference on Electrical Engineering and Informatics (ICEEI), pp. 1–6 (2017). https://doi.org/10.1109/ICEEI.2017.8312434
26. de Carvalho Bragança, D.: Document Automation in ITLingo PSL Excel Template: MSc dissertation. Instituto Superior Técnico, Universidade de Lisboa (2021)
27. Ravindran, A.: Django Design Patterns and Best Practices. Packt Publishing Ltd (2015)
28. Nielsen, J., Landauer, T.K.: A mathematical model of the finding of usability problems. In: Proceedings of the INTERACT 1993 and CHI 1993 Conference on Human Factors in Computing Systems, pp. 206–213 (1993)
29. Breiman, L.: Random Forests. Mach. Learn. **45**(1), 5–32 (2001)
30. Liaw, A., Wiener, M.: Classification and regression by Random Forest. R. News **2**(3), 18–22 (2002)
31. Genuer, R., Poggi, J.M., Tuleau-Malot, C.: Variable selection using Random Forests. Pattern Recogn. Lett. **31**(14), 2225–2236 (2010)

How a Professional Association Can Steer Digital Transformation: Case Study of the Belgian Notary Industry

Ziboud Van Veldhoven⬛, Kani Kiliç, Divya Prakash, Ryan Michael Smith-Cooper, and Jan Vanthienen$^{(\boxtimes)}$ ⬛

Research Center for Information Systems Engineering, KU Leuven, Leuven, Belgium
jan.vanthienen@kuleuven.be

Abstract. Embarking on digital transformation is a key challenge facing many organizations. Especially smaller firms face great difficulty due to lack of financial resources, time, and culture. In this paper, we showcase how a professional association can be the key player to digitalize an industry made of small firms. By using semi-structured interviews and a large-scale survey, we outline how the digital transformation of the Belgian notary industry was steered by their professional association Fednot. Our findings indicate that Fednot has functioned as a proficient driver of digital transformation through a strong emphasis on customer-centricity, network organizational structures, and product ecosystems. Finally, we highlight the success factors, barriers to change, and recommendations for future professional association-led digital transformations.

Keywords: Digital transformation · Professional association · Notary

1 General Introduction

Digital transformation (DT) is a term introduced to talk about the rapid change process happening in the world due to the increased usage of and reliance on digital technologies. This process brings forwards major changes in all industries and societies that demand more research. Numerous definitions exist such as "the process that aims to improve an entity by triggering significant changes to its properties through combination of information, computing, communication, and connectivity technologies" (Vial, p.1, 2019) or as "the increasing interaction between digital technologies, business, and society" (Van Veldhoven & Vanthienen, p.11, 2021).

In recent years, DT research has become a major topic in information systems research and practice with over 2,400 papers published to date (Van Veldhoven, Etikala, Goossens, & Vanthienen, 2021) and more than 80% of global firms indicating that DT is critical to their survival in the coming five years (SAP Center for Business Insight, 2017). However, numerous companies face great challenges when dealing with DT such as lack of leadership (Brock & von Wangenheim, 2019), lack of resources (Cichosz, Wallenburg, & Knemeyer, 2020), or lack of knowledge (Schneider & Kokshagina, 2021). One

J. M. Fernandes et al. (Eds.): QUATIC 2023, CCIS 1871, pp. 163–177, 2023.
https://doi.org/10.1007/978-3-031-43703-8_12

way to deal with these challenges might be at the hands of professional associations. These organizations represent, aid, and protect a certain trade or industry. By grouping knowledge and resources, they might be ideal drivers for DT in sectors that face these challenges. However, research about the role of professional associations on the DT of their sector is missing from the literature.

For this reason, we aim to investigate the DT of the Belgian notary industry led by the professional association Royal Federation of Belgian Notaries (Fednot). Not only is research about notaries lacking, but this unique business environment poses an interesting case study. The Belgian notary industry is not only governed by a professional association, Fednot, but is also an integral part of the Belgian legal system and predates the use of digital technologies. Hence, it is largely rooted in traditional ways of doing business and is primarily composed of small, local, and family-owned firms. Furthermore, their status as legal officers with state delegated powers have thus far kept the notaries relatively well insulated from external threats. Due to various emerging threats, Fednot and its members have embarked on a DT journey. To collect the data, a mixed method approach of interviews, surveys, and tertiary data collection was used.

In the next section, we elaborate on digital transformation and describe the Belgian notary industry in more detail. Afterwards, the interview and survey-based methodology is given in section three. The DT of the Belgian notary industry is given in section four. One of the DT results is the launch of four new digital products as shown in section five. We discuss our findings and the implications for future research in section six and conclude the paper in section seven.

2 Background

2.1 Digital Transformation

DT is about the increased usage of digital technologies in an organization as a response to an ever-changing and ever-digitizing competitive landscape (Saarikko, Westergren, & Blomquist, 2020; Vial, 2019). However, these transformations go beyond that of a strictly technical nature and also align to the overall cultural and organizational shift associated with adopting these technologies (Perkin & Abraham, 2017; Saarikko et al., 2020; Vial, 2019). An important consideration for organizations is that the expectations of both their employees and their customers are shaped by the experiences in their day-to-day life. Hereafter, as their personal lives become ever-increasingly digitized and automated, consumers expect all services and products they consume to be of a similar nature. These newly empowered consumers alter the landscape in which the firms must now operate (Lucas, Agarwal, Clemons, El Sawy, & Weber, 2013; Saarikko et al., 2020; Vial, 2019). In addition, as the technological and sociotechnical possibilities are increasing, so are the number of competitions fronts. Firms must pay close attention to the changes in their sector and act swiftly.

2.2 Professional Associations

Professional associations, also called professional organizations, professional societies, or trade organizations, operate, and interact in a variety of ways within a single industry, profession, or within similar firms. They are often founded and funded by members of the organizations that operate in the respective industry or by the government. The primary objective of these entities is the utilization of their knowledge, capabilities, and resources to control the direction of certain activities with the aim of aligning the outcomes with the interest of the sector (Drahos & Shearing, 2014). Essentially, professional associations aggregate their resources to ensure that their views are heard on topics that affect them (Barnett, 2013). The key role is, therefore, the ability to facilitate an environment in which a specific industry can thrive (Tsui-Auch, 2004).

2.3 The Belgian Notary Industry

The Belgian notarial system is a semi-federal legal profession that was established in the early 19th century to ensure a centralized government-sanctioned institution that oversees and takes record of various civil law agreements. A notary is a public officer appointed by the King and receives their power from the state. However, once appointed, notaries function as an independent entity. Their delegated responsibility covers the three primary legal areas: real estate, family law, and enterprise law. Their activities in real estate include facilitating the purchase and sale of properties and the certification of mortgage loans. For family law, their activities include the authentication of marriage settlements, donations, divorces, and inheritance. For enterprise law, their activities include incorporation, mergers, and acquisitions (Royal Federation of Belgian Notaries, n.d.). Currently, as shown in Fig. 1, there are roughly 1200 individual firms, 1500 notaries, and 8000 notarial staff operating in Belgium (The Federation of Enterprises in Belgium, n.d.).

Fig. 1. The Belgian notary industry at a glance.

The primary responsibility of a notary in Belgium is to provide legal advice to their clients with regards to contract performance pertaining to the aforementioned legal areas and to inform their clients of their rights, duties, and the consequences of their commitment (Royal Federation of Belgian Notaries, n.d.). They also play a critical role in drawing up authentic acts. Additionally, the notaries also ensure follow-up protocols such as registration in the public registers (Royal Federation of Belgian Notaries, n.d.).

The government has effectively created a monopoly-like climate by federally appointing all notaries and mandating their operations. Hence, notaries are prohibited from engaging in price differentiation and other revenue-generating activities. Consequently, the Belgian notarial system is situated between a federal institution and a private institution where the individual notaries themselves act in a private and independent fashion from their peers.

The notaries are supported by the professional association Fednot, founded in 1891. Fednot supports the notaries, invests in research and development, and functions as a buffer between the government and the industry, as shown in Fig. 2. They provide services to their members such as legal advice, HR services, training, and IT solutions.

Fig. 2. An illustration depicting the flow of information from the citizen to the government.

However, the notaries have found themselves in a precarious position because of the many disruptions on legal and technological fronts. Some of these threats are innovative technologies, liberalization of activities, and deregulation of prices. As a result, notaries would no longer be able to benefit from their protected environment. This loss of relevance in key business segments, along with the anticipated rise in external rivalry, has functioned as a wake-up call for Fednot and individual notaries. Therefore, Fednot has embarked on a DT journey in the hopes of protecting the interests of the notaries.

3   Methodology

To investigate the impact of DT on the Belgian notary industry and the role of Fednot, a mixed-method approach was chosen that consisted of interviews, a large-scale survey, and tertiary data collection from online sources. Three types of interviews were conducted. First, we interviewed the chief transformation officer (CTO) at Fednot to better understand the industry and frame the questionnaires for the subsequent interviews. Secondly, we interviewed the marketing director and the strategic advisor of Fednot. The aim was to understand the current digital strategy and the competitive landscape of the Belgian notary industry. Third, to investigate the industry at large, three semi-structured interviews were conducted with distinct notary firms to understand their alignment with Fednot and their digital situation.

The findings of these interviews were used to construct a survey to further investigate the adoption of digital solutions across the industry. This survey was distributed to Belgian notaries and consisted largely of Likert-scale and multiple-choice questions but also included optional open questions. Approximately 14% (n = 215) of all notaries (n = ~ 1500) responded to the survey. However, there exists some variation between the number of questions answered as respondents were free to skip questions. Of these respondents, 70.3% (n = 147) reported being part of a micro-sized firm (0–10 employees), 29.2% (n = 61) from a small-sized firm (10–50 employees, and 0.5% (n = 1) from a medium-sized firm (50 + employees).

4   The Digital Transformation of Fednot and the Notaries

4.1   Pre-digital Strategy of Fednot

Prior to their DT, Fednot's primary objective was to function as a service company to the notary firms. Their activities centered around designing and developing applications as well as tools for the back-office activities of notaries. Moreover, they aimed at *"supporting the offices and building a bridge between the notaries and the government with an emphasis of keeping and transferring the data in a secure way"* while ensuring the efficiency of notarial activities. This strategy was internally focused; notaries were prioritized over consumers and external partners. Additionally, Fednot served as a medium of information flowing between the government and the firms, such as updates to laws, regulations, registration of deeds, and critical news.

4.2   Drivers for Change

Three primary driving forces behind the decision to embark on DT were derived through the interviews. First, the European union is looking into ways to open the notarial activities to other players in the market. Secondly, the European union is trying to make price competition possible. If these two changes occur, external competition from other professions can be expected in each of the three notary domains. For real estate, there is a threat from large real estate agents and developers. It has been stated that over the last few decades, the notaries have lost out on around 80 percent of real estate sales in Belgium. For family law, there is competition from both law firms and banks. For enterprise law, there is a threat from large consulting firms. Thirdly, innovative technologies such as blockchain and artificial intelligence (AI) have the possibility to alter current operations significantly causing major disruptions in the market.

4.3   Competitive Advantages

The key competitive advantage of a professional association is typically its size. The same holds true for Fednot that represents the entire industry and is funded by all notarial studies in Belgium. Therefore, Fednot has access to a financial team, a large law team of 40 lawyers, and a large ICT department of over 100 ICT specialists. Evidently, they have access to more capabilities than single notaries. These capabilities enable Fednot to invest in projects and initiatives that benefit the entire industry.

Another key advantage is the industry's innate network structure. Due to price regulation and marketing restrictions, the internal competition is limited, and the notaries typically work in close cooperation. This network structure makes them more agile in decision making and more flexible to change than a single large firm. Moreover, it allows the notaries to have close knowledge of their customers and an understanding of what technological solutions would work best in practice.

4.4 Infrastructure Changes of Fednot

In 2016, Fednot created a transformation unit with a CTO to lead the DT. This unit was created specifically to drive the DT initiative and was separated from the IT department. Additionally, Fednot has instituted cross-functional project groups, steering committees, and an extended management committee. The transformation projects are cross-functional in nature and include the CTO, product managers, and business managers. However, the institutionalized structure remains hierarchical and department based.

Regarding the IT infrastructure, it was completely managed on premise prior to the introduction of DT initiatives. This has changed dramatically to a cloud-first infrastructure since the initiatives' implementation. Currently, 80% of DT products are hosted on the cloud *"because you need high availability, good monitoring, and that is not something an internal team can deliver"*. The old internal applications (e.g., registers) are still operating on legacy systems on premise.

4.5 Cultural Readiness

Cultural readiness is often a major challenge for companies embarking on DT (Hartl & Hess, 2017). Due to approximately half of Fednot being composed of IT personnel, most of the employees generally exhibited an openness and enthusiasm for the changes regarding their DT. Yet, a major issue was the conceptual nature of their proposed projects as these projects have shifted from being internal applications built in a top-down manner to that of external, customer-centric products built in co-creation with stakeholders, partners, and customers. This also required a shift in culture.

Although Fednot did not have major cultural barriers, cultural inertia was prevalent amongst the notary firms in committing to the digital strategy and developments of Fednot. This was most apparent in considering the short-term benefits of the new digital products. For instance, notaries *"will not adopt it because, in the short term, they cannot see the added value. This is really a challenge for the change management team to try and find those practical situations where we can convince the notary to use it"*. To promote these DT projects, Fednot utilizes an ambassador program composed of enthusiastic notaries to encourage proactivity among the notaries towards DT. In the interviews, there has been an emphasis to dedicate more resources towards this program.

The DT goals at Fednot are communicated down from general management to the employees and the notaries through a series of communication mediums: the internal communication platform called *eNotariaat*, direct mailings, a change team, and their ambassador program. Furthermore, Fednot makes use of "World Cafes" where there is a peer-to-peer exchange between notaries regarding DT and the future of the notary industry to help design their strategy and initiatives.

To cope with the shift to externally facing applications, new roles and skills needed to be considered that were non-existent in Fednot such as UI designers. Fednot opted to fill the gaps by hiring an additional 40–50 new employees, roughly 25% of the current size. It also utilizes external partners. This is largely due to the flexibility external partners provide and because of Fednot's unsuccessful previous move to internalize many of the roles needed due to the subsequent loss of agility. However, training does exist within Fednot and is focused primarily on strategy, people management, and culture.

Fednot also offers webinars, training programs, and change teams to notaries for each project and their effective use. This is important as elicited through the survey: 44.4% (n = 92) of notaries strongly or somewhat agree that skill gaps have hindered or impacted their DT, 26.1% (n = 54) neither agreed or disagreed and 29.5% (n = 61) strongly or somewhat disagreed. Moreover, 53.6% (n = 111) of notaries found the training support offered by Fednot to be of good quality, 22.7% (n = 47) found it to be excellent, 19.3% found it average, and 4.4% found it either of poor or terrible quality. For each solution, there is an associated instructional video as well as informational webinars. To address their internal skill gaps, notaries seem to opt for mandatory training courses and the use of external partners to properly integrate Fednot's solutions into their existing IT infrastructure and workflow.

Adopting agile values is a common practice when embarking on DT (Fuchs & Hess, 2018). The same holds for Fednot who is going from a traditional inward-facing mindset to an agile customer-centric focus: *"Today, Fednot's strategy is based on having an excellent customer experience, collaborative culture, and building ecosystems... These are linked together as the new image of the notary"*. Additionally, Fednot is moving towards other agile principles such as a culture of risk taking, working in iterations for projects, and improving the speed of product delivery. Regarding collaboration, Fednot has embraced cross-functional teams and expanded the management committee and the transformation unit. While the agile values are mostly in place in the IT department, the organization is considering the added value of agile for other departments.

Some key cultural values prioritized at Fednot are a move toward co-creation and employee empowerment. They believe that they *"should evolve to a more coaching leadership and empowering the people instead of a top-down culture. It has to be an empowering culture"*. In addition, the horizontal steering committees must take on more responsibilities to facilitate the necessary culture for Fednot to grow their DT.

4.6 Digital Transformation Strategy

In recent years, the strategy at Fednot changed. *"A few years ago, the strategy was only to make tools for the notaries. It was not a real digital approach. It was a digital approach for the notaries related to how they work in their studies"*. Fednot outlined a digital strategy to strengthen the notary's role as a trusted, neutral, and an expert advisor, and to involve the notary in more parts of the customer journey rather than just as an authenticator of legal documents: *"All the strategy that we have today is to look at the market in a larger way than only the notary"*.

Both these objectives required Fednot to broaden its customer and technology focus. While earlier their entire IT focus was on providing tools and services necessary for connecting the notaries with the government, they now had to focus on serving external customers/citizens and on collaborating with strategic partners as well. This renewed customer centricity necessitated the development of new products and services aimed at the society at large and not just for the internal use by the notaries.

The unique aspect found here is that Fednot is not just driving DT for a single organization but for an entire industry. Additionally, unlike a typical organization, the notaries are not Fednot's employees but independent entities. Therefore, they are not bound to adopt Fednot's strategic vision or developed solutions which complicates the

DT projects rollout: *"If you build a product for notaries but the notaries do not buy and do not sell the product, you cannot launch it. The notary also has a choice and is not completely dependent on Fednot for these kinds of products or services, they could use other brands as well"*. This requires precaution and precisely outlining the products and linking those with the notaries before starting the real development.

4.7 Business Model Innovation

As part of Fednot's DT strategy creation, their planned business model innovation consisted of three key components as shown in Fig. 3. The data-centricity aspect leverages Fednot's role as an information hub using the vast amounts of legal data that they and the industry possess. The collaboration aspect is about investing in a collaborative ecosystem to strengthen their position in the market. The third aspect deals with automation of services and AI-based expertise and novel products. The aim of these components is to produce additional revenue to be used to fund Fednot activities and subsidize the services provided by Fednot to the notaries.

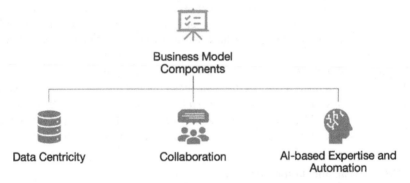

Fig. 3. Business model innovation components of Fednot.

The starting point for the information hub model is the vast amounts of data in the form of legal and supporting documents that the customers provide. Fednot plans to bundle and further enrich this dataset with attributes from open data and geospatial data, in order to provide better services and advice. Another value stream is a digital vault where citizens can upload documents and can automatically access all legal deeds since 2015. With the citizens' authorization, these documents can be accessed by other institutions thereby simplifying the process of submitting physical documents.

For the collaboration aspect, an ecosystem is being developed with consumers and external partners such as notaries, citizens, government agencies, application developers, and other professions such as banks, insurance firms, accountants, and lawyers. *"We want to enter an ecosystem. We need to think for all the markets, who are we going to partner with, and how we are going to expand our offerings"*. The motivation to work in an ecosystem came not just from the desire of the notaries *"taking part in the broader customer journey where they play a role together with other parties"* but also from the pragmatic realization that the notaries cannot beat competition in all areas. The ecosystem consists of a collaboration platform and an API platform that allows both Fednot and third-party applications to seamlessly share data.

To strengthen the notary's role as an expert advisor, Fednot is *"exploring what can we do with the data that we have, and how can we build new services in the area of tomorrow"*. The aim is to enhance their data with data mining and AI-models in two important ways: (a) AI-driven models built on the data hub, such as those for real estate evaluation, to further augment the front-end advisory capability, and (b) an AI-driven document verification solution which aims at automating back-office tasks, thereby freeing up time for the notaries to focus on their core competency as legal advisors.

5 Digital Transformation Products

The source of inspiration for new products developed by Fednot is the notaries themselves. Various workshops are done collaboratively with Fednot and notaries to brainstorm about new services and improvements. This inspiration is used by the innovation lab, a program in which digital experts collaborate to develop and prototype potential products and services that Fednot might offer to the notaries. The lab has considerable leniency and autonomy to experiment with different concepts and is provisioned with an ambitious and flexible budget. The prototypes are then submitted to the board members for approval for further development. Since the beginning of the DT at Fednot, four major products have been developed for use within the industry.

5.1 Biddit

Biddit, launched in 2017, is an online public auction platform for real estate that allows consumers to bid on listed properties and participate in the pricing and valuation of the listed properties. This was Fednot's first DT project after they identified the declining revenue sources from the previous auctioning scheme.

For each product, the survey inquired about its usage and effectiveness. To give one example of the survey results: 198 of 200 notaries indicated they used Biddit of which 39.8% (n = 82) have indicated that they use it always or most of the time. Regarding Biddit's effectiveness, 32.4% (n = 66) consider it extremely successful, 46.1% (n = 94) identified it as somewhat successful and only 3.5% (n = 7) consider Biddit to be either somewhat or extremely unsuccessful. Additionally, 85.9% (n = 176) of the respondents have indicated that they are likely to recommend Biddit to their clients. Moreover, 70.7% (n = 145) of respondents have indicated that they have been effectively trained to use Biddit. An overview is shown in Fig. 4.

5.2 Belgian Notary Network

The Belgian notary network (BNN), launched in 2018, is a private network implemented by Fednot to enable individual notaries to communicate, sign and authorize deeds, and exchange information securely. BNN operates on a closed network in which only licensed parties can participate. Fednot commenced the BNN project to meet the needs of notaries regarding secure digital communication lines. It was delivered by and is operated by external providers.

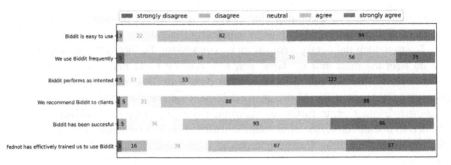

Fig. 4. Notary feedback on Biddit.

5.3 eStox

eStox is an online digital shareholder registry launched in 2019 for small and medium-sized businesses that want to maintain documents of their shareholders list in an easy-to-access online format. It was created in response to regulatory reforms that enabled businesses to use digital channels to keep track of their shareholders' documents. It is a joined notary and accounting product housed in a separate nonprofit organization. The eStox platform also provides the ability to interact with external entities to exchange information on the shareholders' list.

5.4 Izimi

In 2020, Izimi was launched as an online digital repository entrusted with safeguarding individuals' confidential deeds and documents. This secure digital vault is free for the customers of the notaries and allows them to choose which documents to store. While Izimi is strictly speaking a consumer-facing product, it has the capability to integrate with Fednot's existing and future services. An example of this integration is with Naban, which is a digital archiving tool for the notaries. In the future, Izimi will be further integrated in the management software solutions of the notaries.

6 Discussion

6.1 Summary

The Belgian notary industry is an interesting DT case in which the professional association was the main driver of DT. The notaries have come a long way from being a largely pre-digital industry. The notaries are being equipped with new products and skillsets that would help them remain relevant in a business that is under technological and regulatory pressures. With the aid of Fednot, more attention is being paid to novel technologies such cloud computing, data analytics, AI, mobile, and social. This resulted in four new products, Biddit, BNN, Estox, and Izimi, which are being integrated in the management software of the notaries. At Fednot, several organizational changes have taken place to accommodate for this new focus such as a transformation unit and steering groups to manage the DT process, project teams to develop the novel digital solutions, a greater focus on ecosystems with strategic partners, the promotion of agile development methods, and a shift towards a more customer-centric mindset. Table 1 highlights the major impacts of DT in Fednot and the industry.

Table 1. An overview of the DT of the Belgian notary industry.

	Before	After
Organizational structure	Top-down, hierarchical structures	Hybrid structure with cross-functional project teams and a transformation unit
Strategic focus	Improving notary and government coordination	Increasing customer experience and ecosystem integration
It focus	Back-office, efficiency-oriented applications	Agile development of innovative products based on cloud, analytics, AI, mobile and social technologies
Roles & responsibilities	Traditional roles and discrete departments	Emphasis on cross-functional and dynamic roles
Governance	Dictated by the board of administrators and enforced by the C-level executives	IT governance shared with the transformation unit
Industry image	Non-digital, traditional	Modern and customer-centric
Customer experience	Heterogeneous across notaries	Uniform across notaries
Customer-facing digital products	–	Biddit, eStox, and Izimi

6.2 The importance of a Professional Association

The role of a professional association for the DT of their respective sector is an under researched topic in the information systems research community. Yet, their role can be crucial. Thanks to the pooling of resources, Fednot has access to a large ICT team and the resources to innovate. Of the 64 survey responses discussing how DT would look without the existence of Fednot, a substantial proportion of respondents elicited that their DT would have been more limited or non-existent without Fednot (n = 27). Additional responses highlighted that their DT likely would have been slower (n = 11), more difficult (n = 9), and costlier (n = 4). However, some notaries did express less-enthusiastic responses indicating that they believe their DT would have been better (n = 3), more user-friendly (n = 2), cheaper (n = 1), and faster (n = 1) without the orchestrating role of Fednot. Overall, 91.7% (n = 189) of the respondents consider Fednot as either an extremely useful or very useful driver for DT.

In general, Fednot's DT efforts have either completely or somewhat met the notaries' expectations (n = 180) and they are satisfied with its DT efforts. The satisfaction of

Fednot as a driver for DT may be further evidenced by the quick adoption rate seen by the survey respondents. Of these respondents, 10.5% (n = 22) placed in the innovator category, 36.6% (n = 77) in early adopter, 45.7% (n = 96) in early majority, 5.2% (n = 11) in late majority, and 1.9% (n = 4) in the laggard category. However, Fednot states that laggards are free to do so, and they will not convince them to follow the novel approach. If the early adaptors and followers are on board, 70–80% of notaries will follow Fednot's DT efforts. Importantly, the notaries feel that these DT initiatives have projected a positive image of the profession in terms of being tech-savvy and client friendly: *"I think our image has been much more improved and the standard of the professional has been modernized dramatically last years"*.

The role of Fednot as a professional association has expanded from being primarily a service provider to the notaries to also being the primary driver for DT for the whole industry by providing customer-facing solutions. In terms of outcome, the individual notaries are overwhelmingly pleased with the vision and direction Fednot has taken and believe that the industry is much further along than it would have if Fednot was non-existent. Moreover, the financial resources required for hiring 100 + employees for their transformation indicate that the process of DT requires significant investment, something that individual notaries could not afford. This indicates that the pooling of resources from the entire industry may be a smart approach for undergoing resource- and knowledge-intensive processes such as DT.

6.3   Fostering the Proper Culture

Of the four major applications produced since the start of Fednot's transformation, three of them were directed towards the consumer. However, this shift also requires a shift in mindset and culture. Some notaries expressed that they prefer Fednot to focus more on improving internal efficiency rather than addressing citizen pain points. This is a cultural aspect that Fednot should address through change management.

There are other issues related to culture as well. Our results indicate that some of these notary firms may not have the needed digital mindset which leads to reluctance to change. Another important facet of successful transformations is a culture of learning (Vey, Fandel-Meyer, Zipp, & Schneider, 2017). However, while Fednot, at present, has a training program for notaries, they do not specifically address technical training. This presents an issue with the effective use of the applications.

Out of the 48 relevant responses, the notaries expressed that they desired more training (n = 7), more collaboration during solution development (n = 9), more user-friendly designs (n = 7), and better integration between products to avoid excessive double encoding (n = 4). Moreover, some notaries stressed that DT was going too fast (n = 6), that the DT was too focused on the citizen instead of on the notary (n = 4), and that many of the products were too abstract in nature to properly diffuse and promote within the industry (n = 3). One notary elaborates: *"It would be wise, in my opinion, to better calibrate the projects and to ensure that they are bearable by notaries"*. These cultural challenges require close attention for the DT to be successful.

6.4   Barriers, Success Factors and Recommendations

Based on the findings, five recommendations have been derived that can be followed for other professional association-led transformations as shown in Fig. 5:

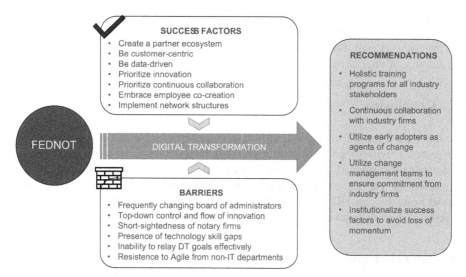

Fig. 5. Success factors, barriers, and recommendations.

6.5   Future Work

Studying the Belgian notary industry has provided unique insights into the DT efforts of both small enterprises and professional associations as a driver for change. Achieving alignment between the companies, which acts as the adopter of digital change, and the professional association, which serves as the driver for change, poses unique challenges requiring more research.

Another interesting research avenue is the impact of product standardization. Products designed by a professional association are launched across the entire sector. While previously each notarial study used to provide services in its own unique way, customer-centric products promoted by Fednot standardize the customer experience across notaries. The long-term impact of standardized products across the industry on competition and competitiveness is unknown and warrants more research.

To develop a deeper understanding of the complex DT steered by a professional association, more case studies must be conducted in other industries comprised of small-sized firms and a professional association that directs them. Such research could be used to draw comparisons on the impact of a professional association as a driver for the industry. In essence, what is now needed is a large-scale research effort to find out if a professional association could be the key element in the successful DT of a sector with many smaller players. And if that is the case, research must be conducted on whether it makes sense for an industry without a professional association to create one.

6.6 Limitations

There have been several limitations that may have inhibited the ability to collect the optimal amount and quality of data. First, when enquiring with the selected notaries about interviewing them, there appeared to be a general reluctance to participate. It is possible that there is response bias towards more tech-forward notaries. This, coupled with the time restrictions and the covid-19 pandemic has led to a non-optimal number of interviews. Lastly, limited literature on DT in professional associations was available to inspire our interviews and surveys or to compare our results with.

7 Conclusion

In this report, the DT of a unique industry comprised of small notaries with federally protected activities that use a central professional association to coordinate their DT efforts was investigated. The findings indicate that the ability of the notaries to pool their resources by use of a professional association has proved advantageous, giving many small firms the capabilities of a much larger organization. However, more research is needed in the role of professional associations in the DT of their sector.

8 Interview and Survey Questions

Link to the interview and survey questions: https://tinyurl.com/FedNot2023.

References

Barnett, M.L.: One voice, but whose voice? Exploring what drives trade association activity. Bus. Soc. **52**(2), 213–244 (2013). https://doi.org/10.1177/0007650309350211

Brock, J. K.-U., von Wangenheim, F.: Demystifying AI: what digital transformation leaders can teach you about realistic artificial intelligence. Calif. Manage. Rev. 110–134 (2019)

Cichosz, M., Wallenburg, C.M., Knemeyer, A.M.: Digital transformation at logistics service providers: barriers, success factors and leading practices. Int. J. Logist. Manag. **30**(2), 209–238 (2020). https://doi.org/10.1108/IJLM-08-2019-0229

Drahos, P., Shearing, C.: Nodal Governance, (May) (2014)

Fuchs, C., Hess, T.: Becoming agile in the digital transformation: the process of a large-scale agile transformation. In: International Conference on Information Systems 2018, ICIS 2018, p. 17 (2018)

Hartl, E., Hess, T.: The role of cultural values for digital transformation: insights from a delphi study. In: AMCIS 2017 - America's Conference on Information Systems: A Tradition of Innovation, 2017-August (August) (2017)

Legner, C., et al.: Digitalization: opportunity and challenge for the business and information systems engineering community. Bus. Inf. Syst. Eng. **59**(4), 301–308 (2017). https://doi.org/10.1007/s12599-017-0484-2

Lucas, H.C., Agarwal, R., Clemons, E.K., El Sawy, O.A., Weber, B.: Impactful research on transformational information technology: an opportunity to inform new audiences. MIS Q. **37**(2), 371–382 (2013)

Perkin, N., Abraham, P.: Building the agile business through digital transformation (2017)

Royal Federation of Belgian Notaries. (n.d.). About the notary and the notarial profession in Belgium | Other languages - Notaris.be

Saarikko, T., Westergren, U.H., Blomquist, T.: Digital transformation: five recommendations for the digitally conscious firm. Bus. Horiz. **63**(6), 825–839 (2020). https://doi.org/10.1016/j.bus hor.2020.07.005

SAP Center for Business Insight. SAP Digital Transformation Executive Study: 4 Ways Leaders Set Themselves Apart (2017)

Schneider, S., Kokshagina, O.: Digital transformation: what we have learned (thus far) and what is next. Creativity Innov. Manage. (May 2020), 1–28 (2021). https://doi.org/10.1111/caim.12414

The Federation of Enterprises in Belgium. (n.d.). Sectoral Federations

Tsui-Auch, L.S.: Bureaucratic rationality and nodal agency in a developmental state: the case of state-led biotechnology development in Singapore. Int. Soc. **19**(4), 451–477 (2004). https://doi.org/10.1177/0268580904047367

Van Veldhoven, Z., Etikala, V., Goossens, A., Vanthienen, J.: A scoping review of the digital transformation literature using scientometric analysis. In: 24th International Conference on Business Information Systems (BIS 2021), p. 12 (2021)

Van Veldhoven, Z., Vanthienen, J.: Digital transformation as an interaction-driven perspective between business, society, and technology. Electron. Mark. **1**(2021).https://doi.org/10.1007/s12525-021-00464-5

Vey, K., Fandel-Meyer, T., Zipp, J.S., Schneider, C.: Learning & development in times of digital transformation: facilitating a culture of change and innovation. Int. J. Adv. Corp. Learn. (IJAC) **10**(1), 22 (2017). https://doi.org/10.3991/ijac.v10i1.6334

Vial, G.: Understanding digital transformation: a review and a research agenda. J. Strat. Inf. Syst. **28**(2), 1–27 (2019). https://doi.org/10.1016/j.jsis.2019.01.003

DQBR25K: Data Quality Business Rules Identification Based on ISO/IEC 25012

Ramón Galera[1,2]([✉]) [ID], Fernando Gualo[1,2] [ID], Ismael Caballero[2] [ID],
and Moisés Rodríguez[2,3] [ID]

[1] DQTeam, Ciudad Real, Spain
rgalera@dqteam.es
[2] Alarcos Research Group, UCLM, Ciudad Real, Spain
{Fernando.Gualo,Ismael.Caballero}@uclm.es
[3] AQCLab, UCLM, Ciudad Real, Spain
mrodriguez@aqclab.es

Abstract. Organizations continuously generate and manage extensive amounts of data for specific purposes, such as making informed decisions or monitoring certain parameters. It is not only essential to obtain the data; how it is obtained, stored, and maintained is equally, if not more, valuable. Data quality is a crucial factor for any organization because if the data does not meet the required level of quality, its use will not yield the best results. To maintain adequate levels of quality, organizations need to identify the data requirements or business rules that their data must adhere to for the intended purpose. The most common problem is organizations' lack of knowledge in identifying business rules adequately. In this regard, a model based on ISO/IEC 25012 enables the assessment of data quality based on an organization's requirements. As a solution, this work presents a methodology to facilitate the identification and classification of business rules for an organization, as well as their association with each data quality characteristic defined by the ISO/IEC 25012 standard.

Keywords: Business Rules · Data Quality · ISO/IEC 25012

1 Introduction

A data quality measurement model aims to quantify the extent to which a dataset in a repository meets the characteristics proposed in a data quality model. Different methods and tools are available to assess data quality properly [1], such as AIMQ: a methodology for information quality assessment [2] or DQA: Data Quality Assessment [3].

Nowadays, when an organization wants to evaluate data quality, it must have or develop a data requirement specification or business rules that the data must comply with based on its intended use within the organization [4]. Although it is not a highly complex process, it does require a certain level of knowledge and fundamentals. If not handled properly, this process can take longer than expected, or the evaluation not be conducted adequately [5].

J. M. Fernandes et al. (Eds.): QUATIC 2023, CCIS 1871, pp. 178–190, 2023.
https://doi.org/10.1007/978-3-031-43703-8_13

This work presents a systematic methodology that assists organisations in obtaining business rules through mechanisms that require less time and effort than the current ones to perform data quality assessment.

The remainder of the paper is structured as follows: Sect. 2 introduces the ISO/IEC 25012 standard and highlights some of its quality characteristics. Next, Sect. 3 explains the technique used to obtain the designed methodology. In Sect. 4, the methodology itself is presented along with its phases. Subsequently, in Sect. 5, the methodology is validated through a case study. Finally, the conclusions and future work are discussed.

2 Background

2.1 ISO/IEC 25012 and ISO/IEC 25024

Among the models and standards developed in recent years for data quality assessment, the ISO/IEC 25012 standard stands out. It defines a quality model with a set of characteristics that should be considered when evaluating a data product's properties [6]. There are a total of fifteen characteristics; however, when performing a data quality assessment, we will focus on the inherent characteristics as they address most situations regardless of the technological context. This approach enables us to conduct an objective and precise evaluation [7]. These characteristics are [8]:

- **Accuracy:** The degree to which data has attributes that correctly represent the true value of the intended attribute of a concept or event in a specific context of use.
- **Completeness:** The degree to which subject data associated with an entity has values for all expected attributes and related entity instances in a specific context of use.
- **Consistency:** The degree to which data has attributes that are free from contradiction and are coherent with other data in a specific context of use. It can be either or both among data regarding one entity and across similar data for comparable entities.
- **Credibility:** The degree to which data has attributes that are regarded as true and believable by users in a specific context of use. Credibility includes the concept of authenticity (the truthfulness of origins, attributions, commitments).
- **Currentness:** The degree to which data has attributes that are of the right age in a specific context of use.

On the other hand, the ISO/IEC 25024 standard presents a set of metrics for measuring such data quality. This standard applies to any data structure within a system [9]. There are numerous properties and ways to measure them. Some examples of these are:

- **Record Completeness:** Compliance with the minimum set of essential features for representing the identity through a registration system.
- **File Completeness:** Level of agreement between the dataset of a data entity and the minimum/maximum range of records intended for that entity.
- **Referential Integrity:** Level of correspondence between each field of a record that is related to an attribute in another data file (e.g., in relational databases: a foreign key), where the value of that field is present in the corresponding attribute of the different file (e.g., in relational databases: there is a referenced primary key) or the value of the foreign key is 'NULL.'

2.2 BR4DQ

The BR4DQ methodology has been developed with the purpose of resolving common problems related to the collection, grouping, and validation of business rules in the context of data quality management within an organization [10]. This methodology aims to overcome challenges such as the lack of organizational agreement on stated business rules and the absence of an explicit statment of business rules as an integral part of an organization's internal approach to data quality management.

BR4DQ represents an improvement over certain other existing methodologies as it incorporates a dedicated phase for the categorization and verification of the business rules pertaining to each data quality characteristic implicated in the evaluation of data quality. The categorization is carried out based on the data quality characteristics that encompass the data quality prerequisites.

This methodology focuses on ensuring that all relevant business rules within an organization are identified and captured comprehensively, and that mechanisms are established for their validation and effective implementation. By implementing this methodology, organizations can enhance their ability to ensure data quality and maximize the value of business information.

However, it is necessary to highlight that this methodology specifically focuses on the internal data quality management system, in contrast to the approach presented in this work, which focuses on providing support for gathering requirements to evaluate an organization, something innovative compared to other evaluation methodologies.

3   Research Method

To conduct a rigorous approach in the research carried out for the proposal of this methodology for the identification and classification of data requirements, this section presents the steps followed based on the principles of design science [11]:

1. **Problem identification and motivation:** After numerous assessments and certifications conducted in recent years to ensure data quality [5], it has been identified that one of the most common challenges is associated with the collection of business rules by the organization seeking evaluation. Poor identification of data rules for an entity, either due to their incomplete nature or imperfect collection, leads to a decrease in the accuracy of evaluation results, as a proper and thorough evaluation is not conducted [12]. The primary motivation is to provide a highly efficient methodology for identifying and classifying business rules based on the ISO 25000 standard, aiming to significantly reduce the time required by stakeholders and minimize ambiguity as much as possible.
2. **Define the goal of the solution:** Since the lack of appropriate business rules for efficient evaluation often stems primarily from stakeholders' lack of understanding and time, the foundation of this solution will be to develop a methodology that facilitates the identification of business rules in a comprehensible and lightweight manner for organizations, as this is the optimal way to achieve a functional solution. This methodology can be integrated with other methodologies, such as ISO/IEC 25040, which is used to certify data quality projects [13].

3. **Design and development of the solution:** Once the problem and objective have been defined, different phases have been designed that are related to the necessary steps to progress from the start of an evaluation, such as identifying its scope to its conclusion and obtaining a quantitative result of data quality.
4. **Validation of the solution:** The validation of the solution will be carried out by applying the methodology in an evaluation of an organisation in a real context. The analysis of the results is presented in Sect. 5.

4   DQBR25K Methodology

DQBR25K is a methodology composed of several phases, to provide support in identifying and classifying business rules during the data quality evaluation process according to the ISO 25012 standard. Furthermore, it seeks to facilitate script generation, evaluation, and support, thereby establishing a structured workflow.

DQBR25K follows a similar structure to the BR4DQ methodology in terms of the logic of business rule identification and capture. Both methodologies are based on the premise that business rules are fundamental to assessing data quality in an organization. However, while BR4DQ focuses on the internal data quality management system, DQBR25K centers around enabling a third party, who may not have in-depth knowledge of the internal system, to identify and comprehend the business rules of the evaluated data.

For each of the phases, their purpose and description, required input products, expected outputs, and activities to be carried out are specified. It is important to note that, depending on the organizational context, performing all the phases may not be necessary, although it is recommended. Instead, only those phases considered necessary to support different activities can be executed. In Fig. 1, an illustration depicting the different phases of DQBR35K can be observed.

Fig. 1. Methodology Overview

4.1   Phase 1: Defining the Scope of the Evaluation

Purpose and Description: The main objective is to identify the data elements that will be part of the data quality measurement and evaluation process [14]. By combining one or multiple repositories, a list of elements will be obtained to form a baseline for work. Figure 2 provides a detailed overview of the current phase.

Input products:

- Organization's data catalog.
- Documentation of information systems subject to evaluation.

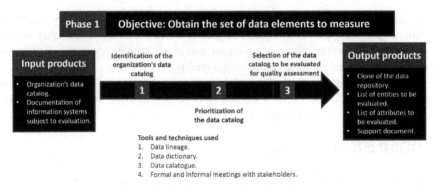

Fig. 2. Detail of phase 1 of the methodology

Output products:

- Clone of the data repository for the evaluation.
- List of entities to be evaluated.
- List of attributes to be evaluated.
- Support document for the evaluation with the different entities and attributes to be evaluated.

Tools and techniques used:

- Data lineage.
- Data dictionary.
- Data catalog.
- Formal and informal meetings with stakeholders.

Activities:

- Identification of the organization's data catalog.
- Prioritization of the data catalog.
- Selection of the data catalog to be evaluated for quality assessment.

4.2   Phase 2: Capturing Business Rules Through Questions

Purpose and description: The main objective of this phase is to identify, determine, and describe the business rules that define the data validity to quantify the extent to which the repository complies with these rules [15]. To improve the management of this phase and achieve better traceability and reduce the required time, based on the experience of various evaluations as described in [5] it was decided to develop a closed questionnaire that contains a series of questions directed toward the organization that wishes to carry out the data quality evaluation. Efforts have been made to minimize the number of questions and limit the possible answers as much as possible, including binary options in several cases. This has been done to avoid redundant questions and ensure that the questions are appropriate [16]. However, some open-ended questions will be necessary as they are fundamental in obtaining sufficient context. Examples of this questions can be found in Phase 2 of the methodology validation, specifically in Fig. 7.

Similarly, due to the different natures of organizations, an open section has been created where data requirements or rules that cannot be classified within any questionnaire question due to their specific domain can be introduced but are still necessary to know. Once these questions have been answered, sufficient information should have been obtained to classify them using the approach of data quality characteristics and properties according to the ISO 25012 model. Furthermore, during the development of this phase, these rules should be validated to identify possible errors introduced by the client organization. This validation will be performed iteratively and always under the supervision of the stakeholders. Figure 3 provides a detailed illustration of the development of this phase.

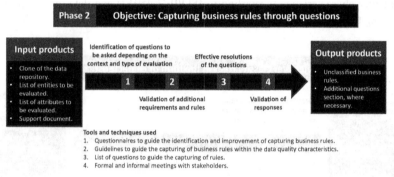

Fig. 3. Detail of phase 2 of the methodology

Input products:

- Clone of the data repository to be evaluated.
- List of entities to be evaluated.
- List of attributes to be evaluated.
- Support document with the entities and attributes to be evaluated.

Output products:

- Support document with the entities and attributes to be evaluated, including the questionnaire with the questions and corresponding responses, i.e., the business rules.
- Section for additional requirements and rules, whenever necessary.

Tools and techniques used:

- Questionnaires to guide the identification and improvement of capturing business rules.
- Guidelines to guide the capturing of business rules within the data quality characteristics.
- List of questions to guide the capturing of rules.
- Formal and informal meetings with stakeholders.

Activities:

1. Identification and selection of questions to be asked depending on the context and type of evaluation.
2. Validation of additional requirements and rules.
3. Effective resolution of the questions.
4. Validation of the responses.

4.3   Phase 3: Classification of Business Rules

Purpose and Description: The main objective of this phase, as shown in Fig. 4, is to classify the identified rules or requirements through the output products of Phase 2 into data quality characteristics (according to ISO/IEC 25012) and data quality properties (according to ISO/IEC 25024).

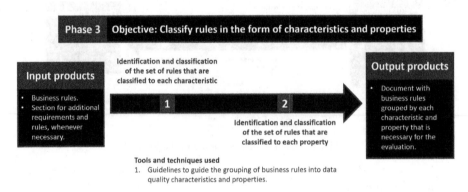

Fig. 4. Detail of phase 3 of the methodology

Input products:

- Business rules.
- Section for additional requirements and rules, whenever necessary.

Output products:

- Document with business rules grouped by each characteristic and property that is necessary for the evaluation.

Tools and techniques used:

- Guidelines to guide the grouping of business rules into data quality characteristics and properties.

Activities:

1. Identification and classification of the set of rules that are classified for each characteristic.
2. Identification and classification of the set of rules that are classified for each property.

4.4 Phase 4: Script Generation and Repository Measurement

Purpose and Description: The main objective is to produce the data requirements validation mechanisms or business rules necessary for data quality measurement and evaluation. In addition, once these mechanisms have been generated, it will be necessary to execute them to obtain a degree of compliance with data requirements and identify strengths and weaknesses in the organization's data repository. Figure 5 provides a detailed outline of this final phase.

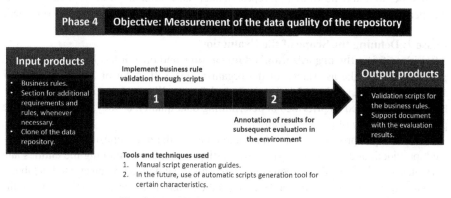

Fig. 5. Detail of phase 4 of the methodology

Input products:

- Document with business rules grouped by each characteristic and property.
- Section for additional requirements and rules, whenever necessary.
- Clone of the data repository where the evaluation will be conducted.

Output products:

- Validation scripts for the business rules.
- Support document with the evaluation results.

Tools and techniques used:

- In the future, use the automatic script generation tool for specific characteristics.
- Manual script generation guides.

Activities:

1. Implement business rule validation through scripts.
2. Annotation of results for subsequent evaluation in the environment.

5 Validation

In order to validate the effectiveness and usability of the presented methodology, a process of measurement and evaluation will be carried out in a real-world context, focusing on a non-governmental organization. This approach will allow for the collection of empirical data that supports the validity of the proposed methodology and its ability to achieve the desired results in a practical environment. This organization contains data about various users, such as studies, nationalities, and assistance.

This case study will focus on the properties of *record completeness, file completeness*, and *referential integrity*. The objective is to explore various examples of question formats and evaluate how these properties are applied to them. The implementation of the methodology will be carried out rigorously, following the different phases detailed throughout this study.

In order to make the validation reproducible, static versions of the repository clone, the measurement scripts and the documents containing the business rules are obtained.

Phase 1: Defining the Scope of the Evaluation

After **identifying the organization's data catalog**, and once it has been analyzed and **prioritized** with the assistance of the organization itself, a set of 16 tables and 227 attributes have been **selected to be evaluated for quality assesment**. These elements have been identified as priorities in determining data quality, as they are crucial for the proper functioning of the organization.

As an output product of this phase, the clone of the data repository has been created, provided, and accessed, and the supporting document containing the entities and attributes to be evaluated has been generated. This document has been created in tabular format, where each row of the table displays the different attributes of an entity, in this case, a database table. An example of the expected results is shown in Fig. 6.

Entity	Attribute
Persona	ID_PERSONA
Persona	FECHA_NACIMIENTO
Persona	ID_PAIS
Persona	IND_RESIDENTE
Persona	SEXO
Persona	NACIONALIDAD
Persona	ESTADO_CIVIL
Persona	ID_CENTRO_ACTIVO
Persona_Nacionalidades	ID_PERSONA
Persona_Nacionalidades	ID_PAIS
Persona_Nacionalidades	IND_DEFECTO
Persona_Nacionalidades	FECHA_ALTA
Persona_Nacionalidades	FECHA_BAJA

Fig. 6. List of attributes of two different entities

Phase 2: Capturing the Business Rules through Questions

Once the entities and attributes to be evaluated have been identified, the next step is to **identify and select the questions** that will be asked, depending on the context and type of evaluation, in order to capture the business rules.. Three questions have been identified to assess the mentioned properties in the work. Two are "*Yes/No*" questions related to the record's completeness and file properties' completeness. The remaining question, corresponding to the referential integrity property, is also boolean-type, but in case of an affirmative response, additional details must be provided. Figure 7 shows the questions mentioned above and their possible answers and details.

N	Question	Answ	Detail
Q1	Must the field always contain a value (no empty fields allowed)?	a) Yes	-
Q1	Must the field always contain a value (no empty fields allowed)?	b) No	-
Q2	Does the value of the field (if any) refer to another attribute contained in another entity?	a) Yes	The value of the field refers to attribute 'X' of entity 'Y'.
Q2	Does the value of the field (if any) refer to another attribute contained in another entity?	b) No	-
Q3	Is the number of records in the table as expected?	a) Yes	-
Q3	Is the number of records in the table as expected?	b) No	-

Fig. 7. Questions to identify business rules corresponding to the properties to be assessed

After obtaining the list of questions to be asked, the organization proceeded to provide **effective resolution of the questions** with the support and supervision of the researchers involved in this work. In this case, there was no need to generate an additional section for additional rules, as all the necessary details for the proper measurement of the properties to be evaluated have been specified. Once the responses have been received, the **resolution is validated** to proceed to the next phase. As an output of this process, a section with all the questions and their corresponding answers has been generated within the evaluation support document, as shown in a fragment in Fig. 8.

Entity	Attribute	Q1	Q2	Detail Q2
Persona	ID_PERSONA	a) Yes	b) No	-
Persona	FECHA_NACIMIENTO	a) Yes	b) No	-
Persona	ID_PAIS	a) Yes	b) No	-
Persona	IND_RESIDENTE	b) No	b) No	-
Persona	SEXO	b) No	b) No	-
Persona	NACIONALIDAD	b) No	b) No	-
Persona	ESTADO_CIVIL	b) No	b) No	-
Persona	ID_CENTRO_ACTIVO	a) Yes	b) No	-
Persona_Nacionalidades	ID_PERSONA	a) Yes	a) Yes	The value of the field refers to the attribute ID_PERSONA of the PERSONA table.
Persona_Nacionalidades	ID_PAIS	a) Yes	a) Yes	The value of the field refers to the ID_PAIS attribute of the MAESTRO_PAIS table.
Persona_Nacionalidades	IND_DEFECTO	b) No	b) No	-
Persona_Nacionalidades	FECHA_ALTA	a) Yes	b) No	-
Persona_Nacionalidades	FECHA_BAJA	b) No	b) No	-

Fig. 8. Questions and answers corresponding to questions Q1 and Q2 of the supporting document

Phase 3: Classification of Business Rules

Thanks to the questionnaire, business rules can be classified more systematically, reducing the time required for identifying and categorizing requirements. Each question or series of questions is associated with specific properties based on ISO/IEC 25012 and ISO/IEC 25024. This ensures a standardized and efficient process for classifying and aligning the rules with the relevant data quality properties. Therefore, the **identification and classification of the business rules** for each feature and property are carried out.

This way, the business rules document is obtained, and the bussiness rules are grouped by characteristics and properties through tables or questions. Figure 9 shows a table from the document with the question *"Must the field always contain a value?"* grouped under the Completeness property and *"Does the value of the field refer to another attribute contained in another entity?"*. This organization of the rules allows for easier reference

Table "Persona_Nacionalidades"	Completeness	Integrity	
	Record Completeness	Referential Integrity	
Attribute	Must the field always contain a value?	Does the value of the field refer to another attribute contained in another entity?	
ID_PERSONA	Yes	Yes	Persona.ID_Persona
ID_PAIS	Yes	Yes	Maestro_Pais.Pais
IND_DEFECTO	No	No	
FECHA_ALTA	Yes	No	
FECHA_BAJA	No	No	

Fig. 9. Questions rated for completeness and integrity characteristics

and analysis, enabling a comprehensive understanding of how each rule relates to the evaluated data quality properties.

Phase 4: Generation and Evaluation of Scripts

In this phase, the necessary **scripts are implemented** to validate the business rules for later evaluation. Furthermore, these scripts are executed.. For example, for the referential integrity of the 'Persona_Nacionalidades' entity, the script in Fig. 10 has been generated, which provides the detailed result shown in the image.

```
select
    count(*)
from
    DWH_CALIDAD_TMP.PERSONA_NACIONALIDADES pn
where
    pn.ID_PERSONA  IN (
        SELECT
            pmp.ID_PERSONA
        FROM
            DWH_CALIDAD_TMP.PERSONA pmp)
    AND pn.ID_PAIS IN (
        SELECT
            mp.ID_PAIS
        FROM
            DWH_CALIDAD_TMP.MAESTRO_PAIS mp)
union
select
    count(*)
from
    DWH_CALIDAD_TMP.PERSONA_NACIONALIDADES pn2 ;
```

Fig. 10. Script and result of the record referential integrity for the Persona_Nacionalidades table

Finally, the **measurement results are annotated** for subsequent evaluation in the supporting document. Based on the results of the different entities for the measured properties, an evaluation can be carried out. Figure 11 provides an example of recording measurement results.

Entity	Record Completeness	File Completeness	Referential Integrity
Persona	0,910	0,975	1,000
Persona_Nacionalidades	0,982	1,000	0,590

Fig. 11. Example of measurement results in supporting document

6 Conclusions and Future Developments

This work presents a valuable contribution to the field of science by introducing a methodology for the identification of business rules and the evaluation of data quality. Unlike other existing methodologies, this proposal stands out for its focus on enabling organizations without prior knowledge to identify and classify business rules.

The methodology designed in this work has been proven effective in real projects, validating its applicability and usefulness in practical contexts. Its main contribution lies in providing a structured and accessible guide for collecting business rules, facilitating the data management and analysis process for organizations. This methodology offers an invaluable solution for those lacking experience in this field, enabling them to effectively progress in identifying and classifying business rules.

Regarding future work, this project plans to expand the covered quality properties to identify all business rules through this methodology. The connection of the rule identification support document with the automatic evaluation script generation program being developed within the organization is also planned. Furthermore, efforts are underway to enhance an existing dashboard application that provides a clear visualization of the degree of compliance for each rule based on the identified quality requirements while applying the methodology proposed in this work.

Acknowledgments. This research has been partially funded by the following projects and grants: Industrial Doctorate (Ref.: DIN2018-009705), funded by the Ministry of Science, Innovation and Universities; ESEDM Project: Evaluation of Master Data Exploitation Systems (Ref.: 13/22/IN/041) funded by the European Regional Development Fund, through the FEDER 2021–2027 Program of Castilla-la Mancha; ADAGIO (Alarcos' Data Governance framework and systems generatIOn) (Ref.: SBPLY/21/180501/000061), funded by the Ministry of Education, Culture, and Sports of the Junta de Comunidades de Castilla La Mancha, Spain, and the European Regional Development Fund (FEDER); and AETHER-UCLM: A Smart for contextualised data analysis focused on quality and safety focused on quality and safety (Ministry of Science and Innovation Innovation, PID2020-112540RB-C42)".

References

1. Batini, C., Cappiello, C., Francalanci, C., Maurino, A.: Methodologies for data quality assessment and improvement. ACM Comput. Surv. (2009)
2. Lee,, Y., Stron,g D., Khan B., Wang, R. AIMQ: a methodology for information quality assessment. Inf. Manage. (2002)
3. Pipino, L., Lee, Y., Wang, R.: Data Quality Assessment, Communications Of The ACM, vol. 45 (2002)
4. Heinrich, B., Hristova, D., Klier, M., Schiller, A., Szubartowicz, M.: Requirements for data quality metrics (2018)

5. Caballero, I., Gualo, F., Rodríguez, M., Piattini, M.: Data quality certification using ISO/IEC 25012: industrial experiences. J. Syst. Softw. (2021)
6. ISO 25000. https://iso25000.com/index.php/normas-iso-25000/iso-25012. Accessed 25 Mar 2023
7. Calabrese, J., Esponda,, S., Pasini A., Boracchia, M., Pesado, P.: Guía para evaluar calidad de datos basada en ISO/IEC 25012. In: XXV Congreso Argentino de Ciencias de la Computación, pp. 696–697 (2019)
8. ISO 25012. https://iso25000.com/index.php/en/iso-25000-standards/iso-25012. Accessed 01 May 2023
9. ISO/IEC 25024:2015 — Systems and software engineering — Systems and software Quality Requirements and Evaluation (SQuaRE) — Measurement of data quality. https://www.iso.org/standard/35749.html. Accessed 06 Mar 2023
10. Caballero, I., Gualo, F., Rodríguez, M., Piattini, M.: BR4DQ: a methodology for grouping business rules for data quality. J. Decis. Syst. 1–31 (2022)
11. Seyffarth, T., Kuehnel, S.: Maintaining business process compliance despite changes: a decision support approach based on process adaptations. J. Decis. Syst. 1–31 (2022)
12. Kumar, P., Anand, K.: Domain-independent method of detecting inconsistencies in SBVR-based business rules, ForMABS (2016)
13. ISO, ISO/IEC 25040 Systems and software engineering - Systems and software Quality, Geneva, Switzerland (2011)
14. Loshin, D.: Enterprise Knowledge Management, Morgan Kaufmann (2001)
15. Watts, S., Shankaranarayanan, G., Even, A.: Data quality assessment in context: a cognitive perspective, Decis. Support Syst. 202–211 (2009)
16. Corea, C., Matthias, T.: Towards inconsistency measurement in business rule bases, pp. 1–8 (2019)

Pitching to the 'Big Fish': Elevating Presentation and Communication Skills in a Software Quality Course

Miguel Morales-Trujillo[1]([✉]) and Ismael Caballero Muñoz-Reja[2]

[1] University of Canterbury, Christchurch, New Zealand
`miguel.morales@canterbury.ac.nz`
[2] Universidad de Castilla–La Mancha, Ciudad Real, Spain
`ismael.caballero@uclm.es`

Abstract. In this work, we present a Software Quality teaching experience based on gamification. In this experience, "A Meeting with the Big Fish", the lecturer and students play different roles in a Shark Tank-like situation. The lecturer (Big Fish) and their sharks maintain a planned meeting with students where harsh and unexpected situations happen to students while presenting a Software Process Improvement proposal. Initial results have shown the effectiveness of the activity in terms of engagement, fun, and authenticity.

Keywords: Gamification in Education · Game-based learning · Pitching · Software Process Improvement · Communication skills

1 Introduction

Gamification proposes to use game thinking and dynamics to increase engagement and stimulate users' active participation, thus enhancing the outcomes [8]. Introducing gamification in educational contexts may benefit student attentiveness and understanding of the course material, lower tension, and boost student morale [10]. As a result, using playful elements in learning environments promotes a powerful learning experience through which to develop knowledge, skills, and/or abilities [8].

In the case of Software Engineering (SE) education, gamification is useful for modeling specific behaviors and for motivating students to apply SE practices and concepts to their development endeavors [9]. However, despite the potential of gamification in SE education in terms of motivating students, few studies offer sound empirical evidence about the impact of gamified applications on user engagement and performance [7].

This innovative and exploratory paper presents as its most important contribution "*A Meeting with the Big Fish*", a gamified activity that aims to improve students' learning experience in a Software Quality course. The 'Big Fish' gamified activity integrates pitching and game elements to present a **Software Process Improvement (SPI)** assignment, so students can practice and enhance their confidence, communication, and presentation skills.

J. M. Fernandes et al. (Eds.): QUATIC 2023, CCIS 1871, pp. 191–199, 2023.
https://doi.org/10.1007/978-3-031-43703-8_14

The remainder of this paper is structured as follows. Section 2 describes the relevant concepts on which the activity is based and the course in which it is developed. Section 3 describes the Big Fish activity, while Sect. 4 presents the discussion. Finally, Sect. 5 presents conclusions and future work.

2   Background and Related Work

2.1   Pitching and Shark Tank

Pitching refers to presenting a product or service to a potential investor to convince them of its viability and value so they fund it. The "pitch" should be concise, and engaging, must highlight the key features of the product/service, and show that it will deliver value. Pitching is usually a targeted, pre-prepared sounding speech addressed to potential investors and accompanied by visual elements (slides, demonstration of promoted objects in action, etc.) [2].

An effective pitch requires clear communication, effective storytelling, showcasing market opportunity, addressing potential risks, and emphasizing the value and uniqueness of the proposal. While pitching encloses soft skills that SE students would benefit to have, communication has not yet received proper coverage in scientific discourse [2].

The "Shark Tank" is a reality television show where participants pitch an idea for entrepreneurial funding [1]. Entrepreneurs pitch their products or services to negotiate investment deals and seek this financial support from the "sharks" (panel of investors), who assess the viability and potential of the product/service.

Following the idea of Shark Tank and pitching, a gamified activity was created in a Software Quality fourth-year course to help students develop and/or improve communication, presentation, negotiation, and persuasion skills, which can benefit them personally and professionally.

Related work has been developed by Haertel et al. [4], where they used "Shark Tank" to improve creativity and entrepreneurship aspects in Engineering students. They found that students tended to avoid radical innovations and risks even in a playful atmosphere. Moore et al. [5] presented the InVenture Challenge, a Shark Tank-based activity that attempts to deliver an authentic experience to introduce students to Engineering. They concluded that it effectively engages students and entrepreneurship through invention.

2.2   The Course: SENG403 – Software Process and Product Quality

The SENG403 – Software Process and Product Quality course introduces fundamental concepts, methodologies, and techniques related to software quality throughout the entire software development lifecycle [3]. Taught at the University of Canterbury, SENG403 is an elective course offered to fourth-year Software Engineering, as well as Computer Science (Hons.) and Master students in Information Systems and Information Technology. The course content has been designed by one of the authors of this paper, drawing upon their experience in the software industry as a business analyst, developer, tester, and project and product manager.

SENG403 pursues ten Learning Outcomes (LOs), being relevant for this paper the following ones:

- LO2 – Apply analysis skills to abstract and devise quality problems affecting process, product, and people (the P's) in software engineering.
- LO3 – Hypothesize specific improvements to make the three P's more effective, efficient, and reliable.
- LO8 – Plan and evaluate, in the form of an experience report, an organizational process or product in terms of quality attributes.
- LO9 – Write, compose, and explain Software Quality Assurance (SQA) outcomes (assessments, audit reports, plans), supported by an oral synthesis to demonstrate effective communication skills both in report writing and presentation.

Course Content. The topics presented in this course include an introduction to the basic concepts of software quality, a review of the industry's most commonly used quality standards and models, and a presentation of several SQA-related tools and techniques. The core topic, in the context of this paper, is *Quality in Software Processes*, where a comprehensive exploration of the obstacles encountered by organizations during software product development and the strategies employed to address them through SPI initiatives is presented. The full description of the course can be consulted at [3].

Assessment. The course assessment is split into three items: two assignments (30% each) and a final exam (40%). In Assignment I, students work in teams and create an SPI proposal from their own practical experience. This assignment allows students to reflect on current software engineering practice critically. Besides, it allows them to evaluate and adapt techniques, methodologies, and practices to their needs. This assessment item addresses LO2, LO3, LO8, and LO9. The Assignment I specification is released during week 5 of the course and should be handed out four weeks later. It is marked, and feedback to students is provided (week 11) so they have the opportunity to improve their SPI proposal. During the last week of the semester (week 12), teams should pitch their SPI proposal during the Big Fish activity.

For completeness, Assignment II is related to a software product assessment in which students are expected to measure specific quality attributes of a product using the ISO/IEC 25010 standard. This assignment is also developed in teams.

3 The Game: A Meeting with the 'Big Fish'

3.1 Activity in Context

A Meeting with the Big Fish is a gamified activity in which students are required to pitch an SPI proposal. The game elements integrated into it are challenges, points, time constraints, and play money. The SPI proposal has been developed in teams of three or four students as part of one of their course assignments (see Sect. 2.2). Each team will act as if they were a startup responding to a Request for Proposals (RFP) launched by a Big Fish organization.

During the pitch, which should last at most six minutes, students will try to convince the Big Fish to contract their services. Each team will role-play to be a startup and will present their proposal to the Big Fish and their team of advisors. The lecturer performs the Big Fish's CEO, and the panel of advisors (sharks) is formed by three or four postgrad students that are familiar with the activity and were asked to act as sharp, brutal, and with little patience sharks. The sharks will play the roles of CTO, CFO, COO, and CMO (optional). In addition to this, several "unexpected" situations can occur at any time, and students are assessed on how they handle these.

The proposals are assessed in terms of *planning* (were the scope, time, and effort specified?), *completeness* (were the required elements defined?), *risks awareness*, *feasibility/appropriateness* (is the SPI doable given the organization's constraints?), *objectivity*, *measurable improvement* (are the defined metrics quantifiable?), *clarity of presentation*, and an *extra aspect* chosen by the sharks (e.g., passion, engagement, innovation). It is important to mention that students know that the meeting will be ruthless but fair, and always under a teaching-innovative and controlled academic umbrella. Teams are assessed before, during, and after their presentations; everything they do or say counts. Each team starts the meeting with 10 "confidence votes" (points), represented by colored balls, and their goal is to keep as many of them as possible. They can lose votes throughout the meeting depending on how they manage the unexpected situations (see Fig. 1).

3.2 Activity Set-Up

The meeting should be held in a room specially arranged for the activity. To make the most of it, the room should not be familiar to students, so they are not aware of what would be available (e.g., a projector, a computer, WiFi access) or how the chairs and tables will be set up.

The week before the meeting, students have had received an email from the Big Fish's personal assistant:

"Dear <startup>,

I hope this email finds you well. I am writing to request a meeting with you to discuss your SPI proposal. The meeting will be held on <date> at <time>. Please be prepared and have everything ready because the CEO has only one hour available. We anticipate a fruitful discussion during our upcoming meeting.

Best regards,"

At this point, students know that:

- The Big Fish is a very busy person. So, for sure, they won't have a one-hour meeting (time constraints).
- The organization has ample financial resources.

- The organization has strict security policies that include access to physical and virtual resources.
- The meeting date and time, and that it will be at the headquarters of the organization.

Regarding the room, the arrangement of chairs and tables should promote a sense of authority, formality, and centrality for the Big Fish, who will lead the meeting. Chairs are placed along the sides of the table for participants, while the Big Fish sits at the head of the table, facing the other participants, giving a sense of authority and importance. The Big Fish will be surrounded by their sharks, which was not something expected by the students.

Name cards should be placed at each seating position to indicate where each student is supposed to sit during the meeting (personalization). Teams should have access to a projector but not WiFi.

3.3   Unexpected Situations

The unexpected situations (challenges) randomly occur to teams before, during, and after the meeting; see Table 1. These are designed to assess students' capability to be creative, tackle and solve problems. Each of these situations is based on real cases the authors of this paper experienced during software projects carried out in different industries.

Before the meeting, students will face three unexpected situations related to access to the building, WiFi, and connecting to the projector. During and after the meeting, students can be bombarded with difficult, malicious, or ill-intentioned questions by the sharks, like questions about the team's capabilities or the "high" cost or complexity of their proposals. Depending on how the students handle these, the Big Fish (and the sharks) will decide how many votes they will lose; if handled well, students will keep their votes. The unexpected situations are the main "learning moments" of the activity, for this reason, after each of them, the lecturer (not anymore as the Big Fish) provides feedback to the team (and individuals) on how these were managed and gives advice.

Once the presentations are finished, the sharks should decide how they will distribute the budget the organization allocated to the project among the teams. Sharks have five tokens representing $100K each (play money) that should allocate to the team(s) of their preference (see Fig. 1). The team which receives the most money and has kept at least three of their confidence votes will win the project (and the activity).

4   Results and Discussion

4.1   Data Collection and Analysis

A Meeting with the Big Fish has been part of the course activities since 2019. Out of the 77 students enrolled in the course in the 2019–2022 period, around 75% of them have participated in the activity; students have the option to opt

Fig. 1. Confidence votes, budget, and unexpected situations cards

out of participation as the activity weighs 0% in terms of the course assessment items. Following the completion of the activity, students answer a standardized questionnaire to evaluate the gamified aspects of the activity using a 5-point scale. The questionnaire results have shown excellent results as the activity is attractive (Average: 4.36; Median: 5); it suits the students' way of learning (4.73; 5); the content is connected to what they have learned (4.73; 5); it is fun (4.91; 5); the level of challenge is adequate (4.45; 5); students would do it again and recommend it to their peers (4.82; 5), and they felt it contributes to their learning (4.73; 5).

The questionnaire also includes a section where students are asked to select the LOs that they believed were addressed during the activity, and, in its last section, students can provide free text opinions regarding their participation experience.

Regarding the LOs, LO2, and LO9 were chosen by 81.8% of the students, while LO3 and LO8 got 72.7% and 54.5%, respectively. The free-text opinions from students are presented in the next subsection.

4.2 Upsides and Downsides

An important part of the activity is the fact that its objective is to make the students live a tense and challenging learning experience (they are aware of it since the lecturer explained it beforehand, giving students the opportunity to ask questions). Nevertheless, this has not been an impediment for being an enjoyable experience that increased student engagement through fun, which is consistent with findings of previous SE gamification studies [6]: *"It was really fun and nerve-wracking. Thank you for organizing such a wonderful event". "I definitely liked the whole setting, having other people there acting as technical*

Table 1. Unexpected situations.

Before the meeting ...
You are entering the headquarters of one of the top-5 richest people in the world. So, immediately after you arrive, you and your team must verify your identity by showing an ID. You are in trouble if you do not have an acceptable proof of identity.
Having sorted the first obstacle, you reached the 20th floor of this state-of-the-art building. You realize you do not have access to the WiFi; the security policies are very strict. If your slides are in the cloud only, you have to wait around 45 min until the IT department grants you access to the internet.

During the meeting ...
One of the organization's experts is a Mr. Wise Guy, but after a couple of interventions, you realize that they are attending the meeting to find your weakest spot and exploit it. Now, he is criticizing you "Why aren't you using the <super duper> model/standard? It is used by many European and US organizations with huge benefits." What would you do if you don't know that model/standard?
The CEO's assistant enters the room to inform them that the city council is on the phone. "Apologies, but I must take that; thank you for coming." You took more than the 6 min allocated to you.

After the meeting ...
Great presentation! The CEO is authentically interested in your solution. But, their "right hand" is whispering to their ear: "We have to get rid of some 'obstacles'" Then, the CEO asks you: "Who should we fire?" What would you do?
You know that you are capable; you have the knowledge and the team to implement the proposal successfully. However, given the small size of your startup and its short history, the CEO asks you: "How will just three/four of you be capable to carry out this millionaire project?" What would you do?

advisors to dissect what you were saying was a fun challenge ... I enjoyed the challenge, and the fast and hard nature of taking the meeting".

The authenticity of the unexpected situations brings realism to the learning experience of the students, and it is much appreciated: "... the use of unexpected scenarios made the exercise more challenging but made you think about potential real-world problems ... it was a good way to prepare us for the kinds of questions we may face in the industry". "Had an awesome experience, one of the most personalized fun experiences I've ever had in a 'standard' lecture .... these will *be some of the educational side memories from uni that I'll remember. I really enjoyed meeting the big fish".*

On the negative side, this type of activity may not be suitable for all learning styles, so this can be a potential cause of students deciding not to participate in it. Although every year the participation rate has been around 75% of the enrolled students and, so far, no negative comments have been received. It is worth mentioning that participants have come prepared and taken the activity seriously. From those students who participated, the main issue they mention is the "lack" of details provided to them: *"I didn't like how unexplained the activity was, was hard to prepare for [the pitch] and there was little documentation about it".* However, one of the activity's goals is for students to be capable of anticipating potential challenges or changes and to build a readiness mindset that enables them to face ambiguous or unpredictable situations with confidence. Overall, the positive feedback and observed effects surpassed the potential negative ones.

5   Conclusions and Future Work

In educational contexts, game elements have shown important benefits to students' attitudes, motivation, and interest, improving their learning experience as a whole. Pitching their own work, in this case, an assignment has contributed to the development of the presentation and communication abilities of students enrolled in a Software Quality course. A Meeting with the Big Fish combines pitching and SPI knowledge into an activity that has been exhibited to be a fun, enjoyable, and meaningful learning experience for students. In future work, we expect to formalize the activity steps so they can be replicated to obtain feedback from other educators.

References

1. Ambrosio, J., Burghardt, M.D., Hecht, D.: Authentic engineering design assessment. In: 2021 ASEE Virtual Annual Conference Content Access (2021)
2. Balakhonskaya, L.V., Balakhonsky, V.V.: Pitching as a communication technology and pitch as a tool for investor relations in the digital environment. In: 2021 Communication Strategies in Digital Society Seminar, pp. 166–172. IEEE (2021)
3. CSSE University of Canterbury: Software Process and Product Quality (2023). https://www.canterbury.ac.nz/courseinfo/GetCourseDetails.aspx?course=SENG403&occurrence=23S2(C)&year=2023
4. Haertel, T., Terkowsky, C., May, D.: The shark tank experience: how engineering students learn to become entrepreneurs. In: 2016 ASEE Annual Conference & Exposition (2016)
5. Moore, R.A., Newton, S.H., Baskett, A.D.: The inventure challenge: Inspiring stem learning through invention and entrepreneurship. Int. J. Eng. Educ. **33**(1), 361–370 (2017)
6. Morales-Trujillo, M.E.: Learning software quality assurance with bricks. In: 2021 IEEE/ACM 43rd International Conference on Software Engineering: Software Engineering Education and Training (ICSE-SEET), pp. 11–19. IEEE (2021)

7. Pedreira, O., García, F., Brisaboa, N., Piattini, M.: Gamification in software engineering-a systematic mapping. Inf. Softw. Technol. **57**, 157–168 (2015)
8. Pesare, E., Roselli, T., Corriero, N., Rossano, V.: Game-based learning and gamification to promote engagement and motivation in medical learning contexts. Smart Learn. Environ. **3**, 1–21 (2016)
9. Souza, M.R.D.A., Veado, L., Moreira, R.T., Figueiredo, E., Costa, H.: A systematic mapping study on game-related methods for software engineering education. Inf. Softw. Technol. **95**, 201–218 (2018)
10. Wortham, T.: Using familiar games in a human factors engineering course. In: Proceedings of IIE Annual Conference, p. 1208. Institute of Industrial and Systems Engineers (IISE) (2008)

Quantum Services Generation and Deployment Process: A Quality-Oriented Approach

Jaime Alvarado-Valiente[1]([✉]) [iD], Javier Romero-Álvarez[1] [iD], Ana Díaz[2] [iD],
Moisés Rodríguez[2] [iD], Ignacio García-Rodríguez[2] [iD], Enrique Moguel[3] [iD],
Jose Garcia-Alonso[1] [iD], and Juan M. Murillo[3] [iD]

[1] University of Extremadura, Quercus Software Engineering Group, Cáceres, Spain
{jaimeav,jromero,jgaralo}@unex.es
[2] Universidad de Castilla-La Mancha, Alarcos Research Group, Ciudad Real, Spain
adiaz@aqclab.es, {moises.rodriguez,ignacio.grodriguez}@uclm.es
[3] CénitS-COMPUTAEX, Cáceres, Spain
enrique@unex.es, juan.murillo@cenits.es

Abstract. Quantum computing technology is revolutionizing the current world and is enabling the creation of advanced applications in various fields, such as healthcare and economics. However, for the industry to carry out mass production of quantum software, it is crucial to ensure an adequate level of quality. However, as quantum technologies move towards practical applications, they face significant challenges. Depending heavily on specific platforms, developers have difficulty creating quantum applications that can run on different quantum providers. Additionally, the lack of mature tools makes the creation of quantum applications a slow and complex process that requires specialized knowledge of quantum mechanics and computer science, where the quality of quantum services can be compromised. This article addresses the need to ensure an adequate level of quality in quantum software, and proposes a process that allows for the improvement of the current generation and deployment of quantum services while evaluating the quality of the created quantum services, using an extension of the OpenAPI Specification and the SonarQube tool.

Keywords: Quantum Computing · Quantum Services · Quantum Software Quality · Process improvement

1 Introduction

Quantum computing is a paradigm that utilizes the principles of quantum mechanics to process information. This new form of computing promises tremendous computational power, enabling the solution of problems that remain unsolved by classical computing in a reasonable amount of time—such as those in the class of problems called BQP [1]. As a result, quantum computing has

J. M. Fernandes et al. (Eds.): QUATIC 2023, CCIS 1871, pp. 200–214, 2023.
https://doi.org/10.1007/978-3-031-43703-8_15

experienced a great surge in popularity, and major technology companies such as Amazon, IBM, and Google are investing heavily in the development of new quantum machines and offering them to users through their cloud platforms [2].

The use of quantum computers through cloud platforms provided by various vendors is reminiscent of classical computing and service-oriented architectures. This means that quantum computing can be utilized through classical-quantum hybrid architectures, where both technologies offer their resources in the form of services [3]. For developers to create quality quantum services and hybrid architectures, tools and techniques that help them obtain the desired quality levels are needed [4].

However, the lack of suitable software engineering techniques for quantum services poses several challenges [5]. These include the low abstraction level at which developers have to work, as well as the lack of mechanisms for the integration, deployment, or quality control of the developed software.

In order to address this problem, alternatives are emerging that aim to close the gap between classical processes and quantum computing [6].

In this context, one of the most relevant aspects of any software development process, including quantum software, is quality. The goal of a quantum service development process must be to ensure that services are reliable, scalable, secure, and efficient. Moreover, it aims to ensure that quantum services meet the required standards of quality to be used in real-world applications [7,8]. Therefore, controlling the quality of new quantum systems is crucial in order to ensure that they function correctly and meet the required levels of effectiveness and efficiency in their processes and operations, as well as the expectations of the different stakeholders [9]. Just as having a quality system in place is crucial to meeting quality standards, government regulations and industry standards in traditional computing, it is even more vital in quantum computing. Because it helps reduce costs, identify and correct problems early, improve the user experience and increase reliability in both the product and the organization. In addition, it helps protect information, preventing data and information security from being compromised, among many other key points. Therefore, controlling and improving the quality of new quantum systems is essential [10].

In order to that, this article proposes the combination of an extension of the OpenAPI Specification and its code generator and an instance of SonarQube[1]. These elements are integrated into a Continuous Deployment process through the use of GitHub Actions[2].

To address these challenges effectively we need answers to some critical questions including: What is needed to ensure an adequate level of quality in quantum software? How can we improve upon existing processes for generating and deploying high-quality quantum services? Furthermore, what metrics can be used to evaluate whether or not a given set up meets required standards?

We propose that our approach using OpenAPI Specification combined with SonarQube integration will lead us towards improved generation/deployment

---

[1] https://docs.sonarqube.org/latest.

[2] https://docs.github.com/en/actions.

processess, while allowing developers obtain desired standards with respect reliability or scalability. We also hypothesize this combination would help bridge gaps between classical-quantum hybrid architectures by allowing both technologies offer their resources as service-oriented architecture.

To present this, the rest of the paper is organized as follows: Sect. 2 analyzes the background of the presented work and discusses the most relevant related works. Section 3 presents the proposal for automatic generation and deployment of quantum services and the supervision of the quality of such services. Section 4 includes the results of the evaluation of proposed method. Finally, Sect. 5 details the conclusions and future work.

2   Background

The use of support tools for software design are a proved way for developers to improve the quality of the produced software. However, in terms of quantum software, there is still a severe lack of this kind of tools. Consequently, the absence of these tools impedes the advancement and maturation of quantum software development, making it more challenging to meet the desired standards of quality and reliability in this rapidly evolving field [10].

Currently, works such a B. Weder et al. [11] propose a quantum software developmentwork such a lifecycle comprising multiple phases to systematically apply software engineering principles and enhance the quality and reusability of quantum applications. This lifecycle ensures the quality of quantum software throughout all development stages, from initial requirements analysis to implementation. However, despite being grounded in software engineering best practices, it lacks conformity to any norms or quality standards, which may pose challenges or limitations when implementing and following this lifecycle in practice.

The assessment of software quality is usually carried out through testing, reviews, static and dynamic analysis, among other quality assurance techniques. It usually involves the measurement and evaluation of software based on different attributes such as functionality, usability, efficiency, etc. Over the past decades, multiple models and standards related to classical software quality have been developed, including ISO/IEC 9126[3], CISQ[4], and ISO/IEC 25000[5], which can be highlighted. In addition, the ISO 25000 standard, also known as SQuaRE (Software Product Quality Requirements and Evaluation), is widely used by organizations worldwide to assess, improve, and certify the quality of classical software. Within this standard, the ISO/IEC 25010 division[6] defines a quality model for software products, consisting of 8 quality characteristics and a set of subcharacteristics related to them [12].

---

[3] https://www.iso.org/standard/22749.html.
[4] https://www.it-cisq.org/standards.
[5] https://iso25000.com/index.php/en/iso-25000-standards.
[6] https://iso25000.com/index.php/en/iso-25000-standards/iso-25010.

In order to determine the quality level of a software product for each of the aforementioned characteristics, a series of metrics are used, which are objective measures that allow for the measurement, evaluation, and control of software quality. However, there is currently no consensus on a model for the measurement and evaluation of quantum software quality. At the metric level, there have been some recent publications [13] that attempt to measure and evaluate quantum circuits, but there are still no metrics available to determine the elements to be controlled in quantum code.

To carry out the measurement of "classical" quality metrics, there are numerous tools available that assist software development teams in identifying potential areas of improvement [11]. Some of these tools include static code analyzers, which analyze the source code of the software for quality issues, automated testing tools, which automate and accelerate the software testing process, performance analysis tools, which measure the performance of the software under different situations and conditions, and architecture analysis tools, which identify potential quality deficiencies related to scalability, maintainability, and portability, among others [14].

Among all the quality measurement tools, it is worth mentioning SonarQube, which is one of the most widely used source code analysis platforms by the software development and evaluation community. SonarQube provides different features to detect potential issues and improvements. Additionally, SonarQube supports multiple programming languages, including those currently used as a basis for quantum program development, and allows for the inclusion of analyses in a continuous integration and deployment process, as intended in this project.

This process of continuous integration and deployment is based on the use of OpenAPI for the generation of quantum services [15]. From a scientific perspective, OpenAPI facilitates the seamless exchange of information across diverse software systems by establishing a shared vocabulary to describe the functionality of APIs. This facilitates the integration of data from multiple sources into research projects or other applications, and allows developers to define and document services in a clear and standardized way. By adapting these tools to work with quantum software we can combine them with SonarQube for the generation of quality metrics [10, 16].

In summary, integrating quality measurement tools into the process of developing quantum services is essential to ensure the quality, efficiency, and security of services, as well as to ensure their interoperability and reuse in different contexts and applications.

3 Generation and Supervision of Quantum Services

In this section, we address the full process of generation, deployment, and validation of quantum services, from the conceptualization of the idea to the evaluation of system performance.

3.1 OpenAPI Specification for Service Generation

To have a fully operational service, developers often add the business logic of the service in a chosen programming language. However, understanding the service's characteristics from documentation or source code alone can be challenging. Nevertheless, using the OpenAPI Specification, the service, and its parameters can be defined using a standard interface that is language-independent for RESTful APIs [17].

In this way, based on the OpenAPI Specification, the source code structure can be generated in different programming languages, facilitating the development of the service.

In this study, the OpenAPI Specification has been applied similarly to how it is used for creating classical services, with the aim of defining and generating quantum services. For this purpose, the OpenAPI Code Generator[7] has been modified, which allows generating server applications from an OpenAPI Specification. This generator has been adapted to support the process of defining and creating quantum services by creating an extension of the OpenAPI Specification, which includes custom properties, and an extension of the code generator, which allows defining and generating code for quantum applications.

With this solution, the process of defining quantum services has been standardized and made possible to automatically generate quantum services from an API specification, and a quantum circuit.

3.2 Workflow for Continuous Deployment

For Continuous Deployment, we have implemented a workflow that integrates automatic code generation of quantum services for different quantum machine providers, and their deployment in containers ready to be consumed by users.

For this implementation, the GitHub code management platform's tool called GitHub Actions has been utilized. It enables developers to specify actions to perform whenever changes are made in the repository. By defining a workflow, developers can outline the sequence of steps to execute after a change is made.

The process is shown in Fig. 1. To start the process, the developer creates one or more quantum circuits using the circuit generation tool Open Quirk[8], or by directly writing the code for the quantum circuit in Python (Step A1)—the primary programming language for quantum computing developed by IBM Qiskit[9]. Subsequently, the developer modifies the YAML file that contains the extension of the OpenAPI Specification and the endpoints of the services (Step A2) including the location of the Python code to be encapsulated or the URL with the designed circuit in Open Quirk.

This extension of the OpenAPI Specification has been designed to allow the developer to include the URL of the quantum circuit that has been designed,

---

[7] https://openapi-generator.tech.

[8] https://algassert.com/quirk.

[9] https://qiskit.org.

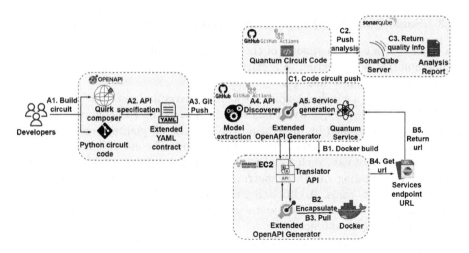

Fig. 1. Workflow for the Continuous Deployment of Quantum Services

and that is to be encapsulated in the service; the provider for which the service is to be generated; the machine on which it is to be executed; and the number of shots—times the circuit is executed on the machine to obtain the results.

At this point, the process of executing the GitHub Actions defined in the repository[10] begins, and the developer's design work ends. Specifically, the process of automatic generation and deployment of the services starts when the developer performs a *commit* to the repository (Step A3). Then, first, it is verified that the repository specification is correctly formatted by generating the services code with the updated version of the OpenAPI code generator (Steps A4 and A5). If the code is generated correctly, the services will be automatically deployed in a container (Step B1), which is done by a request to an API deployed on the AWS server that includes the URL of the YAML file containing the specification and the credentials to configure the execution on the providers. This API receives the call from the GitHub Actions and generates and encapsulates the generated code in a container (Step B2)—which is deployed by exposing it on the first free port (Step B3). Finally, it returns to the developer the URL where the generated services are hosted, which is visible at the end of the workflow execution (Steps B4 and B5).

This Continuous Deployment approach with the use of GitHub Actions is intended to help developers automate time-consuming tasks, reduce the time required to release new versions of software, and automatically deploy services in containers, making them easier for users to access and use. In addition, as explained below, it improves code quality and helps prevent bugs and vulnerabilities which can help improve efficiency and ensure quality in quantum software development.

---

[10] https://github.com/javierrome236/quantumDeployment.

3.3   SonarQube for Quality Supervision

In order to evaluate the quality of the code and identify potential problems and vulnerabilities, a connection to SonarQube has been included in the process, as shown in the workflow in Fig. 1.

SonarQube is a widely recognized tool in industry and research for static code analysis and software quality evaluation. By leveraging the SonarQube parser, an advantage is gained by integrating the analysis of quantum metrics into an established development and analysis environment. The use of SonarQube offers several key advantages, such as integration into the existing workflow, a specific plugin for evaluating quantum metrics, and ease of use and configuration to adapt to project needs. Additionally, the plugin allows for easy integration of quantum software quality measurement from any other initiative, making the proposal more open and accessible.

The aim is to provide quality metrics to identify problems in the code and be able to solve them. To this end, through the workflow, specifically before the generation and deployment of the services, it generates the files that contain only the code corresponding to the circuits (Step C1). These files are stored in a different repository and, by using another GitHub Actions, they are automatically analyzed by the SonarQube tool (Step C2). The integration of GitHub Actions with SonarQube allows us to perform an automatic analysis of the circuit code in each *commit* or *pull request* and receive detailed reports on the quality of that code and potential security issues (Step C3). This helps to ensure that the code that is implemented in production meets the required quality and security standards.

The first step to use this integration is to configure SonarQube on its own server. As mentioned above, in the field of software quality analysis, the SonarQube tool has established itself as one of the most widely used by the community. However, given the lack of a clear definition of metrics for quantum software, this tool does not yet have a specific measurement system for this type of software. To address this issue, in collaboration with the accredited laboratory AQCLab[11], a plugin has been designed and developed that extends the functionality of SonarQube for the measurement of the quantum metrics named in Fig. 2.

This plugin relies on the parser that already has the SonarQube environment, and creates and stores records in its own database to obtain values of the metrics it contains.

Furthermore, the plugin is compatible with the Qiskit syntax—the quantum language developed by IBM—which allows its integration with the Continuous Development, integration, and deployment cycle. Thanks to this, it is possible to carry out a first measurement of the quantum source code, which will allow developers and teams to detect and correct quality problems on quantum software in real-time in the near future.

Once SonarQube and the corresponding plugin are configured, the next step is to add a code analysis task in the GitHub Actions workflow file. For this

---

[11] https://www.aqclab.es/.

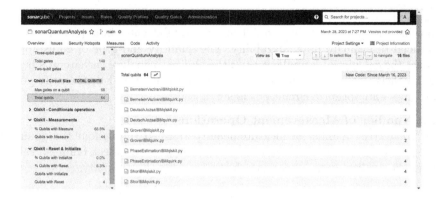

Fig. 2. Quantum metric plugin integrated into SonarQube environment

purpose, the SonarQube actions available in the GitHub Actions *marketplace* have been used. This task automatically executes the code analysis every time a *commit* or *pull request* is made in the repository in order to obtain the analysis results in real-time, mainly from the implemented Qiskit plugin.

3.3.1   Metrics of Quality

In the field of quantum software, a lack of a quality model and metrics for evaluation has been identified. In response to this issue, we have developed an initial proposal of metrics for quantum code [18], based on references from both classical and quantum works, such as [13]. In reference [18] details the metrics implemented in the plugin, which focus on ensuring software maintainability, specifically with an emphasis on analyzability. Although it is still pending publication, the validity and relevance of these metrics to effectively measure and evaluate the quantum software's ability to be analyzed and understood in terms of its structure and functionality have been ensured. This contributes to facilitating its maintenance and future improvements in quantum software.

Taking into account what has been mentioned above, this article describes refined metrics with the aim of improving comprehensibility in the process of measuring the quality of quantum software. Although reference is made to an external publication (reference [18]) to obtain more details about these metrics, the article focuses on providing an overview of their implementation and application in the specific context of quantum software evaluation. This allows readers to become familiar with the relevant metrics and understand how they are used to measure and evaluate the quality of quantum software more effectively.

M1: Circuit Size

The larger the code, the more complex it will be to understand and maintain; therefore, to study this quality property, it is necessary to analyze the metrics width and depth of a quantum circuit. The width is defined as the maximum number of qubits involved in a simultaneous operation. On the other hand, the depth of a quantum circuit refers to the number of gate layers required to complete an algorithm.

M2: Complexity of Gate Operations

Knowing the number of single-qubit and multiqubit gates in a quantum circuit is crucial to evaluate its analyzability. The quantity and type of gates applied impact the calculation complexity and the ability to analyze the circuit's behavior. Furthermore, understanding the quantum architecture helps identify potential issues and optimize circuit efficiency.

M3: Number of Measurement Operations

The greater the number of measurements performed throughout the quantum code, the easier it will be to understand, as well as to detect failures. Table 1 shows the quality metrics necessary for calculating this property.

Table 1. Metrics for 'Number of measurements'

Metric	Description
N QM	Number of qubits with at least one 'Measure' operation
Perc QM	Percentage of measured qubits

M4: Number of Initialization and Reset Operations

This property analyzes the number of initialization operations, which initialize a flexible number of qubits to an arbitrary state, and the number of reset operations, which send the qubits to the $|0\rangle$ state in the middle of a specific computation. Both operations are not gates, as they are not unitary operations and therefore are not reversible.

4 Evaluation

In this section, the evaluation of quantum quality metrics is carried out on recognized quantum algorithms. Specifically, a detailed measurement is conducted to determine the levels of analyzability of these quantum algorithms. To achieve this goal, the SonarQube environment and the metrics plugin are used, which will allow for rigorous measurement. The results obtained from these measurements will serve in the future as a reference and guide for the continuous improvement of quantum algorithms in terms of their performance and effectiveness in solving complex problems in various application areas.

The process to be carried out consists of three main phases. Firstly, a set of quantum algorithms is selected. Subsequently, the necessary services for executing these algorithms in the appropriate environment are generated and deployed. Finally, a detailed measurement of the most relevant quantum metrics regarding the efficiency of the selected algorithms is carried out.

4.1 Study Subjects: Quantum Algorithms to be Serviced

In order to validate the efficacy of our proposal, tests have been carried out with different implementations of 8 quantum algorithms based on quantum circuits.

These algorithms were chosen to cover a wide variety of applications, including both quantum-classical hybrid algorithms and purely quantum ones, which are available in a public repository[12] and are briefly described below.

Bernstein-Vazirani Algorithm

This is an algorithm designed to solve a specific problem where a Boolean function f(x) of n bits is given, and the n bits composing the input x that produce the value f(x) need to be determined.

The Bernstein-Vazirani algorithm has a complexity of $O(n)$, which means that it can solve the problem described above in a time proportional to the number of bits n. For this reason, it presents a significant advantage over equivalent classical algorithms, which have a complexity of $O(2n)$.

Deutsch-Jozsa Algorithm

It is an algorithm designed to solve a specific problem where a Boolean function f(x) can be of two types: constant or balanced. The Deutsch-Jozsa algorithm has a complexity of $O(1)$, which means it is capable of solving the aforementioned problem in a single step.

Grover's Algorithm

This algorithm allows searching an unsorted database of N elements in a time of $O(\sqrt{N})$, instead of the time required by classical algorithms $O(N)$. The Grover's Algorithm—see Fig. 3—is characterized by using quantum superposition to search for the optimal solution in the database, which also allows it to be applied in cryptography and optimization.

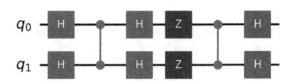

Fig. 3. Representation of Grover's algorithm in Qiskit

Phase Estimation Algorithm

The main objective of this quantum algorithm is to determine the phase of a quantum state on a specific basis. It works by applying successive controlled powers of U to the N-qubit quantum state and using a quantum Fourier transform to determine the phase of the state. The complexity of the Phase Estimation Algorithm—see Fig. 4—depends on the number of qubits used in the input quantum state, resulting in exponential order complexity in the number of qubits.

Shor's Algorithm

This quantum algorithm is designed to factorize large integers in polynomial time. To do so, it relies on the ability of qubits in quantum software to process information simultaneously in multiple states.

---

[12] https://bitbucket.org/spilab/quantum-circuits-code.

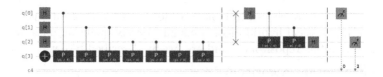

Fig. 4. Representation of the Phase Estimation Algorithm in Qiskit

Simon's Algorithm

This algorithm is focused on finding a function f(x) that is periodic with an unknown period S. Its time complexity is $O(n^2)$, where n is the number of bits required to represent the input.

Quantum Teleportation Algorithm

This is a quantum protocol that allows for the transfer of the quantum state of a qubit between two parties, without the original qubit physically moving from one place to another. This algorithm uses a pair of entangled qubits to transmit the state of the original qubit; however, it requires classical communication between the two parties to construct the state of the original qubit on the destination qubit. Its complexity is difficult to measure, as it depends on the number of qubits and the resources used to generate and maintain the quantum entanglement. Because quantum entanglement is a limited and expensive resource in practice, the complexity of the algorithm is limited by its availability. Although, in general, it is considered a fairly efficient algorithm, it depends on the specific implementation of the algorithm and the quantum system used.

TSP Algorithm

This algorithm presents a possible optimal way to solve the traveling salesman problem using the quantum properties of quantum systems through the use of the quantum Fourier transform. The TSP algorithm requires that the cities be represented as qubits, thus being able to make use of quantum entanglement between the different qubits to find the solution. As for its complexity, it is a polynomial time complexity, compared to the classical algorithm which has an exponential complexity.

4.2 Results

The previously described algorithms are implemented both in Qiskit and using the Open Quirk circuit generation tool, using implementations already available. Therefore, the total number of generated quantum services was 16.

Of these generated services, 12 were deployed correctly and 4 resulted in deployment failures. Based on an analysis of the deployment failures, it was determined that the cause was the lack of consideration in our translation process of certain gates, such as phase gates. The problem therefore lies not in the deployment process itself, but in the fact that certain gate types were not considered in the code generator. To address this issue, we are working on a new version of the generator. After evaluating the quantum algorithms defined in this chapter, a summary of the resulting values obtained for the most relevant quantum metrics is presented in Table 2.

Table 2. Summary of the most relevant results obtained for the metrics after measuring the algorithms

Algorithm	Environment	Metrics						
		Width	Depth	N SQG	N MQG	N QM	N QReset	N IF
Bernstein-Vazinari	Qiskit	4	7	8	3	3	0	0
	Quirk	4	2	8	0	3	0	0
Deutsch-Jozsal	Qiskit	4	5	12	0	3	0	0
	Quirk	4	4	12	0	3	0	0
Grover	Qiskit	2	7	7	1	2	0	0
	Quirk	2	6	7	0	0	0	0
Phase Estimation	Qiskit	4	8	7	11	3	0	0
	Quirk	4	2	7	0	3	0	0
Shor	Qiskit	4	5	5	9	4	4	0
	Quirk	4	3	9	0	4	0	0
Simon	Qiskit	6	2	6	5	3	0	0
	Quirk	6	2	6	0	3	0	0
Teleportation	Qiskit	3	5	8	2	2	0	2
	Quirk	5	2	3	0	2	0	0
TSP	Qiskit	5	4	4	2	3	0	0
	Quirk	3	2	4	0	3	0	0

In general, the results obtained for each of the algorithms suggest that implementing an algorithm in Quirk is simpler and less complex compared to implementation in Qiskit. However, it is important to note that each algorithm is different and their usefulness and complexity vary depending on the problem they solve and the specific characteristics of each algorithm.

In the case of the Bernstein-Vazirani algorithm, there is a clear advantage in terms of complexity when implementing the algorithm in Quirk, suggesting that for similar problems, Quirk could be a more suitable option. On the other hand, for the Deutsch-Jozsa algorithm, lower complexity is also observed in the implementation in Quirk, suggesting that this tool may be more suitable for solving this specific problem.

For the Grover algorithm, although the results in terms of circuit width are similar in both implementations, a significant difference is observed in the measurement at the end of the algorithm. This difference can be important depending on the problem being solved and the data being searched for.

Finally, in the case of the Phase Estimation algorithm, the results obtained do not allow for a direct comparison of the complexity of the two implementations due to differences in the parameters used. However, both results suggest that the implementation of the algorithm in both tools is suitable and can be useful for solving problems related to the determination of phases of quantum states.

Table 3. Ranking of quantum algorithms based on the complexity of their gates

Algorithm	Environment	Metrics	
		N SQG	N MQG
Phase Estimation	Qiskit	7	11
	Quirk	7	0
Shor	Qiskit	5	9
	Quirk	9	0
Simon	Qiskit	6	5
	Quirk	6	0
Deutsch-Jozsal	Qiskit	12	3
	Quirk	12	0
Bernstein-Vazinari	Qiskit	8	3
	Quirk	8	0
Teleportation	Qiskit	8	2
	Quirk	3	0
TSP	Qiskit	4	2
	Quirk	4	0
Grover	Qiskit	7	1
	Quirk	7	0

Based on these measurements, we can proceed to analyze and compare all the measured algorithms based on the complexity of their single-qubit and multi-qubit gates, resulting in the ranking shown in Table 3, which displays the algorithms ordered from highest to lowest quantum gate complexity.

There is evidence that the Phase Estimation algorithm (see Fig. 4) and Shor's algorithm would be the most complex to analyze due to the large number of multi-qubit gates they possess, while Grover's algorithm (see Fig. 3) would be the simplest as it only has a single multi-qubit gate despite having seven single-qubit gates. It is still too early to obtain data on the evaluation, but in future work, these metrics will allow us to obtain quality values based on a quantum model.

5   Conclusions and Future Work

In this paper we have presented a solution for the development and use of quantum services, using techniques and methods from classical service engineering. For this purpose, we have proposed a standardized way of defining quantum services using the OpenAPI Specification, and we have shown how to generate the source code of these services from this specification and a quantum circuit. In addition, we have developed a workflow for the Continuous Deployment of these services in Docker containers using the GitHub Actions tool.

Finally, we have extended this process by incorporating the SonarQube tool, along with a specific plugin to measure the quality of the generated quantum services and detect possible security issues. With the integration of both processes, developers can perform automatic code analysis and receive detailed reports on code quality and potential security issues in real-time. This will help ensure that the code that is deployed in production meets the required quality and security standards. In this way, the application of this environment has made it possible to positively evaluate the source code of some of the most widely used algorithms in the quantum sector, which has been an important step in the validation of their operation. This work has also set the basis for carrying out more exhaustive quality evaluations in the future. Therefore, we hope to facilitate the transition of classical service developers to quantum service development and promote the advancement of this emerging area of technology.

Although there is still much to be done in this field, the results obtained to date encourage us to continue working in this line of research to improve the quality of quantum software. Thus, several lines of future work have been identified to advance in the development and evaluation of quantum services, since it is evident that there are still no clear standards for the evaluation of quantum software quality. Specifically, these lines of work include defining new metrics related to the security evaluation of services, measuring performance in terms of speed and throughput, and expanding test coverage. In addition, other analysis and testing tools can be included to cover important aspects of quantum service development, such as security, scalability, and efficiency.

Acknowledgments. This work is part of grants PID2021-124045OB-C31 and PID2021-124054OB-C32 funded by MCIN/AEI /10.13039/50100011033 and by "ERDF A way of making Europe". The QSALUD project (EXP 00135977/MIG-20201059) in the lines of action of the Center for Technological Development and Innovation (CDTI); and by the Ministry of Economy and Digital Transformation of the Government of Spain through the call for the Quantum ENIA project. The European Union through the Recovery, Transformation and Resilience Plan - NextGenerationEU in the framework of the Agenda España Digital 2025. The Q2SM Project: Quality Quantum Software Model (EXPTE: 13/22/IN/032) financed by the Junta de Comunidades de Castilla-La Mancha and FEDER funds.

References

1. Aaronson, S.: BQP and the polynomial hierarchy. In: Proceedings of the Annual ACM Symposium on Theory of Computing, pp. 141–150, October 2009
2. MacQuarrie, E.R., Simon, C., Simmons, S., Maine, E.: The emerging commercial landscape of quantum computing. Nat. Rev. Phys. **2**(11), 596–598 (2020)
3. Rojo, J., Valencia, D., Berrocal, J., Moguel, E., García-Alonso, J.M., Murillo, J.M.: Trials and tribulations of developing hybrid quantum-classical microservices systems," ArXiv, vol. abs/2105.04421 (2021)
4. Moguel, E., Rojo, J., Valencia, D., Berrocal, J., Garcia-Alonso, J., Murillo, J.M.: Quantum service-oriented computing: current landscape and challenges. Softw. Q. J. **30**(4), 983–1002 (2022)

5. Akbar, M.A., Khan, A.A., Mahmood, S., Rafi, S.: Quantum software engineering: a new genre of computing, November 2022
6. Garcia-Alonso, J., Rojo, J., Valencia, D., Moguel, E., Berrocal, J., Murillo, J.M.: Quantum software as a service through a quantum API gateway. IEEE Internet Comput. **26**(1), 34–41 (2021)
7. Verdugo, J., Rodríguez, M., Piattini, M.: Software quality issues in quantum information systems. In: Q-SET@ QCE, pp. 54–59 (2021)
8. Zhao, J.: Quantum software engineering: Landscapes and horizons, arXiv preprint arXiv:2007.07047 (2020)
9. Mishra, A., Otaiwi, Z.: Devops and software quality: a systematic mapping. Comput. Sci. Rev. **38**, 100308 (2020)
10. Piattini, M., Serrano, M., Perez-Castillo, R., Petersen, G., Hevia, J.L.: Toward a quantum software engineering. IT Prof. **23**(1), 62–66 (2021)
11. Weder, B., Barzen, J., Leymann, F., Vietz, D.: Quantum software development lifecycle. In: Serrano, M.A., Pérez-Castillo, R., Piattini, M. (eds.) Quantum Software Engineering. pp. 61–83. Springer, Cham (2022). https://doi.org/10.1007/978-3-031-05324-5_4
12. Rodríguez, M., Pedreira, Ó., Fernández, C.: Certificación de la mantenibilidad del producto software: Un caso práctico. Revista Latinoamericana de Ingeniería de Software **3**(3), 127–134 (2015)
13. Cruz, J.A., Piattini, M.: "Towards a set of metrics form quantum circuits understandability (2015)
14. Rodríguez, M., Piattini, M., Ebert, C.: Software verification and validation technologies and tools. IEEE Softw. **36**, 13–24 (2019)
15. Romero-Álvarez, J., Alvarado-Valiente, J., Moguel, E., García-Alonso, J., Murillo, J.M.: Using open API for the development of hybrid classical-quantum services. In: Service-Oriented Computing-ICSOC. Workshops **2022**, 364–368 (2022)
16. Gemeinhardt, F., Garmendia, A., Wimmer, M.: Towards model-driven quantum software engineering. In: IEEE/ACM 2nd International Workshop on Quantum Software Engineering (Q-SE), vol. 2021, pp. 13–15. IEEE (2021)
17. Schwichtenberg, S., Gerth, C., Engels, G.: From open API to semantic specifications and code adapters. In: 2017 IEEE International Conference on Web Services (ICWS), pp. 484–491. IEEE (2017)
18. Díaz, A., Rodríguez, M., Piattini, M.: Towards a set of metrics for hybrid (quantum/classical) systems maintainability. J.UCS, p. Submitted pending publication (2023)

External Dependencies in Software Development

Aless Hosry$^{(\boxtimes)}$ and Nicolas Anquetil

Univ. Lille, Inria, CNRS, Centrale Lille, UMR 9189 CRIStAL, 59000 Lille, France
`{aless.hosry,nicolas.anquetil}@inria.fr`

Abstract. Successful software requires constant modifications. To guarantee the continuous proper functioning of the applications, developers need to understand them well, particularly by having an accurate map of the dependencies between the parts they are modifying. However, some of these dependencies are not easily identified. For example, in an Android application, there are dependencies between the Java source code and XML parts, some of which are materialized by a generated "R" Java class. We call such dependencies external because they are introduced by some agent external to the source code. On top of the categorization of dependencies defined in the literature, we define restrictions on the *External Dependencies* that allow us to verify the source code and identify possible flaws. We created a common approach relying on reusable patterns to search for containers and entities that are part of such dependencies and implemented it in a prototype that we validate on two different projects from GitHub and developed using different frameworks.

Keywords: External dependency · Cross language · Multi-language · Multi-tier

1 Introduction

Repeated modifications are necessary for successful software. This cycle of modifications is known as software evolution. When performed by developers or tools (e.g., refactoring tools) without enough knowledge of the applications, maintenance will lead to decreased software quality. The knowledge required involves identifying all incoming and outgoing dependencies of a software artifact to be modified. We define dependency as the need for one artifact to rely on another artifact in order to fully operate as expected. Developers are more likely to miss *External Dependencies* than explicit dependencies and introduce bugs into software [19].

Yu and Rajlich [20] call hidden dependencies, data dependencies between two modules that are not readily apparent in the source code. As such, these dependencies are considered design faults. We are more interested in dependencies

J. M. Fernandes et al. (Eds.): QUATIC 2023, CCIS 1871, pp. 215–232, 2023.
https://doi.org/10.1007/978-3-031-43703-8_16

introduced by external tools or agents like Android. GWT[1], J2EE[2], ODBC[3], etc. Contrary to Yu et al. definition, such dependencies are inevitable and therefore not design faults. We call them *External Dependencies*: a dependency between two artifacts that is created through an external agent. Often the two dependent artifacts will be in two different source files, but "external" refers to the fact that the dependency is introduced by an external agent, not to the fact that the artifacts are external. For example, a GUI framework like JavaFX will offer widgets like a Button and callbacks on these widgets (`setOnAction(EventHandler)`). The dependency between a button and its handler is not clear in the source code if one does not know how JavaFX works. It is handled *externally*, even if both artifacts are defined in the same file.

Examples of such "external agents" are frameworks working with a variety of programming languages suited for different objectives such as building user interfaces, handling logic, and querying databases. Other frameworks allow different projects to collaborate, for example in client/server (multi-tier) applications.

We found that there is no clear, unique definition in the literature of what a hidden dependency is. That's why we introduce the notion of *External Dependency*. Also, most of the available tools only consider specific types of *External Dependencies* in specific contexts. The majority focuses on identifying the dependencies, ignoring other perspectives like detecting errors due to missing dependencies or excessive dependencies.

As a result, we will go over the following points that outline our strategy in this paper to detect all possible types of *External Dependencies*, built on top of the earlier work of Hecht et al. [6]:

1. We list in this paper all the types of *External Dependencies* we found in the previous works [6,20], in addition to the exceptions;
2. We list the commonalities we found that lead to a single approach for *External Dependency* detection;
3. We explain the restrictions for those commonalities following each type and how they lead to the detection of errors;
4. We validate our approach with a tool that works using common search patterns by experimenting it for a first implementation of two applications developed in two different frameworks.

The paper is structured as follows: In Sect. 2 we list all the previous works in the literature. Section 3 lists different categories of *External Dependencies*, then lists the cardinalities found for each one. Our tool *Adonis* is presented in Sect. 4, followed by two experiments and results Sect. 5. Finally, we end up with a conclusion Sect. 6.

---

[1] Google Web Toolkit gwtproject.org.

[2] Java 2 Platform, Enterprise Edition oracle.com/java/technologies/appmodel.html.

[3] Open Database Connectivity wikipedia.org/wiki/Open_Database_Connectivity.

2   Related Work

In the literature, many solutions exist for analyzing different types of *External Dependencies*. We first present the different publications found before proposing a classification scheme for them.

2.1   Existing Tools

Yu and Rajlich [20] are discussing "hidden dependencies", but they use a definition (classes having a data dependency that is not readily apparent in the source code) different from what we are discussing in this paper.

DeJEE developed by Shatnawi et al. [16], is able to generate automated analysis for J2EE solutions in order to identify a dependency call graph of a given J2EE application using the KDM metamodel; They use static analysis to build a KDM model of the software and match it with XML artifacts through rules with lexical matching.

BabelRef is a tool developed by Nguyen et al. [12]. It detects automatically the dependencies between generated client artifacts (HTML and JavaScript) and generated server artifacts (PHP). It relies on dynamic analysis with a single tree-based structure called the D-model using object matching.

EdgeMiner is a tool developed by Yinzhi et al. [2] to automatically detect callbacks for Android framework applications, whether they are created in Java source code. The analysis is performed statically on the source code and returns a list of callbacks that were identified using object matching, for example, when callbacks are introduced by an implemented Java interface. The authors also provided a different method of implementing callbacks using XML resources in Android applications, although their strategy does not address their detection.

Hecht et al. [6] developed another approach that detects dynamically the dependencies established in J2EE applications using codified rules. This is the only work we found that aims for a generic approach, considering different types of dependencies (callbacks, multi-language, multi-tiers). Still, it is limited to the J2EE framework.

Polychniatis et al. [15] proposed a static method for detecting cross-language links based on matching lexically common tokens between two possibly dependent modules. The detection algorithm is then followed by applying specific filters, such as filtering frequent tokens and omitting one-character tokens.

Grichi et al. [4] made a study on 10 Java Native Interface (JNI) open-source multilanguage systems to identify dependencies between Java and C++ using the Static Multilanguage Dependency Analyzer (S-MLDA) to detect static cross-language links and the Historical Multilanguage Dependency Analyzer (H-MLDA) based on software co-changes to identify links that could not be detected statically.

GenDeMoG, which is a tool developed by Pfeiffer and Wąsowski [13], allows specifying intercomponent dependency patterns statically for artifacts in heterogeneous systems. The tool relies on parsing languages, querying source code objects each time, and retrieving the possible dependencies between different artifacts.

Mayer and Schroeder [8] created a generic approach to understanding, analyzing, and refactoring cross-language code by directly specifying and exploiting statically semantic links in multi-language programs. Their tool, XLL, was developed using QVT-Relations (QVT-R), where a set of rules for cross-language links per language is defined as a relation inside a transformation block, after parsing the source code, and introduces for the first time the idea of cross-language link correctness.

Dsketch is a tool created by Cossette and Walker [3] and used by developers to specify patterns and match blocks of code in any programming language using lexical matching. After identifying the artifacts, Dsketch starts looking statically for possible links between the languages of these artifacts, following a set of steps predefined by the author.

Soto-Valero et al. [18] suggested a new automatic approach to identify third-party Java dependencies statically in Maven projects, remove unneeded classes, repackage used classes into a different dependency, and regenerate the XML configuration file to refer to the new dependencies. The objective of their approach is to create a minimum project binary that only contains code required for the project and eliminates "bloated dependencies". As such, they introduce the notion of dependency correctness (or incorrectness in the case of bloated dependencies).

Kempt et al. [7] introduced an approach that could be applicable to enhance the refactoring of cross-language links between Java and Groovy. Their approach is completely static and relies on searching over source code objects, as Groovy and Java can easily interact with each other. In order to accelerate the searching engine, the authors propose filtering the classes on which, for example, the method call is executed, creating a hierarchy scope, and starting a second search following the method inside the limiting hierarchical scope.

2.2   Categorization of the Tools

We classify the presented work in different categories (summarized in Table 1[4]):

Dependency type: Many of the papers are considering dependencies existing in *cross-language* applications, like between Java source code and an XML configuration file, *multi-tier* like between a client application and a server one, *callbacks* from external libraries, or *generated files* like the R class in Android or the files generated by J2EE, or HTML and Javascript generated by PHP;

Analysis: We saw that both *static* and *dynamic* analyses could be used by the tools;

---

[4] For completion, we include Yu et al. in the table although, as already said, they consider a different type of dependency.

Matching strategy: There are two different strategies used: *Object matching* works on a model of the application and looks for specific objects in the model, *lexical matching* works directly on the source text (Java, XML, . . .);
Engine: Finally, some approaches are based on user defined *rules* to identify dependencies, while others *automatically* discover them.

Table 1. Existing approaches (dependency types)

Name	Dependency Type	Analysis	Matching strategy	Engine
Yu and Rajlich [20]	*Data dependencies*	*Static*	*Object*	*Rule*
EdgeMiner [2]	Callbacks	Static	Object	Automatic
Dsketch [3]	Cross-language	Static	Object	Rule
Grichi et al. [4]	Cross-language	Static	Lexical	Rule
Hecht et al. [6]	all[a]	Dynamic	Object	Rule
Kempf et al. [7]	Cross-language	Static	Object	Rule
XLL [8]	Cross-language	Static	Object	Rule
BabelRef [12]	M-tiers[b], Gen.[c]	Dynamic	Object	Rule
GenDeMoG [13]	Cross-language	Static	Object	Rule
Polychniatis et al. [15]	Cross-language	Static	Lexical	Automatic
DeJEE [16]	Cross-language	Static/Dyn	Lexical	Automatic
Soto-Valero et al. [18]	Cross-language	Static	Object	Automatic

[a]Multi-tiers, generated files, callbacks, cross-language
[b]Multi-tiers
[c]Generated files

We can see that only one paper considers multiple dependency types (Hecht et al. [6]: cross-language, multi-tiers, callbacks, and generated files). Also, two papers, Pfeiffer and Wąsowski [13], and Soto-Valero et al. [18], consider dependency correctness by identifying when a dependency should not exist. Additionally, we found that some approaches are generic [3,8,13,15], while others work only for specific languages and frameworks [2,4,6,7,12,16,18,20].

3   Structuring the Domain

Having reviewed the literature on dependencies introduced by agents external to the source code, we will now discuss more in-depth the different categories of these *External Dependencies* that were introduced in the preceding section. We also discuss dependencies correctness and how an *External Dependency* detection tool can help, not only in understanding the software, but also in pointing out possible flaws.

3.1   Categorization

Different kinds of *External Dependencies* exist in software where artifacts are written in different languages or tiers need to interact:

Cross-language dependencies are those between artifacts written in different languages. For example, in the GWT framework where XML can be used to define the UI and Java is used to handle the behavior. The dependency between Java and CXML appears in the Java code with annotations such as @UiField and @UiHandler. If any change affects the XML artifact, the developer must apply in parallel the same change on the dependent Java artifacts, otherwise the dependency is broken and the application might fail at runtime. This seems to be the kind of *External Dependencies* most studied (see Table 1) Such dependencies may be difficult for the developers to detect as they imply a good understanding of the framework used [10]. For example, Android also expresses the GUI in an XML file and the behavior in Java code, but the dependencies are not materialized in the same way. Examples are not limited to GUI, other Cross-language dependencies can be found when an SQL query (in a String) references the tables and columns of an external database.

Multi-tiers dependencies appear in applications with a distributed architecture. For example, they can access data on one or more database servers, the business logic runs on an application server, the presentation logic is deployed on a web server, and the user interface runs on a web browser [11]. Thus, in a call established between a client and server application using Java RMI, the client program must be aware of the structure of interfaces that extend java.rmi.Remote in order to invoke its methods and make a successful call to the server tier. Again, such calls between tiers depend on the communication framework used, yet changes to one tier could require in parallel updates to the second.

Callback dependencies are often used by libraries to allow the user to get back control from library's elements. For example, in the JavaFX graphical library, a Button widget can give back control to the application upon end-user interaction through the setOnAction(EventHandler) callback. Kempf et al. [7] mention it for the Android framework. Again, each framework has a different set of callbacks that must be known to adequately identify the dependencies.

File generation dependencies appear when a framework or tool generates additional files, predefined in configuration files and parsed on deployment time, able to generate additional components linked with the existing ones of the project [6]. Such dependencies are hidden until the project is deployed or executed, and during the analysis phase, a developer or an analysis tool may not be aware of their existence. These dependencies may be accompanied by other kinds, for example, Android generates a R class that allows to link the Java code to XML artifacts (Cross-Language dependencies). In the context of J2EE, Hecht et al. use dynamic analysis to detect these File generation dependencies.

Documentation dependencies exist when the documentation refers to the source code. For example, the JavaDoc has special annotations to refer to classes, methods or their parameters. Some refactorings are able to detect and modify the comments when an artifact is renamed. These dependencies might be considered less critical because they don't affect the behavior of the application. Yet they are important for the readability and understandability of the source code. In this case, the "external agent" introducing the *External Dependencies* might be considered to be the human reader.

As noticed above, these categories are not mutually exclusive and actually frequently co-existent. We saw the example of Generated file dependencies and Cross-language dependencies, but a Multi-tier dependency will often come with a Callback dependency to allow one tier to answer to events in another tier.

3.2   Dependency Correctness

A dependency exists between two artifacts (or entities) that we will call *reference* and *Resource*. Following Pfeiffer and Wąsowski definitions: "*a [Resource entity]*[5] *is a fragment of code that introduces an identifiable object, a concept, etc.*", and "*a [Reference entity]* is a location in code that relates to a *[Resource entity]*". The definitions need to be more generic as we are not dealing solely with source code (XML files, documentation), but we will mostly restrict ourselves to *External Dependencies* which involve some source code, although we sometimes also consider dependencies between CSS specifications and HTML documents, which are typically not considered source code.

Most of the work cited in Sect. 2 focuses on identifying the *External Dependencies* to help fully understand the application and preserve the quality of the modified source code. We saw that Soto-Valero et al. [18] went one step further by considering the correctness of dependencies. Also, Pfeiffer and Wąsowski [14] state that the dependencies are always many-to-one between Reference entities and Resource entities.

The issue of correctness is important as it allows for checking (and possibly preserving) the quality of the application. The idea of cardinality (many-to-one) is an obvious candidate to express possible restrictions on the *External Dependencies*. However, although the many-to-one is the most frequent, we found the statement of Pfeiffer and Wąsowski to be incorrect in some cases; not all *External Dependency* are many-to-one.

We consider the cardinality of *External Dependencies* independently from the Reference side and the Resource side.

Resource side: The Resource entity might be mandatory or optional.

    Mandatory: This is the most common case, the Resource entity referenced must exist or there will be an error at compilation or execution time.

---

[5] They call them "key".

Optional: Less common examples can be found in HTML tags (e.g., a specific `div`) considered as Resource entities. A CSS file can reference ("depend on") a non existent HTML tag, a JavaScript function could similarly look for the optional existence of a given node in the DOM of an HTML page.

Reference side: A Reference entity can be mandatory or optional, single or multiple:

Multiple: This is the most common case, a Resource entity can be referenced by multiple Reference entities.

Single: In specific cases such as ORM[6], there can be only one object referring to any element defined in a database.

Optional: Most of the time, Reference entities are optional. For example, one may not use a possible callback offered by a library.

Mandatory: There are cases where a Reference entity is mandatory. Its absence will often not produce a compilation or execution error, but it still denotes a flaw or a lack of understanding of the framework used. In the worst cases, this lack of understanding is circumvented by the developers with some needlessly complex and non-standard constructions in the source code.

The cardinality for any *External Dependency* is fixed by the framework considered.

Stating the cardinality of an *External Dependency* allows a tool to not only identify the dependencies (to help analyze the application), but also to verify them (to help discover flaws). We will see in our examples (Sect. 5) that we did find such flaws.

We propose two main categories of flaws/errors:

Excessive dependencies: They characterize a Resource entity that was created but never referred to [8]. In multi-tier applications, we had the case where many services were declared on the server side but never used on the client side. They were not possible extensions to be used by other client applications, but old code that ceased to be used ("dead services"). Other possible cases are when the developer made a mistake and the Reference entity points to a wrong (similar) Resource entity. Soto-Valero et al. [18] call them "bloated dependencies" when removing unused Java classes from imported jar files.

Missing dependencies: They characterize Reference entities that are referring to Resource entities that do not exist. Such dependencies are uncommon since most applications cannot run properly if resources are not available. Such dependencies have a higher chance of existing in the case of HTML and CSS, or comments. In this case, they would result in a wrong/unappealing rendering of a web application, and misleading comments. Note that wrong web page rendering can lead to an unusable web application in some cases.

---

[6] Object Relational Mapping wikipedia.org/wiki/Object-relational_mapping.

4   External Dependencies Detection

This section explains how we implement a generic *External Dependency* detector. We first decompose the problem into two sub-problems, which allows us to develop a small library of reusable patterns. We then give the general architecture of our solution.

4.1   Requirements

Going back to the categorization of work proposed in Sect. 2, we want a generic solution that allows us to identify dependencies with the following properties:

Dependency types: No limitation, we are interested in *External Dependencies* coming from multi-tier programming, cross-language programming, the generation of files during the installation process, and libraries making use of callbacks.

Matching strategy: The object matching strategy (on a model of the application) allows to identify more complex structures than lexical matching, for example searching for "a method in a class implementing a given interface and carrying a given annotation". This is why many publications have used it. However, building a model of an application may be a complex task, for example for less commonly used programming languages for which there is no generic parser and symbol resolver available. In these cases, lexical matching is a simpler solution, fast and flexible to implement [5].

We will allow both solutions, taking advantage of whatever tools are already available for a given language.

Engine: Some publications propose automatic solutions that are able to discover dependencies without the user specifying where to look for them. All of these are specific to one given framework except Polychniatis et al. [15] which may produce many false positives.

We will prefer a rule-based engine where we specify for each framework where to look for dependencies. This is the preferred solution in the domain (see Table 1).

Analysis: As for any software analysis approach, one can use static or dynamic analysis. The static approach is usually favored. It is easier to apply across various programming languages (and other languages too) and across application contexts.

We will use this solution too.

File generation dependencies have been covered dynamically by Hecht et al. [6]. That could be a limitation of our approach for this dependency type.

4.2   Decomposing the Problem

To simplify the implementation of a generic solution, we decompose the dependency identification problem into two parts: First, we look for *Containers*, software artifacts that may contain a Reference entity or a Resource entity. Containers are usually large artifacts, such as an entire file. Second, within a potentially interesting container, we look for *Entities* that will be either Reference entities or a Resource entities. For example, a (Reference) container in the GWT framework could be any Java class that contains the annotation `@uiField` or `@uiHandler`. These annotations are used in the GWT framework to establish the link between Java and XML.

This decomposition can help specifying the rules when using lexical matching.

We limit a container to be written in any single language, like a Java container, an XML container, etc. This simplifies the work of searching for entities in a container. Note that this may lead to a non-obvious situation where an SQL string inside a Java file or a comment inside any source code is considered a different container because the language is not the same. It may not be very important for lexical matching rules, but it is key for object matching rules that are based on models: They would require an SQL or a comment model to search in.

In the literature, many approaches search for some kind of "container" [4,7–9,13,17] by declaring specific search patterns or by discovering them with some heuristics. Thus, Kempt et al. [7] propose first filtering containers that may contain such dependencies to accelerate the research.

There are two kinds of containers: Reference containers and Resource containers. In the GWT example above, the Java class containing the annotation is a Reference container and the Resource container will be an entire XML file describing the GUI.

Within these containers, we apply matching patterns to find the entities involved in *External Dependency*. Again, for the GWT example, inside the Reference container, we will be looking for specific attributes of methods carrying the GWT annotations.

4.3   Reusable Patterns

Decomposing the problem into containers and entities allows us to have reusable patterns. For example, searching for an XML element according to one of its attribute names can be done whether this is an XML configuration file, or an XML layout file. It would therefore be applicable to *External Dependencies* detection in J2EE or GWT.

For a given language, the patterns can be used for container or entity detection. Each pattern can be expressed declaratively given the object type and its properties in form of key-value pairs. Consider the below pattern description for finding annotations in Java model: (i) the type of the object that we're looking inside is a `FamixJavaModel` (ii) in order to extract the annotations we use `allAnnotationTypes` property (iii) the pattern accepts annotation name parameter associated to value property of `FamixJavaAnnotationType` to search for annotations we are interested in (i.e. 'UiField') (iv) the pattern returns the container name where the previously specified attribute is found, using `FamixJavaAttribute` parentType property, also expressed declaratively in the same pattern by using Temporary variables (i.e. '@ClassObject')

This is especially important for object matching patterns, where we need to build a model of the source code. Working with this decomposition and reusable patterns allow to more easily add new frameworks.

4.4   Adonis

Our solution is implemented in a tool called Adonis (https://github.com/ alesshosry/Adonis). First, Adonis takes as input two elements: the code to analyze and the framework identification (eg. GWT or RMI). The framework must be known by the tool: (i) programming language importer if we want to use object matching; (ii) detection rules for Reference containers, Resource containers, Reference entities, and Resource entities. This follows from the definition of *External Dependencies*, where one needs to know the usage rules of a framework to be able to identify the dependencies it introduces. Detection rules for a given framework can be based on reusable patterns for the considered programming language. That is to say, a pattern to detect a given Java class can be used by rules for the GWT or RMI framework (and any framework based on the Java programming language).

Second, Adonis offers two "engines": lexical and object based matching, depending on the rules describing the framework to analyze. The selection of an engine depends on the availability of meta-models and importers to generate source code models.

Third, Adonis applies the rules of the framework to identify Reference and Resource containers/entities. It maps Reference entities to their Resource entities, leading to the generation of *External Dependencies* that were implicit in the framework. By considering the restrictions defined in Sect. 3.2, it can also identify possible flaws.

5   Validation

We validate our approach on two projects taken from GitHub. The objective is to evaluate whether (i) the approach can identify *External Dependencies*, (ii) it works for different types of dependencies, (iii) we can reuse patterns across frameworks, and (iv) it can detect flaws (missing or excessive dependencies).

5.1   Validation Setup

We are interested in how our approach can be adapted to different frameworks, if possible with different kinds of dependency types (cross-language, multi-tier, etc.). For practicality reasons, we chose two frameworks involving the same languages: Java and XML. Thanks to the Moose platform [1], we already have a Java importer and meta-model on which we can easily express object matching patterns. Building an XML model is easy since there are many libraries to parse XML.

Cross-Language Experiment. For the cross-language example we will focus on GWT, a framework to develop Web applications using a combination of Java and XML. In GWT Java artifacts (class attributes or methods) are "linked" to widgets described in XML files through the annotations `UiField` and `UiHandler`. For example, Listing 1.1 shows how an attribute on line 3 is referring to a Window defined in Listing 1.2 as an XML element (lines 1 to 5). Similarly, the Java method on line 5 is linked to the Button widget on lines 2 to 4 of the XML file. GWT requires that the Java and XML files be located in the same folder and have the same name (without their respective extensions: `.java` and `.xml`).

Listing 1.1. GWT Java

```
1  public class ApplicationSettingsDialog implements Editor<
       ApplicationSettings> {
2    @UiField
3    protected Window window;
4    @UiHandler("saveButton")
5    public void onLoginClicked(SelectEvent event) {
6      window.hide();
7    }
8  }
```

Listing 1.2. GWT XML

```
1  <gxt:Window ui:field="window" pixelSize="300, 110" modal="true"
       headingText="Global Settings" focusWidget="{saveButton}">
2    <gxt:button>
3      <button:TextButton ui:field="saveButton" text="Save" />
4    </gxt:button>
5  </gxt:Window>
```

The cardinality of these *External Dependencies* is many-to-one, as several Java associations can refer to the same XML attribute. The XML attributes (Resource entities) are mandatory, the Java ones (Reference entities) are optional, i.e. Java part is not required to refer to all XML widgets.

We manually counted the number of Reference containers (i.e. some java classes), Resource containers (i.e. `.xml` files); Reference entities in the Java code; Resource entities defined in the XML files; and *External Dependencies* found (i.e. the number of Reference entities with a matching Resource entity).

Multi-tier Experiment. For the multi-tier example, we will focus on the RMI[7] framework that is also based on Java. RMI allows to build distributed applications where a client part can call server methods running in a different JVM.

A Java interface is needed (`TheRemoteInterface` in the example below). It extends `java.rmi.Remote` and declares methods that can throw `java.rmi.RemoteException`.

---

[7] Remote Method Invocation.

On the server side, a class (`TheServerClass`) implements this interface and defines the service methods (line 1 in Listing 1.3). An instance of this class is registered in the RMI registry (lines 3 and 4 in Listing 1.3).

Listing 1.3. RMI server code

```
1  public class TheServerClass implements TheRemoteInterface { ... }
2  ...
3  Registry registry = LocateRegistry.createRegistry(<port number>);
4  registry.bind("rmi://localhost/TheServerClass", new TheServerClass());
```

On the client side, an instance of this interface is obtained from the RMI registry (Listing 1.4) and calls to its methods will be forwarded to the server application.

Listing 1.4. RMI client code

```
1  Registry registry = LocateRegistry.getRegistry(<number>);
2  TheServerInterface instance = (TheServerInterface) registry.lookup("rmi
      ://localhost/TheServerClass");
```

Again, we manually counted the number of Reference containers (i.e. some java interfaces), Resource containers (i.e. java classes); Reference entities in the Java classes; Resource entities defined in the java interfaces; and *External Dependencies* found (i.e. the number of Reference entities with a matching Resource entity).

5.2 Use Cases

For the cross-language experiment, we chose the Traccar project[8] that uses the GWT framework. It was created in 2012, has 100 commits, and in total 34 Java classes, and 13 XML files. We counted the containers and entities manually and found in total 10 Reference containers out of the 34 Java classes and 10 Resource containers out of the 13 XML files. Some of the Resource entities (in XML) are not referred to in Java, and multiple Reference entities (in Java) may refer to the same Resource entity. The number of Resources, Referred Resources and External Dependencies are presented in Table 2. Each row in the table is for a pair of matching .java and .xml files (i.e. Reference/Resource containers).

For the multi-tier experiment, we chose the UniScore solution[9]. It was created in 2020 and has a track record of more than 100 commits. Uniscore-Server is the server part sub-project of the UniScore solution. It is composed of two interfaces and 41 classes. Uniscore-Client is the client part sub-project of the UniScore solution. It has one interface and 50 classes. We manually counted the number of Resource containers that is, interfaces extending `java.rmi.Remote`. There is only one such interface in the project that declares 54 methods which are the Resource entities. In parallel the Reference containers are classes that use

---

[8] https://github.com/traccar/traccar-web/tree/legacy.
[9] https://github.com/redhawk96/UniScore.

Table 2. GWT (cross-language) experiment

Containers	Resources	Referred Resources	External dependencies
ApplicationSettingsDialog	5	4	4
ApplicationView	12	4	4
ArchiveView	14	11	11
DeviceDialog	6	5	5
DeviceView	16	12	17
LoginDialog	6	5	6
StateView	5	4	4
UserDialog	7	6	6
UsersDialog	10	6	8
UserSettingsDialog	5	4	4

an instance of the Resource container. We found 14 such classes out of the 50 classes in the client part. For each Reference container, we also manually counted the number of entities, that is to say methods invoking Resource entities. The number of Resources, Referred Resources and External Dependencies are presented in Table 3. Each row in the table represents a Reference container.

5.3   Rules and Patterns

We developed patterns for Java and XML languages used by the two frameworks of our experiments. We defined two XML patterns and 12 Java patterns in all. Our strategy consists of filtering containers and finding entities inside each one.

For the cross-language experiment (GWT framework), we used one rule to find Resource containers (XML files): It looks for all XML files having a name matching a Java file. For the Resource entities, we use one rule: It looks for all XML nodes having a `UIField` or `Field` attribute. This rule uses twice the same XML pattern that looks for XML nodes having a given attribute.

We used one rule to find Reference containers (Java classes): It looks for all Java classes using a `@UiHandler` or `@UiField` annotation. This rule uses twice the same Java pattern that looks for annotation instances having a given name. For the Reference entities, we use one rule: It looks for the argument value of all `@UiHandler` or `@UiField` annotations in the container. Again, this rule uses twice the same Java pattern to look for annotation instances.

For the multi-tier experiment (RMI framework), we used one rule to find Resource containers (Java interfaces): It looks for all Java interfaces extending the `java.rmi.Remote` interface. This rule uses a Java pattern that looks for all implementations of a given Java interface. For the Resource entities, we use one rule: It looks for all Java public methods that declare throwing `java.rmi.RemoteException`. This rule uses two Java patterns, one looking for

Table 3. RMI (multi-tier) experiment

Containers	Resources	Referred Resources	External dependencies
SubmissionContentPanel	54	1	1
DashboardContentPanel	54	7	7
ExamContentPanel	54	8	9
LogoutNavigationPanel	54	1	1
LoginContentPanel	54	4	8
UniScoreClient	54	2	2
RemoveQuestionNotifier	54	2	2
DisplayQuestionsContentPanel	54	2	2
CreateQuestionContentPanel	54	2	2
DisplayQuestionContentPanel	54	2	2
StudentContentPanel	54	4	4
ModuleContentPanel	54	1	1
QuestionnaireContentPanel	54	4	4
SubmissionMailer	54	3	3

public methods and the other looking for methods declaring to throw a given exception.

We used one rule to find Reference containers (Java classes): It looks for all Java classes that use instances of at least one of the Resource containers. This rule uses one Java pattern to look for instances of a given interface and this pattern is called repeatedly for each of the Resource containers found. For the Reference entities, we use one rule: It looks for invocations of any of the Resource entities found. This rule uses a Java pattern to look for invocations of a given method.

5.4   Results

We ran Adonis for both experiments to detect the number of containers, entities and *External Dependencies* and compare them with what we found by manual count.

For the GWT experiment, Adonis was able to correctly detect the 10 containers (rows of Table 2). It also correctly detected all Resources and References.

The analysis of "Resources" and "Referred Resources" columns shows that multiple Resource entities are defined in XML but never referred to in Java. For example, for the `DeviceView` containers, only 12 out of 16 Resource entities were referred to. This is allowed in the GWT framework and is not considered a flaw.

Moreover, the comparison between "Referred Resources" and "External Dependencies" columns shows that the number of *External Dependencies* can be larger than the number of referred Resource entities, indicating that some Resource entities are referred by several Reference entities. For example, for the

`UsersDialog` containers, there are 8 *External Dependencies* for only 6 Reference entities. Two references to `removeButton` and `addButton` can be found in the source code. Again, this is allowed in the GWT framework and is not considered a flaw.

For the RMI experiment, Adonis was able to correctly detect the 14 Reference containers (rows of Table 3). It also correctly detected all Resources and References entities.

The analysis of "Resources" and "Referred Resources" columns shows that multiple Resource entities are defined in the server but never referred to in the client. For example, in `DashboardContentPanel` container, we can see that only 1 out of 54 Resource entities is referred to.

In total, we found that only 26 Resource entities out of 54 were referred, which results the existence of 28 excessive dependencies. Moreover, the comparison between "Referred Resources" and "External dependencies" shows that the number of referred Resource entities can be less than the number of *External Dependencies*. For example, for the `DashboardContentPanel` class, we can see that none of the Resource entities was referred more than once, which is not the case for `ExamContentPanel` class, where we found `addLogActivity` was referred twice. This explains why we found 9 *External Dependencies* instead of 8.

6   Conclusion

Various frameworks are used to create various types of software. These frameworks rely on a set of rules specific to each one to establish dependencies. We conclude the existence of multiple types of *External Dependencies* such as multi-tiers, callbacks, and cross-language links in polyglot programming. We also state that even if each framework connects its languages or tiers in a unique way, a common approach emerges. This approach is based on finding the correct containers that lead to the identification of specific entities defined according to the framework's rules. Additionally, this approach defines restrictions that lead to error detection, making it important to know how to proceed with the re-engineering work. To design a detector that can achieve the usage goals successfully, we established a set of requirements and based on them, we developed our tool *Adonis* with the flexibility of defining or using existing patterns to limit the number of containers, detect entities, and link them following each framework rules that we experimented with two different projects.

References

1. Anquetil, N., et al.: Modular Moose: a new generation of software reverse engineering platform. In: Ben Sassi, S., Ducasse, S., Mili, H. (eds.) ICSR 2020. LNCS, vol. 12541, pp. 119–134. Springer, Cham (2020). https://doi.org/10.1007/978-3-030-64694-3_8
2. Cao, Y., et al.: EdgeMiner: automatically detecting implicit control flow transitions through the android framework. In: NDSS (2015)

3. Cossette, B., Walker, R.J.: DSketch: lightweight, adaptable dependency analysis. In: Proceedings of the Eighteenth ACM SIGSOFT International Symposium on Foundations of Software Engineering, pp. 297–306 (2010)

4. Grichi, M., Abidi, M., Jaafar, F., Eghan, E.E., Adams, B.: On the impact of interlanguage dependencies in multilanguage systems empirical case study on Java native interface applications (JNI). IEEE Trans. Reliab. **70**(1), 428–440 (2020)

5. Griswold, W.G., Atkinson, D.C., McCurdy, C.: Fast, flexible syntactic pattern matching and processing. In: WPC 1996. 4th Workshop on Program Comprehension, pp. 144–153. IEEE (1996)

6. Hecht, G., et al.: Codifying hidden dependencies in legacy J2EE applications. In: 2018 25th Asia-Pacific Software Engineering Conference (APSEC), pp. 305–314. IEEE (2018)

7. Kempf, M., Kleeb, R., Klenk, M., Sommerlad, P.: Cross language refactoring for eclipse plug-ins. In: Proceedings of the 2nd Workshop on Refactoring Tools, pp. 1–4 (2008)

8. Mayer, P., Schroeder, A.: Cross-language code analysis and refactoring. In: 2012 IEEE 12th International Working Conference on Source Code Analysis and Manipulation, pp. 94–103. IEEE (2012)

9. Mayer, P., Schroeder, A.: Automated multi-language artifact binding and rename refactoring between Java and DSLs Used by Java frameworks. In: Jones, R. (ed.) ECOOP 2014. LNCS, vol. 8586, pp. 437–462. Springer, Heidelberg (2014). https://doi.org/10.1007/978-3-662-44202-9_18

10. Mushtaq, Z., Rasool, G., Shehzad, B.: Multilingual source code analysis: a systematic literature review. IEEE Access **5**, 11307–11336 (2017)

11. Neubauer, M., Thiemann, P.: From sequential programs to multi-tier applications by program transformation. In: Proceedings of the 32nd ACM SIGPLAN-SIGACT Symposium on Principles of Programming Languages, pp. 221–232 (2005)

12. Nguyen, H.V., Nguyen, H.A., Nguyen, T.T., Nguyen, T.N.: BabelRef: detection and renaming tool for cross-language program entities in dynamic web applications. In: 2012 34th International Conference on Software Engineering (ICSE), pp. 1391–1394. IEEE (2012)

13. Pfeiffer, R.-H., Wąsowski, A.: Taming the confusion of languages. In: France, R.B., Kuester, J.M., Bordbar, B., Paige, R.F. (eds.) ECMFA 2011. LNCS, vol. 6698, pp. 312–328. Springer, Heidelberg (2011). https://doi.org/10.1007/978-3-642-21470-7_22

14. Pfeiffer, R.-H., Wąsowski, A.: TexMo: a multi-language development environment. In: Vallecillo, A., Tolvanen, J.-P., Kindler, E., Störrle, H., Kolovos, D. (eds.) ECMFA 2012. LNCS, vol. 7349, pp. 178–193. Springer, Heidelberg (2012). https://doi.org/10.1007/978-3-642-31491-9_15

15. Polychniatis, T., Hage, J., Jansen, S., Bouwers, E., Visser, J.: Detecting cross-language dependencies generically. In: 2013 17th European Conference on Software Maintenance and Reengineering, pp. 349–352. IEEE (2013)

16. Shatnawi, A., et al.: Static code analysis of multilanguage software systems. arXiv preprint arXiv:1906.00815 (2019)

17. Shen, B., et al.: Cross-language code coupling detection: a preliminary study on android applications. In: 2021 IEEE International Conference on Software Maintenance and Evolution (ICSME), pp. 378–388. IEEE (2021)

18. Soto-Valero, C., Harrand, N., Monperrus, M., Baudry, B.: A comprehensive study of bloated dependencies in the maven ecosystem. Empir. Softw. Eng. **26**(3), 45 (2021)

19. Vanciu, R., Rajlich, V.: Hidden dependencies in software systems. In: 2010 IEEE International Conference on Software Maintenance, pp. 1–10. IEEE (2010)
20. Yu, Z., Rajlich, V.: Hidden dependencies in program comprehension and change propagation. In: Proceedings 9th International Workshop on Program Comprehension. IWPC 2001, pp. 293–299. IEEE (2001)

Measuring Team Effectiveness in Scrum

Kars Beek[1,2(✉)], Gerard Wagenaar[1], Laura Kester[2], Sietse Overbeek[1],
and Evert de Rooij[2]

[1] Faculty of Science, Department of Information and Computing Sciences, Utrecht University,
Princetonplein 5, 3584 CC Utrecht, The Netherlands
{g.wagenaar,s.j.overbeek}@uu.nl
[2] Info Support, Kruisboog 42, 3905 TE Veenendaal, The Netherlands
{kars.beek,laura.kester,evert.derooij}@infosupport.com

Abstract. Teams have become building blocks of organizations, leading to an exponential increase in team studies, including team effectiveness studies in Scrum software development. However, research on measuring Scrum team effectiveness based on objective measures, contrary to self-reporting with Likert scales, is absent. Through a design science research methodology with literature review, focus groups, interviews, and an expert panel, 29 objective measures were identified contributing to seven team effectiveness concepts. All measures can be quantified or directly derived from work management systems, such as Jira or Azure DevOps. Examples include the number of solved retrospective items after a new sprint, contributing to the team effectiveness concept 'Continuous Improvement', and the number of times a sprint goal has been achieved, contributing to both 'Team Morale' and 'Stakeholder Satisfaction'. In this way, the study offers proof of the benefits of agile, especially Scrum, software development through effective teams as well as providing practitioners a first insight in benchmarking their Scrum team effectiveness.

Keywords: Team Effectiveness · Scrum · Objective measures

1 Introduction

Scrum is one of the most popular methods in software development [14]. The Scrum framework consists of a framework that offers a way of team collaboration for solving complex problems [20]. As a result of the popularity of Scrum, research on the topic of teams has grown exponentially in the last decade, leading also to an increase in team effectiveness studies in Scrum [12]. However, observations show that all studies that address the topic of Scrum team effectiveness measure team effectiveness based on self-reporting. In other words, providing a personal opinion on a situation or question. A symptom of self-reporting is a Likert scale. A Likert scale is a rating scale that expresses the subjectivity of individuals [9]. Subjectivity in measures can bring limitations [8]. First, subjective measures are difficult to aggregate and interpret because they are often expressed on ordinal scales. Moreover, it has been noticed that these measures are not

J. M. Fernandes et al. (Eds.): QUATIC 2023, CCIS 1871, pp. 233–247, 2023.
https://doi.org/10.1007/978-3-031-43703-8_17

correlated with facts from the field. As a result, subjectivity in measures has limitations, according to research [8]. Therefore, the objective of this research is to find out:

RQ: To which extent can team effectiveness in Scrum be measured based on objective measures?

In this paper, measures that quantify team effectiveness in Scrum will be presented. Previous findings on the topic of team effectiveness will be discussed in Sect. 2. In Sect. 3, the research design is described. Section 4 presents the findings of the research. In Sects. 5 and 6 the findings will be discussed, and validity threats will be examined. Last, in Sect. 7, the conclusions of this paper will be presented.

2 Previous Findings

This section discusses previous findings on the definition of team effectiveness in the literature. In addition, related work will be used to compile information on the different methods to measure team effectiveness in other research areas and in Scrum.

2.1 A Definition of Team Effectiveness

There is a significant amount of ambiguity regarding the concept of team effectiveness [3]. This is mainly since different organizations have different views on what defines "effectiveness" [1].

Without giving a formal definition, Hackman [6] states that in addition to performance outcomes, such as speed to solution and the number of errors, other outcomes should also be taken into account, for example, group cohesiveness and member satisfaction, to determine the effectiveness of a team. A general observation was that literature addressed the above-mentioned criteria for team effectiveness. However, a general definition of Team Effectiveness is often lacking.

One of the few definitions of 'team effectiveness' found has been given by Fransen et al. [5], and defines team effectiveness as, *"the quality of team performance, as well as the perceived satisfaction with individual needs of team members"*. This definition addresses team effectiveness at the team level (that is, performance) and the individual level (that is, satisfaction of team members). As a result, the definition of Fransen [5] can be applied in a broader context and has therefore been used during this research.

2.2 Measuring Team Effectiveness

Since the authors found no studies on measuring team effectiveness in Scrum based on objective measures, other disciplines have been visited. In this case, an exploratory literature review has been done in the fields of healthcare and engineering. These two research areas comprised the majority of team effectiveness studies. Following the number of team effectiveness papers, it can be assumed that the papers in these research areas have a respectable level of team effectiveness maturity.

Healthcare. Two meta-review studies provide an overview of measuring team effectiveness within the healthcare discipline. One of the first studies in this research area [11], reviewed 22 studies and concluded that all 22 studies applied objective measures and only 4 of the 22 studies also used subjective measures. A follow-up study [2] shows that this trend has not changed. Examples of objective measures can be categorized into patient outcomes (e.g., the functional status of a patient), and organizational outcomes (e.g., costs). Although no numbers are provided in studies that applied subjective or objective measurement, the study advised that research on the topic of team effectiveness in healthcare includes outcomes less frequently used, such as professional well-being, that is, staff satisfaction, and focuses on identifying possible deadly combinations between outcomes.

Engineering. For engineering, the studies done only contained subjective measures. Multiple studies have been conducted [25, 4, 7], and all of these studies applied Likert scales and therefore subjective measures to measure team effectiveness. Unfortunately, these papers do not elaborate on why they contain only subjective measures.

The general conclusion of this section is that there are a variety of methods of measuring team effectiveness in the areas of engineering and healthcare research. Although most healthcare research teams measure the effectiveness of the team based on objective measures, most effectiveness studies of engineering teams apply subjective measures.

2.3 Measuring Team Effectiveness in Scrum

The first study to address the topic of team effectiveness in Scrum was by Moe et al. [13]. In this study, to evaluate team effectiveness in Scrum, the "Big Five" teamwork [19] has been applied. Although this paper included a small case study and is already more than 15 years old, it provides a good understanding of the relationship between team effectiveness and Scrum. Furthermore, the findings of Moe et al. [13] form the basis for future research in the area of team effectiveness in Scrum, such as the paper by Verwijs [22]. Teamwork is only one component of the overall picture of team effectiveness [22]. Therefore, Verwijs concluded that seven factors contribute to team effectiveness in Scrum. These factors are continuous improvement, stakeholder concerns, team autonomy, responsiveness, management support, team morale, and stakeholder satisfaction. In the paper, these concepts have been measured using Likert scales. A Likert scale gives quantitative value to qualitative data [9]. Therefore, the study does not address objective measures to measure team effectiveness, which can be implied as a research gap. Delgado et al. [3] explain why most team effectiveness studies contain subjective measures instead of objective measures. He states that in most studies, subjective measures are used to measure performance effectiveness and behavioral outcomes, as data are often unavailable for objective measurement. As a result, it is difficult to make comparisons of the different characteristics of the team [3].

3 Research Design

In this study, the design science research methodology created by Peffers et al. [15] will be followed. Different phases are shown in Fig. 1. Each phase consists of activities.

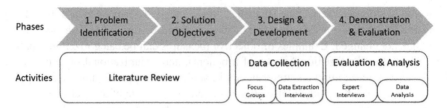

Fig. 1. Design Science Process Model adapted from Peffers et al. [15]

3.1 Literature Review Protocol

Before the different stages will be discussed, a literature review protocol will be elaborated to guide the literature review. This protocol was derived from Kitchenham et al. [10] and was tailored for this research. The first step of this protocol was to apply search terms in different search engines. These terms have been derived from the research question and the defined problem statement. 'Team Effectiveness Scrum' and 'Productivity Scrum' are the main search terms derived from the research question and problem statement. This step led to a selection of papers in which inclusion and exclusion were applied. The exclusion criteria contained three elements. Studies written in another language than English were excluded. Textbooks and papers that include student experiments were also excluded. Papers were excluded if they have been published at conferences that are grouped into categories less than C based on the core conference ranking. After the exclusion criteria, the inclusion criteria were applied. These contained also of three steps. First, the titles were being screened. The papers were selected if the title contained 'team effectiveness' and 'Scrum' or 'productivity' and 'Scrum'. Second, the abstracts of the papers that were selected after the first inclusion criteria step were analyzed. As a third step, the selected papers from the second inclusion criteria step were thoroughly read. Only papers were included that describe/discuss at least one of the following elements: Team effectiveness in Scrum, Productivity in Scrum, Method to calculate team effectiveness productivity, or team effectiveness productivity metrics in Scrum teams.

Ultimately 24 papers were derived from the protocol that can been considered suitable for this paper.

3.2 Problem Identification and Solution Objectives

The main part of the Problem Identification & Solution Objectives is to identify the problem and research gap and formulate objectives for the final created artifact. The problem identification of this research is described in Sect. 1, and the Solution Objectives phase has been elaborated in Sect. 2.

3.3 Design and Development

The Design & Development phase consists of the data collection process, which is elaborated in Sect. 4. There were several activities involved in the data collection process. First, two focus groups were organized to generate objective measures related to team effectiveness and Scrum. In the first focus group, five Scrum experts were asked to generate measures with objective measures related to Scrum and team effectiveness, taking into account the definition of team effectiveness by Fransen et al. [5]. *"the quality of team performance, as well as the perceived satisfaction with individual needs of team members"*.

In the second focus group, the aim was to link the objective measures generated in the first focus group with the seven concepts of team effectiveness, defined by Verwijs et al. [22]. Verwijs proved that these seven concepts form the basis of Scrum team effectiveness. Linking them to a certain team effectiveness concept indicated that the measures can be applied in measuring Scrum team effectiveness. Furthermore, the second focus group was also applied to review the measures that were generated from the first focus group. The last phase of data collection was to indicate whether the measures derived from the focus groups could be measured in a practical setting. For this, work management system interviews were conducted with Scrum masters to indicate whether a measure can be quantified in work management systems, such as Jira or Azure DevOps.

3.4 Demonstration and Evaluation

During focus groups in the previous phase, measures were collected and linked to the seven concepts of team effectiveness. Expert interviews were conducted to define the exact influence of a certain measure on team effectiveness, since this has not been specified yet. As a result, information was collected on how a certain measure influences team effectiveness, which is described in Sect. 5. In addition, these experts had at least five years of experience in Scrum projects. The structured interview method was used during these interviews. This method involves scheduling questions in which the researcher will ask each respondent the same questions in a similar way [17]. For each expert interview, the following question was asked, taking into account the definition of team effectiveness by Fransen et al. [5]:

How does this measure influence team effectiveness?
The last step of this phase is an analysis of the interviews. Each measure contains several opinions on whether the measure affects team effectiveness. The purpose of the analysis was to obtain information on whether the four opinions were on the same line. Therefore, a coding scheme was applied in which a specific color was applied to each measure. The end result was an overview that includes the expert's perspective on each measure. Additionally, a color-coded analysis was also performed to indicate whether experts were on the same line about the influence of each measure on team effectiveness.

4 Generating Objective Measures

In total, two focus groups have been conducted to generate objective measures. In addition, six interviews have been conducted to indicate whether the measures generated from the focus groups, can be measured in a work management system.

4.1   Focus Group 1

The first focus group consisted of five participants, in which each participant had at least five years of experience in Scrum projects. In total, 54 measures were derived from the first focus group session. After removing the duplicate measures, 54 measures have been reduced to 39 measures. In addition to removing duplicates, the measures needed to be divided into objective and subjective measures. Although participants were asked to mention the objective measures down, the evaluation showed that there were also subjective measures involved. As a result, a check was needed to remove the subjective measures. This process was carried out by the researcher and validated by the focus group participants. In this process, the 39 measures have been reduced to 30 measures. Ultimately, 30 objective measures were collected after the first focus group.

4.2   Focus Group 2

The second focus group consisted of six participants. Similarly to the first focus group, the objective was to gather participants who have more than five years of Scrum experience. However, one participant had less than five years of Scrum experience. Participants in the second focus group were asked to relate 30 objective measures, from the first focus group, to the seven concepts of team effectiveness. As mentioned in Sect. 2.3, the seven concepts were continuous improvement, stakeholder concern, responsiveness, management support, team autonomy, team morale, and stakeholder satisfaction. In addition, participants could add objective measures to the concepts, as most of the participants did not participate in the first focus group. In total, 10 measures were added, which resulted that the number of measures grew from 30 to 40 unique measures. However, there was noted that measures were applicable to multiple concepts. In total, 10 of the 40 measures were applied to two concepts. As a result, 50 measures, of which 10 duplicate measures, were distributed across the seven concepts. Table 1 provides an overview of the Team Autonomy team effectiveness concept and the measures related to the concept. The first column shows the team effectiveness concept that is related to the measures, and the second and third columns show the measure and the definition of the measure. The fourth column indicates whether the measures were derived from the first focus group, or were added in the second focus group. An overview of all team effectiveness concepts and their associated measures will be provided in Table 3 in Sect. 5.2.

4.3   Data Extraction Work Management Systems

The last part of the results section dives deeper into the objective measures that are currently measured in work management systems such as Jira or DevOps. In total, six interviews were conducted with four Scrum masters, a software engineer, and a delivery manager. The purpose of the interviews was to review the measures and determine whether they can be measured in work management systems. During interviews, it became evident that it was not always that straightforward whether a measure can be quantified in a work management system. As a result, five categories have been created, in which each category contains a color.

Table 1. Objective measures linked to the Team Autonomy team effectiveness concept.

Team Effectiveness Concept	Objective measure	Definition	Derived from 1st focus group session
Team Autonomy	The amount of technical debt in a sprint/release	The number of trade-offs during a sprint. Technical debt is the consequence that software projects face when they make trade-offs to implement lower quality, less complete solutions to meet budget and schedule constraints imposed by business realities	Yes
	The number of scrum teams working together on the same product	The number of teams working together on the same product	Yes
	The number of reviews/acceptance tests executed by external parties	The number of reviews and acceptances given by external people outside the scrum team	No
	The number of software releases	The number of releases of a scrum team within a certain period/sprint	Yes
	The number of user stories/items executed by a minimum of 2 scrum team members	The number of tasks that are executed by at least 2 scrum team members	No

- The measure can be quantified in a work management system. (GREEN)
- The measure can be quantified, but not in Jira or Azure DevOps. (BLUE)
- The measure cannot be directly derived from the work management system. However, data points are available in the system. (YELLOW)
- The measure can be counted manually and put into the work management system. (ORANGE)
- The measure can neither be quantified nor visualized in a work management system. (RED)

The first three categories contain measures that can already be computed in work management systems or the data available to compute the measure. The last two categories are measures in which a large adjustment has to be made to the system to compute the measure, or it is not possible to compute the measure. The number of measures and the percentage of the total number of measures, which is 40, attached to a certain category are shown in Table 2. The first column indicates the category. Columns 2 to 7 show the number of measures and the percentage related to the category, according to the interviewee. Column 8 provides insight into the average percentage per category. Table 2 shows that a variety of responses have been provided to determine whether a measure can be quantified. Since the knowledge of the work management system differs

Table 2. The number of measures related to a category.

Category	Interview						Avg. % Category
	1	2	3	4	5	6	
The measure can be measured in a work management system	12 (30%)	10 (25%)	19 (47.5%)	20 (50%)	10 (25%)	8 (20%)	32.9%
The measure can be computed, but not in Jira or Azure DevOps	7 (17.5%)	1 (2.5%)	1 (2.5%)	1 (2.5%)	1 (2.5%)	2 (5%)	5.4%
The measure can not be directly derived from the work management system. However, the data points for indicating the measure are available in the system	11 (27.5%)	6 (15%)	2 (5%)	5 (12.5%)	2 (5%)	13 (32.5%)	16.3%
The measure can be counted manually and put into the work management system	6 (15%)	4 (10%)	5 (12.5%)	5 (12.5%)	3 (7.5%)	3 (7.5%)	10.8%
The measure can be neither measured nor visualized in a work management system	4 (10%)	19 (47.5%)	13 (32.5%)	9 (22.5%)	24 (60%)	14 (35%)	34.6%

among the interviewees, the most optimistic scenario has been chosen. This means that whenever an expert mentions that the measure can be quantified, it is assumed that the measure can be quantified. Table 3, one page 11 provides a more detailed overview of whether a measure can be quantified taking into account the most optimistic scenario mentioned above.

Table 3. Overview of each measure and color codes from the evaluation and data extraction research phases.

Measure	Color Code Evaluation	Color Code WMS	Contributes to TE?	TE Concept
The number of retrospective items solved after a new sprint			Yes	CI
The number of bottlenecks visualized by a value stream map			Yes	CI
Measuring software quality with SonarQube			Yes	CI
The number of bugs/defects within a sprint			Yes	CI
Test time			Yes	CI/R
Built time			Yes	CI/R
Release time			Yes	CI/R
The number of changes to the product/sprint backlog after a sprint review meeting			Yes	CI/SC
Response time stakeholders to requests			Yes	SC/R
Business value			Yes	SC/SS
The number of stakeholders attending sprint meetings			No	SC/TM
The number of acceptance tests 'first time right'			No	SC
The number of times the same feedback is addressed by stakeholders			Yes	SC
The difference between the items/stories that are created in this sprint compared to the previous sprints			No	SC
The time it takes to execute an integration			Yes	R
Done work			Yes	R
Review time			Yes	R
Lead time release/story			Yes	R
The number of software releases			Yes	R/TA
Cycle time			Yes	R
The ratio between the working hours and meeting hours			No	R
The number of managers attending a sprint review meeting			No	MS
Response time of management to requests			No	MS
Availability and recognizability of management			No	MS
Resources (euros)			No	MS
The amount of technical debt during a sprint/release			Yes	TA
The number of scrum teams working on the same product			Yes	TA
The number of reviews/acceptance tests executed by external parties			No	TA
The number of user stories/items executed by a minimum of 2 scrum team members			Yes	TA
User story age			Yes	R/TM
The number of backlog items			Yes	TM
The number of times the sprint goal has been achieved			Yes	TM/SS
The number of scrum team formation changes			Yes	TM
The number of releases to production without bugs			No	TM
The number of team events at least two members are present			No	TM
Average velocity previous X sprints			Yes	SS
The number of uncommitted features delivered within a release/sprint			Yes	SS
The finished user stories compared to the predicted number of user stories			Yes	TM/SS
Downtime			Yes	SS
The lead time of a feature compared to the expected delivery time of a feature			Yes	SS

5   Evaluation of the Team Effectiveness Measures

In this section, the evaluation of the findings will be discussed. Additionally, measures that contribute to measuring team effectiveness will be presented.

5.1   Expert Interviews

In total, four expert interviews were conducted to evaluate whether a measure provides information on team effectiveness. In addition to the answers of the experts, a link has been made to scientific literature to find out if the influence of a certain measure on team effectiveness has already been investigated. However, not all measures could be linked to scientific literature.

The analysis of the opinions on each measure showed that there is still much discussion among experts on whether a measure influences team effectiveness. Therefore, categories have been assembled to distinguish measures.

- The color *GREEN* has been used if all experts agree that the measure has an effect on team effectiveness.
- If the color is *BLUE*, this means that an expert disagreed and three experts agreed that the measurement had an impact on team effectiveness.
- If two experts agree, *YELLOW* is used if the measure influences team effectiveness.
- The color *ORANGE* was applied if three experts disagreed and one expert agreed on whether a measure influences team effectiveness.
- *RED* has been used if all experts state that the measure does not influence team effectiveness.

In general, it can be concluded that measures in the first and second categories, the colors Green & Blue, strongly influence team effectiveness. It could be argued that there is too much debate on whether the measure impacts team effectiveness for the measures that contain, the Yellow, Orange & Red colors. Due to this discussion, it has been assumed that there is no direct relationship between the measure and team effectiveness.

Ultimately, 35 of the 40 measures were assigned to the first and second categories and thus influence or strongly influence team effectiveness.

5.2 Relating the Evaluation Phase to the Work Management Data Extraction Phase

The aim of this section is to indicate whether a measure provides information on team effectiveness and can be measured in a work management system. The previous section provided information on what measures can be related to measuring team effectiveness. In this section, a link will be made between the evaluation of the measures and the extraction of data from the work management systems.

The colors Green & Blue in Sect. 5.1 state that the measure influences or strongly influences team effectiveness. For Sect. 4.3, Data extraction Work Management Systems, the color Green, Blue & Yellow indicate that a measure is measurable in a work management system. Whenever a measure is attached to both categories mentioned above, the measure provides information on team effectiveness, and the measure can be quantified in a work management system. In other words, the objective measure contributes to measuring team effectiveness in scrum. In the previous section, there was described that 35 measures out of the 40 measures influence or strongly influence team effectiveness based on the Green and 'Blue colours. These 35 measures will be taken to the expert interviews column. This column shows that out of the 35 measures, 29 measures also have the Green, Blue or Yellow colour. This means that, according to the expert interviews, and whether a measure can be quantified in a work management system, 29 measures contribute to measuring Team Effectiveness. These measures contain a Yes, in the Contributes to TE? column. A complete overview of whether a measure contributes to measuring scrum team effectiveness is shown in Table 3, which provides the name of the measure, the evaluation color, the color to indicate if the measure can be quantified in a Work Management System[1], whether the measure contributes to measuring Team Effectiveness[2] and the concept(s), Continuous Improvement[3], Stakeholder Concern[4], Responsiveness [5], Team Autonomy[6], Management Support[7], Team Morale[8], Stakeholder Satisfaction[9], of team effectiveness to which the measure is linked, based on the second focus group.

6 Discussion

In this section, the 29 measures that contribute to team effectiveness will be examined at the concept level, which is described in Sect. 2.3. Furthermore, observations during the second focus group will further discuss the generated measures.

---

[1] WMS
[2] TE
[3] CE
[4] SC
[5] R
[6] TA
[7] MS
[8] TM
[9] SS

The second focus group showed that 40 unique measures were related to the seven concepts of team effectiveness. The evaluation phase showed that 29 of the 40 measures ultimately contribute to measuring team effectiveness in scrum. This shows that these measures could provide a broad overview of measuring team effectiveness as a whole. However, further analysis shows that not all concept can be fully measured. Verwijs [22] states that there are seven concepts important in scrum team effectiveness. To ensure that all concepts are covered in measuring team effectiveness, objective measures are linked to the seven concepts of team effectiveness.

An analysis was performed to identify differences in the measurability of concepts. In other words, whether a concept can be quantified. The analysis shows that two concepts, stakeholder concern and management support, are the most represented. Three of the seven measures (42.9%) related to stakeholder concerns do not contribute to measuring team effectiveness. Four of the four measures (100%) related to management support do not help measure scrum team effectiveness. For team morale, team autonomy, and responsiveness these percentages are 25%, 20%, and 8.3% respectively. This indicates that there is still a great difference in the measurability at the concept level. Verwijs [22] concluded that all these concepts influence team effectiveness. It is important to note that not all seven concepts can be fully measured on the basis of objective measures. Therefore, this should be taken into account when measuring team effectiveness based on these measures. Table 4 provides an overview of the measurability of each concept.

Table 4. Measurability overview concepts

Team Effectiveness Concept Measurability	(%)
Continuous Improvement	100%
Stakeholder Satisfaction	100%
Responsiveness	91.7%
Team Autonomy	80%
Team Morale	75%
Stakeholder Concern	57.1%
Management Support	0%

In addition to the difference between concepts, another interesting note on measures can be derived from discussions in the second focus group.

The discussion dealt with the idea that numbers alone do not mean anything. In other words, if a measure provides a number, what does this number mean? Several studies discuss the importance of providing meaning to a number [21, 24]. First, these studies concluded that the meaning of vague quantifiers and numerical values can vary greatly. Also, the problem with people is that each individual has his or her own internal scale to make judgments. As a result, numbers can be interpreted differently and can create confusion. During the focus group, a solution was already suggested. According to a focus group participant, *"to determine whether a given number is high or low, a comparison should be made to, for instance, a predefined goal or a certain trend"*, in other studies, benchmarking is defined as 'enabling and motivating one to determine how well one's current practices compare to other practices [18, p 786]'. By applying benchmarking, a number of a measure can be understood and helps to understand what the number means for certain standards or for a trend [16]. To apply this matter to this study. As the authors point out, the 29 metrics identified may be related to team effectiveness, but as they are just numbers they are not of use. In order to assess team effectiveness and make comparisons, these measures will have to be converted into indicators, with thresholds that determine when the team has a low, medium or high level, for example.

In general, Sect. 5.2 shows that 29 of the 40 measures help measure team effectiveness. Although this is the majority of the measures generated from the focus group, it does not mean that mapping these measures provides a complete picture of measuring team effectiveness. There is still a great difference in the ability to measure the seven concepts of team effectiveness. Furthermore, the measures have to be seen in series or in a trend, or a certain benchmark has to be applied to provide context to a number of a measure.

6.1 Validity Threats

In this section, threats to validity will be discussed. This concerns internal, conclusion, and external validity threats [23].

The internal validity threat is related to the expertise of the participants and interviewees in this research. However, for all interviews and focus groups, the participants had multiple years of Scrum project experience. However, different groups formations were used during both focus groups. As a result, most participants of the first focus group did not participate in the second focus group. This harms the internal validity.

The conclusion validity threat relates to the sample size of the focus group and the number of expert interviews. This can be seen as rather small.

The external validity threat relates to the generalizability of this research. This research took place at one organization. Although this threatens generalizability, all participants were consultants who also worked with or at other companies. As a result, experiences derived from other organizations were also indirectly taken into account. Therefore, this limits the external validity threat.

7 Conclusions and Future Research

In this research, results were presented on whether it is possible to measure team effectiveness based on objective measures. Focus groups and interviews were conducted to answer research questions:

"To which extent can team effectiveness in Scrum be measured based on objective measure?"

We identified 29 measures that contribute to measuring team effectiveness in Scrum. This signals that team effectiveness can indeed be measured to a large extent on the basis of objective measures. However, a few notes have to be taken into account. First, a number on its own of a certain measure has no meaning. Therefore, benchmarking or a trend in numbers has to be applied to provide meaning or context to a number of a measure. Furthermore, there is a variety in the measurability of team effectiveness concepts. For example, for one concept, all linked measures do not provide meaning to team effectiveness or cannot be measured in a work management system; for another concept, all linked measures are related and can be measured in a work management system. Although not all concepts can be fully measured, five of the seven concepts can be measured for at least 75%, providing a solid basis for measuring team effectiveness. Last, this research can be considered an exploratory study on the topic of measuring team effectiveness based on objective measures. The outcomes provide a first insight into this topic, which can be built on.

Future works should focus on extending this research to other software companies that apply scrum principles. This can result in new insights and new measures that can be applied to measure team effectiveness. Furthermore, it would be interesting to apply the measures in practice. As a result, feedback can be collected for new measures or current measures can be reexamined.

References

1. Benders, J., Van Hootegem, G.: Teams and their context: moving the team discussion beyond existing dichotomies. J. Manage. Stud. **36**(5), 609–628 (1999)
2. Buljac-Samardzic, M., Doekhie, K.D., van Wijngaarden, J.D.: Interventions to improve team effectiveness within health care: a systematic review of the past decade. Hum. Resour. Health **18**(1), 1–42 (2020)
3. Delgado Pinã, M.I., María Romero Martínez, A., Gómez Martínez, L.: Teams in organizations: a review on team effectiveness. Team Perform. Manage. Int. J. **14**(1/2), 7–21 (2008)
4. Doolen, T.L., Hacker, M.E., Van Aken, E.: Managing organizational context for engineering team effectiveness. Team Perform. Manage. Int. J. **12**(5/6), 138–154 (2006)
5. Fransen, J., Kirschner, P.A., Erkens, G.: Mediating team effectiveness in the context of collaborative learning: the importance of team and task awareness. Comput. Hum. Behav. **27**(3), 1103–1113 (2011)
6. Hackman, J.R., Morris, C.G.: Group tasks, group interaction process, and group performance effectiveness: a review and proposed integration. Adv. Exp. Soc. Psychol. **8**, 45–99 (1975)
7. Imbrie, P., Maller, S., Immekus, J.: Assessing team effectiveness. In: 2005 Annual Conference, pp. 10–229 (2005)
8. Jahedi, S., Méndez, F.: On the advantages and disadvantages of subjective measures. J. Econ. Behav. Org. **98**, 97–114 (2014)
9. Joshi, A., Kale, S., Chandel, S., Pal, D.K.: Likert scale: explored and explained. Br. J. Appl. Sci. Technol. **7**(4), 396 (2015)
10. Kitchenham, B.: Procedures for performing systematic reviews **33**, 1–26 (2004)
11. Lemieux-Charles, L., McGuire, W.L.: What do we know about health care team effectiveness? A review of the literature. Med. Care Res. Rev. **63**(3), 263–300 (2006)
12. Mathieu, J.E., Gallagher, P.T., Domingo, M.A., Klock, E.A.: Embracing complexity: reviewing the past decade of team effectiveness research. Annu. Rev. Organ. Psych. Organ. Behav. **6**, 17–46 (2019)
13. Moe, N.B., Dingsøyr, T.: Scrum and team effectiveness: theory and practice. In: Abrahamsson, P., Baskerville, R., Conboy, K., Fitzgerald, B., Morgan, L., Wang, X. (eds.) XP 2008. LNBIP, vol. 9, pp. 11–20. Springer, Heidelberg (2008). https://doi.org/10.1007/978-3-540-68255-4_2
14. One, V.: 14th annual state of agile development survey. Version One, INC. (2020). https://stateofagile.com/#ufh-c-7027494-state-of-agile

15. Peffers, K., Tuunanen, T., Rothenberger, M.A., Chatterjee, S.: A design science research methodology for information systems research. J. Manag. Inf. Syst. **24**(3), 45–77 (2007)
16. Purwanto, A.: Benefit of benchmarking methods in several industries: a systematic literature review. Syst. Rev. Pharm. **11**(8), 508–518 (2020)
17. Rashidi, M.N., Begum, R.A., Mokhtar, M., Pereira, J.: The conduct of structured interviews as research implementation method. J. Adv. Res. Des. **1**(1), 28–34 (2014)
18. Raymond, J.: Benchmarking in public procurement. Benchmarking Int. J. **15**(6), 782–793 (2008)
19. Salas, E., Sims, D.E., Burke, C.S.: Is there a "big five" in teamwork? Small Group Res. **36**(5), 555–599 (2005)
20. Schwaber, K., Sutherland, J.: The Scrum Guide, vol. 21, p. 1 (2011)
21. Scissons, E.H.: All numbers are not created equal: measurement issues in assessing board governance. Corp. Gov. Int. J. Bus. Soc. **2**(2), 20–26 (2002)
22. Verwijs, C., Russo, D.: A theory of scrum team effectiveness. ACM Trans. Softw. Eng. Methodol. **32**, 1–51 (2023)
23. Wohlin, C., Runeson, P., Höst, M., Ohlsson, M., Regnell, B., Wesslén, A.: Experimentation in Software Engineering-An Introduction. Kluwer Academic Publishers, Doedrecht (2000)
24. Wright, D.B., Gaskell, G.D., O'Muircheartaigh, C.A.: How much is 'quite a bit'? Mapping between numerical values and vague quantifiers. Appl. Cogn. Psychol. **8**(5), 479–496 (1994)
25. Yang, M.C., Jin, Y.: An examination of team effectiveness in distributed and colocated engineering teams. Int. J. Eng. Educ. **24**(2), 400 (2008)

Author Index

A
Abreu, Fernando Brito e   1
Almeida, Duarte   1
Alvarado-Valiente, Jaime   200
Anquetil, Nicolas   215

B
Barletta, Vita Santa   76
Barrocas, André   147
Beek, Kars   233
Boon, Gijsbert C.   130

C
Caballero Muñoz-Reja, Ismael   191
Caballero, Ismael   178
Caivano, Danilo   76
Condori-Fernandez, Nelly   121

D
da Silva, Alberto Rodrigues   147
de F. Carneiro, Glauco   1
de Rooij, Evert   233
Díaz, Ana   200
dos Reis, José Pereira   1

E
El-Baz, Yassin   130

G
Galera, Ramón   178
Garcia-Alonso, Jose   200
García-Rodríguez, Ignacio   200
Gualo, Fernando   178

H
Hackenberg, Georg   15
Heikkinen, Sanna   30
Hosry, Aless   215

J
Jäntti, Marko   30

K
Kester, Laura   233
Kiliç, Kani   163

L
Lako, Alfred   76
Lopes Margarido, Isabel   106

M
Marchetto, Alessandro   90
Miranda, Eduardo   60
Moguel, Enrique   200
Morales-Trujillo, Miguel   191
Münch, Jürgen   45
Murillo, Juan M.   200

O
Overbeek, Sietse   233

P
Pal, Anibrata   76
Prakash, Divya   163

R
Ricca, Filippo   90
Rodríguez, Moisés   178, 200
Rohmah, Arini Nur   121
Romero-Álvarez, Javier   200

S
Saraiva, João   147
Smith-Cooper, Ryan Michael   163

J. M. Fernandes et al. (Eds.): QUATIC 2023, CCIS 1871, pp. 249–250, 2023.
https://doi.org/10.1007/978-3-031-43703-8

Stettina, Christoph J.   130
Stocco, Andrea   90

T
Trieflinger, Stefan   45
Tukiainen, Markku   30
Tüzün, Alican   15

V
Van Veldhoven, Ziboud   163
Vanthienen, Jan   163
Visser, Joost   130

W
Wagenaar, Gerard   233
Weiss, Lukas   45

Printed in the United States
by Baker & Taylor Publisher Services